SELECTED SATIRES
OF LUCIAN

EDITED AND TRANSLATED BY

LIONEL CASSON

W · W · NORTON & COMPANY

New York · London

To Albert Billheimer, teacher and friend

W.W. Norton & Company, Inc.
500 Fifth Avenue, New York, N.Y. 10110
www.wwnorton.com
W.W. Norton & Company, Ltd.
Castle House, 75/76 Wells Street London WIT 3QT

W. W. Norton & Company, Inc., is the publisher of *The Norton Anthology of English Literature*, edited by M.H. Abrams *et al.*; *The Norton Anthology of Poetry*, edited by Alexander W. Allison *et al.*; *The Norton Anthology of American Literature*, edited by Nina Baym *et al.*; *The Norton Anthology of Short Fiction*, edited by R.V. Cassill; *The Norton Reader*, edited by Arthur M. Eastman *et al.*; *The Norton Anthology of Modern Poetry*, edited by Richard Ellmann and Robert O'Clair; *The Norton Anthology of Literature by Women*, edited by Sandra M. Gilbert and Susan Gubar; *The Norton Anthology of World Masterpieces*, edited by Maynard Mack *et al.*; and the Norton Critical Editions.

ISBN 0-393-00443-0

PREFACE

Lucian's genial mockery, aimed at man's omnipresent failings, is never out of date: the jabs he gave the hypocrites, grandstanders, fakers, and boobs of the ancient world can just as appropriately be administered to their counterparts of the modern.

But it is hard for the English reader of today to find this out. No volume of representative selections in translation is in print. There are satisfactory versions of the complete works (which would fill four books this size), but the reader who takes this long and not consistently interesting route will lose a good deal of the sting of Lucian's needle. Besides, the translators have been rather virginally shy at calling a spade a spade (which would no doubt have made Lucian hoot with glee). I hope this book will meet the need.

In making the selection, my first step was to eliminate almost all the pieces that belong to Lucian's career as a professional lecturer: speeches, formal introductions, short essays. This still left me with too little room to include all that stood high on most critics' lists or even all I wanted to include myself. In the next round of elimination I followed my own taste with this one limitation: I tried to illustrate the full range of Lucian's subject matter and various literary forms.

In translating I followed the principles I used in my *Masters of Ancient Comedy*. My prime purpose was to catch the spirit of the Greek rather than its literal meaning. My language throughout is somewhat less formal than Lucian's. This is deliberate: a more formal rendering, though closer to the meaning of the original, was, I felt, further from its spirit. Here and there, in places where translating Lucian's words would have produced something lifeless and wooden, I did not hesitate to paraphrase

—but only here and there; I have fought hard against the temptation to tell these pieces my way instead of Lucian's. Nor have I hesitated to change allusions or doctor jokes to make them intelligible to modern readers. The renderings in verse reproduce the meters of the original (though I have substituted our five-beat line for the six-beat line of Greek iambics).

Two people gave me invaluable aid in writing this book. My father, as always, read and reread every page of the manuscript. The dialogue throughout has profited from his fine feeling for idiom, and the exposition from his uncompromising insistence on clarity. My wife, too, read the manuscript, and her thoughtful comments and suggestions have improved many a passage.

Rome
March 1961

CONTENTS

MAN'S WORLD

Men

Maids

Philosophers

INTRODUCTION

"In the second century of the Christian Aera, the empire of Rome comprehended the fairest part of the earth, and the most civilized portion of mankind. The frontiers of that extensive monarchy were guaranteed by ancient renown and disciplined valor. The gentle, but powerful, influence of laws and manners had gradually cemented the union of the provinces. Their peaceful inhabitants enjoyed and abused the advantages of wealth and luxury . . . During a happy period of more than fourscore years, the public administration was conducted by the virtue and abilities of Nerva, Trajan, Hadrian, and the two Antonines."

These are the words with which Edward Gibbon opens his monumental history. They paint a picture of material well-being whose colors are bright but not false: government was efficient and honest; people were prosperous, and Western civilization was enjoying the longest period of peace in its history.

Politically the West was one world, all under the rule of the Roman Empire. Any inhabitant could make his way from the heat of Mesopotamia to the fogs of England without crossing a frontier. As you would expect under such circumstances, economic health was, in general, sound: in most places business was good and people were making money. There was a steady climb up the lower rungs of the social ladder into the middle class. Moreover, since in government as well as business, careers were open to talent, more and more from the middle class moved up, too, becoming millionaires and entering the ranks of the political or social elite. Men who, a generation back, had been slaves now built themselves impressive homes, sent their sons to college, gave handsome donations to their home towns, and held office as aldermen or mayors.

But, on the spiritual side, things were not so rosy. Gibbon says in a famous sentence: "The various modes of worship which prevailed in the Roman world were all considered by the people as equally true; by the philosopher as equally false; and by the magistrate as equally useful." There is point to his cynicism. The spirit had gone out of the traditional religions of Greece and Rome: worshiping Zeus or Jupiter was, like our saluting the flag, a matter of form rather than religious feeling. What people did to fill the void, to satisfy their emotional needs, depended on their background: the educated took to philosophy, the others to cults and superstition.

All over the empire religions with highly charged emotional content, with elaborate and impressive rites, flourished: the worship of Isis with its grand ceremony, of Mithras with its holy banquet held in a small and dimly lit chapel, of Cybele with its bouts of frenzy, of Demeter and Persephone with the special initiation and other secret hocus-pocus of the Eleusinian Mysteries. And superstition, always strong, was now rampant; people gaped in wonder at self-styled magicians, patronized all the ancient seats of prophecy, flocked to astrologers and fortune-tellers.

For those who considered all this so much claptrap there was philosophy. Every major city had its university where students could attend the lectures of well-known teachers—all students able to afford the tuition, not just the sons of the socially acceptable. The government, eager to promote culture, actually endowed professorships for the four major philosophical sects: the Stoics—who counted even Emperor Marcus Aurelius in their number, Academics (disciples of Plato), Peripatetics (disciples of Aristotle), and Epicureans. Students—or anyone, for that matter— could also listen at no cost to the soapbox lectures of the ubiquitous Cynics. The university town par excellence, the Oxford or Cambridge of the ancient world, was, as always, Athens. But whether in Athens or elsewhere, whether a highly paid professor was lecturing or a grimy Cynic orating, there was precious little creative thought. Much debate, much logic-chopping, much acrimony, and no lasting contributions.

This was the world into which, around 120 A.D., Lucian was born. It made his successful career possible. It is mirrored on many of his pages.

Lucian came, not from Rome or Athens, not even from Alexandria or Antioch, but from Samosata, a remote town on the banks of the Euphrates near the eastern outskirts of the empire. He is not only an example of the local boy who made good but the ancient equivalent of Joseph Conrad: the population of Samosata was mostly Syrian, and the first language this master of Greek talked was Syriac.

Just about all we know of Lucian's life comes from remarks he drops in his writings. His family was apparently lower middle class—some uncles ran a statue-making shop —so, when he finished his elementary education, he was supposed to learn a trade (cf. p. 3). In the world of the second century A.D. there was nothing to stop even a poor Syrian boy from setting his sights higher than a mason's hammer. He evaded his parents' plans for him and, as he puts it, "a mere boy, still talking a foreign language and wearing the next thing to native Syrian costume," took off for Ionia on the west coast of Asia Minor. In Lucian's day the open sesame to a professional career was public speaking; once a man had the rhetorician's arsenal at his command the way was open to riches and reputation as lawyer or lecturer. There were first-rate universities providing such training in Ionia at Ephesus and Smyrna, but Lucian probably couldn't afford the tuition. However, by some means or other, in his teens and early twenties he not only kept himself alive but gained his superb command of Greek, saturated himself in the literature of Greece, and mastered the art of public speaking.

His first career was the bar (cf. pp. 347, 349), but he soon abandoned it for the lectern. The traveling lecturer of those days could make money and a name by entertain-

ing the well-fed, culturally minded burghers of the pros-
perous cities that dotted the Roman Empire. Lucian left
Ionia and spent a number of highly successful years lec-
turing in Greece, Italy, and Gaul (ancient France); in
Gaul he may even have held one of the well-paying gov-
ernment professorships.

About 160 or so he returned to Ionia and, a wealthy
man and a celebrity, paid a visit to his home town (cf.
p. 3). He stayed in the east for a while (he was in
Antioch in 162 or 163) and then, about 165, made up his
mind to settle down at Athens. Like a dutiful son he took
his father and other members of the family with him (cf.
p. 295) to share in his good fortune. Somewhere along the
way he must have married since he mentions having a
young son.

Athens was a turning point. It was here that he gave
up his successful career as lecturer to become an artist,
that he subordinated the rhetorician to the writer. For the
first decade of his stay, say roughly from 165 to 175, he
devoted full time to his pen and turned out his finest
work, including almost all the pieces in this collection.
Then, for some reason, he took to the platform again.
When he was quite an old man, Emperor Commodus
(180–192) appointed him to a lucrative government job in
Egypt. This is the last we hear of him.

Lucian as a thinker is consistent and honest (most of
the time) but no great intellect. His point of view, influ-
enced in the main by the writers of Athens' golden age,
the fifth and fourth centuries B.C., was relatively simple
and clear-cut: an undeviating rationalism plus its counter-
part, hardheaded skepticism. Anything to do with the su-
pernatural is anathema to him: there are no gods; there
is no providence; all oracles are *ipso facto* fakes. All sham
is equally anathema: the prophet who pretends to powers
he cannot possibly possess, the tyrant who clothes vicious-
ness with noble-sounding words, the philosopher who
won't practice what he preaches. Lucian's treatment of

philosophy—and philosophers walk through page after page of his works—shows how superficial his thought can be. To Lucian all philosophy is worthless. Is this because he has grappled with the problems it tries to solve, weighed the solution offered by each school, and found them all wanting? Not at all—it's because, in his experience, the practitioners are a bunch of hypocrites.

Another element in Lucian's outlook, along with his rationalism and skepticism, is a fearless candor:* he goes after his pet hates with every weapon at his command. But his method of attack reveals that he is no Pope or Swift whose scathing satire welled up inexorably from the core of their beings. Lucian is more genial and easygoing; he will take time to amuse and entertain as well as to point out the error of men's ways. Moreover, by turning toward literature instead of life, as he so often does, he generalizes and enlarges his moralizing; this makes it less immediate, although just as telling, and more in line with his relaxed point of view. A Juvenal will direct his broadsides at the worship of Isis or Cybele or other cults that were favorites in his day; Lucian directs his against the gods of Homer. A Johnson will lament the sad state of civilization and draw examples from the streets of London; Lucian preaches the same sermon but illustrates it from books written over half a millennium before.

It is as literary artist, not moralist, that Lucian lays claim to fame. His intellect may have been ordinary, but his wit, humor, irony, exuberant comic fantasy, and craftsmanship with words most certainly are not. He has his faults: there is still plenty of rhetoric in even his best pieces, for he could never completely shuck off his platform manner; a man of books, he cannot resist an opportunity

---

* We all change when we get old. Toward the end of his life this brandisher of the flag of free speech accepted a government post—and the Roman government, though efficient and benign, was a thoroughgoing autocracy. Lucian, naturally, was touchy on the point and wrote a not very convincing defense of his action.

for a quotation particularly from his beloved Homer; he has no objection to using over and over the same ideas, jokes, phrases, even whole sentences. Yet all this gets lost in the blaze of his genuine talents. Above all, he shares the true artist's gift of creating scenes that burn themselves into a reader's memory. Charon and Hermes perched on their peaks, Wealth courteously delivering his devastating logic, Menippus grimly cheery among the skeletons, Peregrinus approaching his pyre, harried Zeus listening nervously to the philosophers (a perfect role for Edward Everett Horton, if Hollywood were ever to do Lucian)— I first read these pages thirty years ago and they have never left me. The mockery amuses—but there is more here than mere amusing mockery.

One of Lucian's foremost contributions to literature is the satiric dialogue. He took Plato's dialogue, which Plato had created to enliven the presentation of his ideas, infused it with the spirit of the spoken dialogue of comedy, and wrought an instrument capable of playing any tune. Lucian's dialogue can be light and airy (*Dialogues of the Courtesans, Dialogues of the Gods*), sophisticated and witty (*Prometheus, Zeus the Opera Star*), thought-provoking and cutting (*A Voyage to the Underworld, Charon*). A second instrument he wields masterfully is narrative. He can give any tale he tells unflagging drive and startling vividness, whether the straightforward account of the cockeyed adventures of *A True Story*, the charming recollections of *My Dream*, or the intricate, carefully worked-out scenography of *The Death of Peregrinus*. Dialogue and narrative are the twin pillars of Lucian's stylistic genius.

One more achievement Lucian gets credit for: he carried off a dazzling tour de force. The language he wrote was not the Greek spoken around him; it was an imitation, almost perfectly done, of what had been written over five hundred years before his time by the great names in Greek literature. It's as if an author today were to compose in the language of Shakespeare and do it so successfully only an Elizabethan or an expert could tell it wasn't the real thing.

Lucian's mocking laughter did not die with him. It has re-echoed down the centuries in the works of a host of subsequent writers.

One of the first to translate him was no less a personage than Erasmus, who rendered some of the best pieces into Latin. Erasmus' own *In Praise of Folly,* one of the great books of all time, is Lucianic in spirit through and through. Sir Thomas More, taking his cue from Erasmus, also did some renderings into Latin, and his celebrated *Utopia* owes a debt to *A True Story.* By the sixteenth century most of Lucian's works were available in Latin and some even in English and other modern languages, which enlarged many times the field of his influence. All the Elizabethans felt his spell. Marlowe's famous line about Helen's face is a paraphrase of one by Lucian (cf. p. 205); Ben Jonson's *Volpone* has many a reminiscence of the *Dialogues of the Dead;* Shakespeare's *Timon of Athens* (whatever of his hand is in it, that is) is based on Lucian's *Timon,* and the famous grave scene in Hamlet echoes the *Dialogues of the Dead.*

England, France, Germany—Lucian has left his mark on practically all of Western literature. In France *A True Story* inspired Cyrano de Bergerac (*Histoire comique des états et empires de la lune*) and, through him, Jules Verne, while the dialogues influenced a whole galaxy of writers: Boileau, Fontenelle, Fénelon, Voltaire. In England *A True Story* has Gulliver in its debt, and the dialogues can claim Walter Savage Landor's *Imaginary Conversations* and Andrew Lang's *Letters to Dead Authors* as descendants. In Germany both Schiller and Goethe felt the influence of the dialogues, while Baron Münchhausen's adventures include gobs taken wholesale from *A True Story.*

Painters have fallen under Lucian's spell no less than writers. Botticelli's two interesting pieces, *Calumny* and *Centaur Family,* are illustrations of word-pictures from

Lucian. Raphael, Mantegna, Michelangelo, Dürer, all in one way or another drew ideas from his pages. And the ubiquitous *Dance of Death* (generally attributed to an original by Holbein) was inspired by the *Dialogues of the Dead*.

I have spoken enough for Lucian. Let him speak for himself now.

A BIT OF AUTOBIOGRAPHY

My Dream

MY DREAM
[1–2]

When he was thirty-five or forty, Lucian, by then a well-known public lecturer, paid a visit to his home town —the local boy who had made good. This piece is presumably an address he delivered at the time.

No sooner had I stopped going to school—I was by then well on in my teens—when my father held a conference with his friends about the next step in my education. Most of them argued against higher education: since it involved lots of trouble, time, and expense, it was for families with handsome incomes and not for ours whose budget, being tight, needed some fairly quick bolstering. However, they pointed out, if I took up some ordinary trade, straight off I'd get enough to feed myself, and a big oaf like me wouldn't have to keep living off my father; then, before long, I'd be making him very happy by adding steady earnings to the family finances. This led to the raising of a second point for discussion: which trade was easy to learn, suitable for the son of a respectable family, cheap so far as equipment was concerned, and sure to provide a decent income. Well, each person had a different one to recommend, depending on his point of view and experience. An uncle of mine, my mother's brother, was present, a statue maker with a very good reputation and one of the best stonecutters in the business. My father turned to him and said, "With you here, it wouldn't be right to pick any other trade. Take him (and he pointed toward me); take charge of him, and teach him to be a good stonecutter, mason, and statue maker. He's capable, and you know yourself he's got a talent for the work." My father had gotten this notion from the tricks I used to play with wax. You see, whenever school was over, I used to scrape the wax from my tablets[1] and mold it into cows or horses or even human figures—very lifelike ones, my father thought. These would bring me a whipping from my teachers, but at this moment they were bringing me acclaim for a natural gift, and hopes were high that, because of this knack of mine for modeling things, I'd quickly pick up the trade.

As soon as a suitable day was agreed upon for apprenticing me to my craft, I was handed over to my uncle. I give you my word, I wasn't overly troubled by what was happening. As a matter of fact, it looked to me like an entertaining pastime and one that would give me a chance to show off to the other boys—they could be my audience as I carved gods and made little figurines for myself and any particular favorites present. But the first thing to happen was what usually happens to beginners. My uncle handed me a chisel and told me to come down lightly on a slab that was lying between us, giving me at the same time the old saw about "well begun" being "half done." Since I had had no experience, I came down too hard and it broke. He flew into a rage, grabbed a stick lying nearby, and put me through an initiation ceremony that was neither gentle nor encouraging. As a result, the preface to my career was a flood of tears. I ran out the door and came home, bawling all the way, with the tears running down my cheeks. There I told the whole story of the whipping and showed my welts. Then I launched into a denunciation of my uncle as a monster of cruelty, adding that he had done this to me because he was jealous: he was afraid I'd turn out better at the craft than he. My mother got very angry and heaped abuse on her poor brother. Night came at last and I fell asleep, still in tears and with that stick very much on my mind.

What I've told you so far has been amusing and childish. The sequel, however, is not something to be dismissed lightly; it deserves, gentlemen, your closest attention. For, to put it in Homer's words, there

> came unto me as I slumbered, a dream sent by heaven
Through the ambrosial night,[2]

so clear it was all but real. Even now, after so much time
has passed, the shapes that appeared to me then still re-
main before my eyes and the words I heard still echo in
my ears. That's how vivid it was.

Two women had me by the hands, and each was trying
with all her might to drag me toward her. Such a struggle
was going on between them that I was nearly ripped in
half. First one would get the upper hand and almost have
me to herself, and then I'd find myself in the other's
clutches. And they kept shouting back and forth: "He be-
longs to me and you're trying to take him away"; "You're
going after other people's property and you're not going to
get away with it." One was a working woman, a mannish
type, with unkempt hair and calluses on her hands; she
had her dress tucked up and was covered with stone dust
just the way my uncle looked when he was chipping
marble. The other had a lovely face, carried herself well,
and wore a mantle smartly draped.

Finally they left it to me to decide which I wanted to
be with. The rough, mannish one spoke first. "My boy,"
she said, "I'm the craft of statue making which you started
to learn yesterday. You know me; I'm a relative of yours,
one of the family. Your grandfather (and she named my
mother's father) was a stonecutter, and your two uncles
owe their fine reputation to me. If you're willing to stay
away from the jibber-jabber of this one here (and she
pointed to the other woman) and follow me and spend
your life with me, first and foremost, you'll eat heartily
and have broad shoulders, and second, you'll be free of
any bitterness at your lot and you'll never leave your
birthplace and family to go gallivanting abroad. Everybody
will praise you—but for works, not words. Don't turn up
your nose at my shabby appearance and dirty clothes.
After all, from a start like this the great Pheidias went on
to create his Zeus, Polycleitus to carve his Hera, Myron
to gain everyone's acclaim and Praxiteles everyone's ad-
miration.[3] People worship these men the way they do gods.
And, if you follow in their footsteps, you too will make a

name for yourself among all men; it can't help but hap-
pen. You'll make your father a person to be envied and
your fatherland a place to be remembered."

All this and a good deal more the Lady of Statue Mak-
ing said, speaking Greek like a foreigner[4] and stumbling
painfully. She rushed along, simply stringing words to-
gether in her effort to convince me. But I can't recall them
any more; most of them went in one ear and out the other.

When she had finished, the second woman started and
said more or less the following: "My dear boy, I am edu-
cation. We've already spent some time together and you
know me, even though you haven't yet tried me to the full.
This lady has pointed out the advantages of becoming a
stonecutter. Here's what they add up to. You'll be a work-
man doing hard manual labor, with all your prospects in
life invested in just that. You yourself will be a dull-witted
nobody earning a few paltry pennies. You'll cut no figure
in public; friends won't seek you out; enemies won't fear
you; neighbors won't envy you—you'll be just a workman,
that's all, a face in a crowd, always there to bow and
scrape before the man who's a leader, always the lackey
of the man who can use words, a steppingstone in the
path of your betters. It will be a dog's life. Even if you
become a Pheidias or a Polycleitus and create wonderful
masterpieces, the world will acclaim your art—but not one
of your admirers, if he has any sense, would ask to be in
your shoes. Whatever sort of person you may be, people
will still think of you as a workman, a manual laborer, a
man who makes his living with his hands.

"On the other hand, if you listen to me, to begin with,
I will reveal to you what has been done by the great men
of old; I will report their many marvelous deeds and
words to you; through me you will come to know virtually
all there is to know. Your soul, the part that is supreme in
you, I will deck with a multitude of the finest adornments,
with good sense, justice, reverence, gentleness, reasonable-
ness, understanding, strength, love of the good things in

life, and desire to strive for the ideal—for all these are truly
the purest adornment the soul can have. Next, all that has
happened in the past, all that must happen in the pres-
ent, will be made known to you; even more, I will help
you foresee the future—in a word, all things that are,
whether of god or man, I will teach you before many days
have passed. Today you are a poverty-stricken boy, son of
some nobody, with thoughts of entering the lowliest of
trades. Tomorrow you will be the object of everyone's envy
and jealousy, honored, acclaimed, a man of the highest
reputation, looked up to by the leaders in social standing
or wealth, wearing clothes such as these (and she pointed
to those she had on; she was splendidly dressed), accorded
public recognition and public office. And if you travel, even
abroad you will not be unknown and unnoticed; I will
place upon you such marks of distinction that everyone
who lays eyes on you will nudge his neighbor, point to you,
and say, 'That's him!' If some great event befalls your
friends, or even the whole nation, you will be the one all
will look to. Wherever you happen to make a speech, the
crowd will listen openmouthed; they will marvel; they will
congratulate you on the power of your words and your
father on the good fortune of having such a son. They say
that some men become immortal. I will make this come
true for you: even after you leave this life, you will con-
tinue to be the companion of people of culture and to ad-
dress your words to the finest minds. Who ever heard of
the great Demosthenes' father? Yet look what I made of
the son! Aeschines' mother played a tambourine for a liv-
ing, yet look how I made King Philip pay him court![5]
Socrates himself was brought up by Lady Statue Making
here,[6] but, as soon as he knew better, he deserted her and
defected to me, and you know how his praises are sung
on all sides. Yet you intend to turn your shoulder on such
great men, on celebrated deeds, noble words, a fine figure,
honor, reputation, admiration, public recognition and office,
power, fame as an orator, and acclaim as a man of under-

standing. Instead you are going to put on a filthy apron, become a slave to all outward appearance, and busy your hands with crowbars and gravers, hammers and chisels. Hunched over your work, your eyes and mind on the ground, low as low can be, you will never lift your head to think the thoughts of a true man or a free spirit. All you will think of is how to give grace and form to your work—how to give grace and charm to yourself will be the last thing on your mind; you will make those blocks of stone of yours worth more than your own self."

While these words were still on her lips, without waiting for her to finish what she had to say, I rose and declared myself: with joy in my heart I crossed over to Lady Education and turned my shoulder on the ugly drudge—particularly since there flashed through my mind the thought of that stick and of the rather sound beating she had handed me yesterday, my very first day at her trade. For a while she carried on terribly at being abandoned, clenching her fists and gnashing her teeth. Finally, like Niobe in the story, she became rooted to the spot and turned into stone.[7] An unbelievable thing to have happened, but you must not doubt my word; dreams can work magic, you know. Then the other turned to me and said, "You have made the right decision and I shall repay you for it. Come, get into this carriage right now (and she pointed to a winged vehicle drawn by horses that looked like Pegasus). I want you to see for yourself the great things you were going to miss by not becoming my disciple." I got in, and she took the reins and drove off. High in the sky I traveled the whole circuit from east to west, looking down upon cities, tribes, and nations and, like Triptolemus, scattering seeds of some sort over the earth.[8] What kind I no longer recall. I only remember that men applauded when they looked up, and all whom I came upon in my flight cheered me on my way.

When my guide had finished revealing all this to me—and me to my well-wishers—she brought me back home.

But I no longer had on the clothes I was wearing when I left the ground; my impression was that I returned looking pretty grand and glorious. She found my father standing about waiting, and she pointed out to him the new clothes and the figure I cut as I came in; she even gave him a gentle reminder of the plans he had almost put into effect for me.

This is the vision I remember came to me when I was still a boy—perhaps because I was so emotionally disturbed by that beating I had received.

While I was talking, did I overhear one of you say, "My god, what an interminable dream! And so long-winded!"? Or did someone interrupt to remark, "Must have been a winter dream when the nights are longest. Or maybe it took three nights, like Heracles' conception.[9] What's come over him? Why does he give us this drivel? Why bring up a night in his childhood and dreams that are ancient history? Stale nonsense! What's he take us for—professional dream analysts?" No, my dear sir, I do not—and neither did Xenophon when he told how he dreamed that his father's house was on fire and so on—you all know the story.[10] He told it, not to have it interpreted or with the deliberate intention of talking drivel—it was during wartime; a battle was on; the enemy was on all sides, and things were desperate—but because telling it served a useful purpose. So I too have told you this dream of mine for a reason: to turn our young men toward the better course and get them to strive for education, particularly those who, because they are poor, are afraid to take a chance and are inclining toward lesser goals to the ruin of a fine talent. Their resolution will be stiffened, I'm sure, if they hear my story, if they hold me up as an apt example, if they contrast the boy who didn't flinch before the poverty he once faced but set forth on the road to the finest things in life and pursued the goal of education with the man who has now come back to you—a man who, if nothing more, is at least as famous as any stonecutter!

NOTES

[1] I.e., the waxed tablets he used in school to write on, as children of a few generations ago used slates.

[2] *Iliad* 2.56–57. At this point Lucian the autobiographer leaves the stage and the public lecturer takes over. What follows is an imaginative reworking of a well-known story told by Xenophon (*Memorabilia* 2.1.21–34) plus some reminiscences of the debate between the Just and Unjust Arguments in Aristophanes' *Clouds* (889–1023).

[3] Pheidias, Polycleitus, and Myron were the great sculptors of the fifth century B.C. and Praxiteles one of the greatest of the fourth century B.C. The Zeus was the colossal statue in the temple at Olympia. The Hera stood in the temple to Hera at Argos.

[4] The native language of Samosata, where Lucian was born, was Syriac.

[5] Demosthenes' father was "in trade" to be sure, but his trade was running a sizable sword factory; the family was well-to-do and far from lowly. The great orator did all he could to save Athens from the schemes of Philip of Macedon. Aeschines, a bitter rival, spoke for the pro-Macedonian party and was consequently made much of by Philip. Aeschines' mother was a priestess in some not very reputable cult—if Demosthenes can be believed.

[6] His father was a sculptor, and Socrates is said to have followed the trade in his early years.

[7] Niobe, who had many children, boasted that she was superior to Leto, the mother of only Apollo and Artemis. For this indiscretion her children were slain and she was turned to stone.

[8] Triptolemus, by scattering seeds from a winged chariot supplied by the goddess of grain, introduced agriculture to men.

[9] When Zeus had the assignation with Alcmena that led to the birth of Heracles, he arranged to have the night prolonged to three times its normal length.

[10] *Anabasis* 3.1.11.

TWO ROMANCES

A True Story

Lucius, the Ass

A TRUE STORY
[1.1–2]

A True Story *is Lucian's tall-tale travelogue to end all
tall-tale travelogues.*

*Lucian, with Odysseus' fabulous adventures in mind,
brands Homer as the founder of this literary form. That
seems unfair: epic poets make no claim to be roving re-
porters. A more likely candidate is Herodotus who, though
called the "Father of History," wasn't above telling tales
of ants bigger than foxes, dog-headed men, and other such
forerunners of the Abominable Snowman. He inspired a
whole school of Greek Baron Münchhausens, such as the
Ctesias and Iambulus whom Lucian mentions by name,
none of whose writings, however, have survived.*

*In the present elaborate spoof there are many things we
can recognize: the parodies of passages from Homer and
Herodotus; a mimicking of the way Xenophon describes
a land battle and Thucydides a sea battle; the quoting of
the terms of a treaty verbatim à la Thucydides, and so on.
We can guess that at times Lucian is poking fun at popu-
lar legends such as the versions known to him of Jonah
and the Whale or of Sindbad and the Roc. Had we the
works that have been lost, very likely we could identify a
parody behind almost every one of his exuberant inven-
tions.*

PART I

No athlete or body-building enthusiast thinks only of
exercising and being in condition. He thinks also of relaxing
when the occasion calls for it and, as a matter of fact, he
considers this the most important part of training. In my
opinion the same holds for book enthusiasts: after poring
over a lot of serious works, they ought give the mind a

rest to get it into even better shape for the next workout. The most suitable way for them to spend the interval is with light, pleasant reading which, instead of merely entertaining, furnishes some intellectual fare as well—and this I think they'll agree is true of the present work.

It is a work that will appeal to them not only because of the exotic subject matter, the amusing plot, and the way I've told all sorts of lies with an absolutely straight face, but because I've included comic allusions to all our noted poets, historians, and philosophers of old who have written so many fabulous tall stories. I don't need to name names: you'll recognize them yourselves as you read along. Ctesias of Cnidus, the son of Ctesiochus, has written things about India and the Indians that he neither saw himself nor heard from anyone who had any respect for the truth. Iambulus has written a lot of unbelievable stuff about the ocean; everyone knows he made it all up, yet, for all that, he has put together an amusing account. Lots of other writers have shown a preference for the same technique: under the guise of reporting their travels abroad they spin yarns of huge monsters, savage tribes, and strange ways of life. The arch-exponent of, and model for, this sort of tomfoolery is Homer's Odysseus telling the court of Alcinous about a bag with the winds in it, one-eyed giants, cannibals, savages, even many-headed monsters and magic drugs that change shipmates into swine—with one such story after another he had those simple-minded Phaeacians goggle-eyed.[1]

Now, I've read all the practitioners of this art and I've never been very hard on them for not telling the truth—not when I see how common this failing is even among those who profess to be writing philosophy.[2] What I have wondered at, though, is the way they're convinced they can write pure fable and get away with it. Since I'm vain enough myself to want to leave something behind to posterity and since I have nothing true to record—I never had any experiences worth talking about—in order not to be the only writer without a stake in the right to make up tall tales, I, too, have turned to lying—but a much more honest lying than all the others. The one and only truth you'll hear from me is that I *am* lying; by frankly admitting that there isn't a word of truth in what I say, I feel I'm avoiding the possibility of attack from any quarter.

Well, then, I'm writing about things I neither saw nor heard of from another soul, things which don't exist and couldn't possibly exist. So all readers beware: don't believe any of it.

Some time ago I set out on a voyage from the Straits of Gibraltar. A favorable breeze carried me into the Atlantic Ocean, and I was on my way. The basic reasons for the trip were my intellectual curiosity, my thirst for novelty, and the desire to find out what formed the farther border of the ocean and what peoples lived there. I had consequently put aboard a large stock of provisions and plenty of water and had taken on as crew fifty acquaintances who shared my interests; I had also laid in a good supply of weapons, induced—by the offer of a handsome salary—the best navigator available to go along, and had our vessel, a fast brig, made shipshape for a long and hard stay at sea.

For a day and a night we sailed before a wind that was favorable but not strong enough to carry us out of sight of land. At dawn of the following day, however, the wind made up, the sea began to run, and the sky grew dark. There wasn't even time to take in sail; we gave up and let the ship scud before the gale. For the next seventy-nine days we were driven along by a furious storm. Suddenly, on the eightieth, the sun broke through and we saw, fairly near, a hilly island covered with forest. The sound of the surf was not too loud; by now the storm had mostly subsided. We made for the shore, disembarked, and for hours just lay on the ground, a natural thing to do after such a long ordeal.

Finally we got up and decided that thirty of us would

stand by to guard the ship while I took the other twenty
to reconnoiter the island. We had advanced about a third
of a mile through thick forest when we came upon a bronze
shaft. It was inscribed in Greek, and the legend, dim and
worn, read: "This marks the spot reached by Heracles and
Dionysus." And, pressed in the rock nearby, were two sets
of footprints, one a hundred feet long, the other some-
what less. I figured the smaller were Dionysus' and the
larger Heracles'. We paid our respects and pushed on.

We hadn't proceeded very far when we came upon a
river, not of water, but of wine, which had the very same
taste as our vintage Chian. The stream was so wide and
deep that in places it was actually navigable. In view of
such tangible evidence of a visit from Dionysus I was now
much more inclined to believe the inscription on the shaft.
I decided to track down the source of the river and walked
upstream. Here I found no signs of any spring but, instead,
a large number of enormous vines full of grapes. The roots
of each were oozing drops of clear white wine, and these
formed the river. Under the surface we could see a good
many wine-colored fish which, it turned out, also tasted
like wine; in fact, we got drunk on some that we caught
and ate. (Naturally, when we cut them open we found
them full of dregs.) Later, having given the matter some
thought, we mixed them with fresh-water fish and thus
made our sea-food cocktails less potent.[3]

After fording the river at a narrow point, we came upon
vines of a fabulous type. The part growing out of the
ground, the stalk proper, was well set up and thick. But
the part above that was a perfect replica of a female body
from hips to head, looking somewhat like Daphne in those
paintings where she's shown turning into a tree as Apollo
lays his hands on her.[4] The women had branches bearing
clusters of grapes growing out of the tips of their fingers
and, instead of hair, actual shoots with leaves and grapes.
They called out to welcome us as we came up, some in
Lydian, some in Indian, but most in Greek. They also

started kissing us on the lips, and everyone they did this to immediately became drunk and began to reel. We weren't able to pick the grapes because, as we pulled them off, the women would cry out in pain. They were burning with desire to have intercourse with us. Two of my men tried it—and couldn't be pried loose: they were held fast by the penis; it had grown into, become grafted onto, the vines. Soon the pair became entwined in a network of tendrils, sprouted shoots from their fingers, and looked as if even they were ready to bear fruit. We abandoned them and fled back to the ship where we gave the men who had stayed behind a report of everything, including the vinous intercourse of their two shipmates.

We then broke out the water jars, watered up—and also wined up from the river—and, after spending the night on the beach, sailed off at dawn before a moderate wind. Around noon, when the island had dropped out of sight, a typhoon suddenly hit us. It spun the ship around and lifted it about thirty miles high in the air. But, before it could let us drop back into the water, as we hung suspended in the sky, a wind filled our sails and carried us along. For seven days and nights we sailed the air. On the eighth we sighted a large land mass like an island in the sky. It was round and, illuminated by some immense light, shone brightly. We put in there, anchored, and disembarked, and, upon reconnoitering the countryside, found it was inhabited and under cultivation. During the day we could see no other land about but, when night came on, we saw a good many other islands the color of fire, some bigger than ours and some smaller. Below was another land mass with cities, rivers, seas, forests, and mountains; we guessed it was our own earth.

I decided to push farther inland. En route we ran into what is called locally the Buzzard Cavalry and were taken captive. Now the Buzzard Cavalry is made up of men who ride on buzzard back; they use birds the way we do horses. Their buzzards, you see, are enormous creatures, mostly three-headed; to give you an idea of their size I need only point out that any one of their wing feathers is longer and thicker than the mast on a big cargo vessel. This Buzzard Cavalry has orders to run patrol flights over the countryside and bring before the king any aliens they find. So we were arrested and brought before him. He looked us over and, guessing from the way we were dressed, said, "You are Greek, gentlemen?" We nodded. Then he said, "How did you get here with all that air to cross?" We told him our whole story and he, in turn, told us all about himself. His name was Endymion[5] and he, too, had come from earth: some time in the past he had been snatched up in his sleep, brought here, and made king of the place.

He explained to us that the land we were in was what appeared to people on earth as the moon. He told us, however, not to worry or be apprehensive, that we were in no danger, and that we would be given everything we needed. "Once I win this war I'm involved in against the people living on the sun," he added, "you can stay here with me and live happily ever after." We asked him who his enemies were and how the disagreement had come about. "Phaëthon,"[6] he told us, "is king of the people living on the sun—the sun, you see, is inhabited just like the moon —and he's been at war with us for a long while. It all started this way. Some time ago I got the idea of collecting the poorest among my subjects and sending them out to found a colony on the Morning Star, which is completely bare and uninhabited. Phaëthon out of spite called out his Ant Cavalry and intercepted the expedition before it had gone halfway. We were beaten—we were no match for his forces at the time—and turned back. Now I want to take the offensive again and establish my colony. If you're willing, come, join our army. I'll supply each of your men with one buzzard from the royal stables plus a complete outfit. We leave tomorrow."

"If that's what you want, why, of course," I replied.

We stayed the night with him as his guests. At the crack

of dawn his lookouts reported that the enemy was approaching, and we rose and took our positions. Endymion had 100,000 troops, not counting supply corps, engineers, infantry, and contingents from foreign allies. Of the 100,-000, 80,000 were Buzzard Cavalry and 20,000 Saladbird Cavalry. The saladbird is an enormous bird covered all over with salad greens instead of feathers; its wings look exactly like lettuce leaves. Alongside these were units of Peashooters and Garlickeers. He also had some allied forces from the Big Dipper: 30,000 Fleaborne Bowmen and 50,-000 Windrunners. The Fleaborne Bowmen are mounted on huge fleas—hence the name—each as big as twelve elephants. The Windrunners, though ground forces, are able to fly through the air without wings. This is the way they do it: they wear shirts that go down to their feet; by pulling these up through the belt and letting them belly before the wind like sails, they're carried along the way a boat would be. In battle they serve for the most part as mobile infantry. There was talk that 70,000 Ostrich-Acorns and 50,000 Crane Cavalry were expected from the stars over Cappadocia, but they never showed up so I didn't see them and, consequently, haven't dared to describe what they're like—the fabulous things I heard about them are unbelievable.

So much for the make-up of Endymion's army. The equipment was standard throughout: a helmet made from a bean (enormous, tough beans are grown there), a breastplate of overlapping lupine husks (since the husks of the local lupines are very hard, like horn, they are made into armor by being stitched together), and a sword and shield of the Greek type.

At the appropriate moment Endymion drew up his forces for battle. The Buzzard Cavalry together with the king and his elite guard (including us) were on the right, the Saladbird Cavalry on the left, and, in the center, the cavalry units from the foreign allies, each disposed as it chose. The infantry, numbering about 60,000,000, he positioned as follows. He ordered the local spiders—they are numerous and big, any one of them larger by far than the average Aegean island—to span the air between the moon and the Morning Star with a web; as soon as they finished, he stationed the infantry on the plain so formed, with General Nightly Goodday and two others in command.

On the enemy side the Ant Cavalry with Phaëthon in command formed the left wing. This arm uses enormous winged beasts similar to our ants in every respect except size, for the largest can run upwards of two hundred feet in length. The mount as well as the rider fights, principally by using its feelers. Their number was reportedly 50,000. On the right wing were the Aerognats, bowmen astride huge gnats, also 50,000 in number, and, behind them, the Aerojumpers. These, although light-armed infantrymen, are especially dangerous because they have slings that fire elephantine radishes capable of inflicting in whomever they hit a gangrenous wound which spells instant death; rumor has it these missiles are tipped with mallow juice.[7] On the Aerojumpers' flank were 10,000 Stalk-and-Mushroomeers, heavy-armed troops for hand-to-hand combat, so called because they use mushrooms for shields and asparagus stalks for spears. Nearby were 5000 Dog-Acorns, dog-faced men who fought mounted on winged acorns; they had been sent by the inhabitants of Sirius. According to reports, Phaëthon had other allies who were late—the Cloud-Centaurs and a detachment of slingers he had summoned from the Milky Way. The Cloud-Centaurs arrived after the battle had been decided. (How I wish they hadn't gotten there at all!) The slingers never showed up, and I've heard say that Phaëthon was so angry he subsequently laid their country waste with fire.

Such was the make-up of the force attacking us. The standards were raised; donkeys—the substitute in these armies for trumpeters—brayed the charge on both sides; the lines clashed, and the battle was on. The sun's left immediately fled without waiting to engage our Buzzard

Cavalry; we pursued, slaughtering as we galloped. Their right, however, overpowered our left, and the Aerognats gave chase all the way to where our infantry was drawn up. The infantry came to the rescue, and the Aerognats, well aware that their left had been defeated, gave way and ran. The retreat turned into a full-scale rout: our men killed or captured huge numbers. Streams of blood spilled over the clouds, drenching them and turning them the scarlet color they take on at sunset. Quite a lot dripped down on earth—which makes me wonder whether something similar hadn't occurred centuries ago and Homer simply jumped to the conclusion it was Zeus sending down a shower of blood to honor Sarpedon's death.[8]

As soon as we returned from the pursuit we erected two monuments, one on the cobwebs to commemorate the infantry battle, the other on the clouds for the air battle. Before we had finished, our lookouts reported the approach of the Cloud-Centaurs, the forces which were to have joined Phaëthon before the battle. Sure enough, they came into view, an absolutely incredible sight: each was a combination of man and winged horse, the human part as tall as the upper half of the Colossus of Rhodes and the equine as big as a large cargo vessel. I won't put down their number; it was so great I'm afraid no one will believe it. Sagittarius, the archer from the Zodiac, was in command. When they realized their allies had been defeated, they sent word to Phaëthon to return to the attack and, lining up in battle formation, charged. The Moonmen who, because of the chase and subsequent search for plunder, had broken ranks and scattered all over, were routed to a man; the king himself was pursued to the walls of his capital, and most of his birds were killed. After tearing down our two monuments, the Cloud-Centaurs overran the entire plain woven by the spiders and, in the process, took me and two of my shipmates prisoner. When Phaëthon arrived on the scene, monuments were again erected—this time for his side.

The very same day we were carried off to the sun, our hands tied behind our backs with a strip of cobweb. The enemy decided against laying siege; instead, on the way back they set up a barricade in mid-air, a double wall of cloud, which cut the moon off completely from the sun's light. The moon consequently went into total eclipse and remained in the grip of perpetual night. Greatly upset, Endymion sent a message to the Sunmen imploring them to tear down the structure and not force his subjects to live their lives in pitch-darkness. He said he was ready to submit to taxation, furnish military aid when required, and enter into a nonaggression pact, and he volunteered to supply hostages to guarantee performance. Phaëthon and his people held two referendums: in the first they were as bitter as ever, but in the second they changed their minds[9] and agreed to a treaty of peace worded thus:

The Sunmen and their allies hereby agree to a treaty of peace with the Moonmen and their allies on the following terms:

The Sunmen shall tear down the barricade they erected, shall hereafter never make war on the moon, and shall return all prisoners at a ransom to be determined for each;

the Moonmen shall grant autonomy to all other stars and shall not bear arms against the sun;

each party shall render aid to the other in the event of aggression by a third party;

the king of the Moonmen shall pay to the king of the Sunmen an annual levy of 10,000 jars of dew and provide 10,000 hostages from his own subjects;

both parties shall co-operate in founding the colony on the Morning Star; interested nationals of any other country may take part;

this treaty shall be inscribed on a tablet of silver and gold to be erected in mid-air at the common frontier.

Sworn to by
> Firestone
> Heater
> Burns
>> for the sun;
> Nighting
> Moony
> Allbright
>> for the moon.

Peace was made on these terms, and the moment it took effect the wall was torn down and the prisoners, including us, released. When we arrived back on the moon, our shipmates and Endymion himself came out a little way to meet us and welcomed us with tears in their eyes. Endymion asked us to stay on and take part in founding the colony, promising to give me his own son in marriage (there are no women on the moon). I was not to be persuaded and requested instead to be sent back down to the ocean. When he realized my mind was made up he let us go after a week's entertainment as his guests.

I want to describe the strange, new phenomena I observed during this stay on the moon.

The first is that males and not females do the childbearing. Marriage is with males, and there isn't even a word for "woman." Men under twenty-five are the wives, men over, the husbands. The embryo is carried not in the belly but in the calf. Once conception takes place, the calf swells up; after a due period of time it is cut open and the child, not yet alive, extracted. Life is induced by placing the child, mouth wide open, toward the wind. It's my opinion that the Greek word for calf, which literally means "belly of the leg," came to us from the moon, since there the calf and not the belly serves as the region of gestation.

I shall now describe a second phenomenon which is

even stranger, namely the race called "tree people." The procreation of tree people is as follows. A man's right testicle is cut off and planted in the ground. This produces a huge tree of flesh with a trunk like a penis. It has branches and leaves and, as fruit, bears eighteen-inch acorns. When ripe, these are gathered, the shells cracked open, and men are hatched from them.

Moonmen have artificial penises, generally of ivory but, in the case of the poor, of wood; these enable them to have intercourse when they mount their mates.

They never die of old age but dissolve and turn into air, like smoke.

The diet is the same for everyone: frog. Every time they light a fire they grill frogs on the coals because there's such a plentiful supply of these creatures flying about. While the cooking goes on, people seat themselves in a circle around the fire as if at a table and have a banquet sniffing in the smoke that's given off. Frogs provide their food; for drink they compress air in a cup to produce a liquid resembling dew.

They don't urinate or defecate. They have no rectal orifice so, instead of the anus, boys offer for intercourse the hollow of the knee above the calf, since there's an opening there. A bald pate or no hair at all is considered a mark of beauty; they can't stand men who wear their hair long. (Among the inhabitants of the comets, on the other hand, the opposite is true, as some natives who were visiting the moon informed me.[10]) They do, however, wear beards which grow a little above the knee. Their feet terminate in a single toe, and they have no toenails. Above the rump grows a cabbage which hangs down like a tail; it's always ripe and doesn't break off even when they fall on their backs.

Their nasal discharge is a very bitter honey. When they work or exercise they sweat milk from every pore; by adding a few drops of the honey, they can curdle this into cheese. They make oil not from olives but onions, a rich grade that smells as sweet as myrrh. Their vines, which are plentiful, are a water-producing variety since the grapes are a form of hailstone; it's my theory that, when the wind blows and shakes the vines, the clusters burst and this produces hail on earth.

They use the belly as a pocket, putting into it whatever they need to carry with them, for it can be opened and closed. No liver is visible inside, only a rough, furry lining; infants consequently snuggle in there during cold weather.

The wealthy wear clothes of flexible glass and the poor of woven copper. The country is rich in copper; it's worked the way we work wool, by being soaked in water.

I am going to describe the kind of eyes they have, though I hesitate to do so since you're sure to think I'm lying. They have removable eyes: whenever they want they take them out and keep them safe until they need them; then they put them back and have sight again. Many who have lost their own borrow other people's, and some men, all well-to-do of course, own a good supply of spares. Everybody has ears of plane-tree leaves except the men hatched from acorns; theirs are of wood.

Another marvel I saw was in the royal palace. Here there is an enormous mirror suspended over a rather shallow well. If you stand in the well, you hear everything said on earth; if you look at the mirror, you see each city and nation as clearly as if you were standing over it. When I took a look, I saw my own homeland and my house and family; I can't say for sure whether they saw me.

Any person who doesn't believe that all this is so need only go there himself. He'll quickly discover I'm telling the truth.

When the time came, we bid farewell to the king and his court, embarked, and set off. Endymion gave me as a good-by gift two glass and five copper shirts and a suit of lupine-husk armor, all of which I left behind in the whale. He also sent a thousand of the Buzzard Cavalry to escort

us for the first fifty miles. On the way we passed a number
of other countries but didn't stop till we came to the Morn-
ing Star, which we found in the course of being colonized.
Here we disembarked and took on water. Boarding ship
again, we entered the Zodiac and passed the sun close to
port, almost touching the shore. We didn't land, although
my men were very anxious to, because the wind was foul.
We could see, however, that the countryside was green
and fertile, well-watered, and full of good things. The
Cloud-Centaurs, who are in Phaëthon's pay, spotted us
and came after our ship but, on learning we were pro-
tected by the treaty, turned back. Our Buzzard Cavalry
escort had left us earlier.

We continued sailing that night and the next day and,
toward evening, when we had already begun the slant
down to earth, arrived at Lampville. This city is located
in mid-air halfway between the Pleiades and the Hyades,
at a much lower altitude than the Zodiac. On going ashore,
we found no humans but only great numbers of lamps
scurrying about or lounging around the main square and
the water front. Most were small, the lower classes as it
were; a few, the rich and influential, were conspicuously
bright. The lamps had each their own house and bracket,
bore names the way we do, and were capable of speech
(we heard them talking). They did us no harm but actu-
ally offered hospitality; we, however, were afraid, and not
one of us had the courage to accept their invitations to
dine or spend the night. Downtown they have a city hall
where the mayor, sitting in judgment all night, calls up
each lamp by name. Those who don't answer are con-
sidered deserters and receive the death penalty, namely
snuffing out. We stood around watching the proceedings,
listening to the lamps defend themselves and submit their
reasons for being late. At one point I recognized my own
lamp. I spoke to it and asked how things were back home,
and it gave me a full account.

We stayed the night there and the following day raised

sail and set off again. By this time we were down among
the clouds. We sighted Cloudcuckooland[11] and wondered
about it but couldn't put in because of an unfavorable
wind. We did receive word, however, that Jay Crow was
on the throne. I was minded how people had foolishly
been skeptical of what the playwright Aristophanes had
written; he was a wise man who told the truth. Two days
later we could see the ocean clearly. No land was visible
except, of course, the islands in the air, and these now had
a fiery bright aspect. On the third day, toward noon, the
wind slackened off to a gentle breeze, and we landed on
the surface of the sea. The moment we touched water we
went hysterical with joy; we celebrated as best we could
under the circumstances and then jumped overboard for a
swim since the day was calm and the sea smooth.

But the prelude to worse trouble often wears the guise
of a change for the better. We sailed along under ideal
conditions for just two days. Toward sunrise of the third
we suddenly sighted a host of sea monsters and whales,
one of which, the biggest there, was over a hundred and
fifty miles long. It came at us, churning up the sea far in
front and making the water foam along its sides; the gap-
ing jaws revealed a set of ivory-white teeth, each one of
which was sharp as a stake and longer than our large phal-
lic poles. We bid each other farewell, embraced, and
waited for the end. By now the monster was on top of us
and drank us in with a gulp, ship and all. But, before it
could grind us to bits, the ship slipped through one of the
gaps between the teeth and tumbled safely into its insides.
There it was pitch-dark at first and we could see nothing;
later, however, when the creature opened its mouth, we
made out a vast cavity, big enough on all four sides, and
high enough, to accommodate a town of ten thousand peo-
ple. Lying about were the mangled remains of all sorts of
fish and other sea creatures, large and small, as well as of
anchors and spars, items of cargo, and human bones. To-
ward the center was a hilly land mass, the result, I imag-

ine, of the settling of silt the monster had swallowed. As a matter of fact, a forest with all kinds of trees had taken root in it, garden truck had come up, and the whole expanse looked like a farm area. The coast was twenty-seven miles around. Sea birds—gulls and kingfishers—could be seen nesting in the trees.

At first we did nothing but weep. After a while I got my comrades on their feet and we took care of the ship by propping it up and of ourselves by rubbing sticks together to make a fire and cooking a meal out of what was available. There was all we wanted of every kind of sea food scattered about, and we still had some of the water we had taken on at the Morning Star. The following day, after getting up, whenever the monster opened its mouth we would catch sight sometimes of mountains, sometimes of sky alone, often of islands; this made us realize that the creature was rushing along into every part of the ocean.

By now we had become used to our new mode of life so, since I was curious to investigate everything, I took seven of my comrades and made my way into the forest. Before we had gone half a mile we came upon a shrine dedicated, as its inscription showed, to Poseidon; a little further on was a spring of clear water and a number of graves marked by tombstones. In addition we heard a dog barking, and smoke was visible in the distance. We guessed there was some sort of habitation about. We quickened our pace and came upon an old man and a young man hard at work tilling a garden plot and irrigating it with water piped from the spring. We stopped in our tracks, delighted, yet at the same time frightened. They, reacting probably in the same way, stood there speechless. Finally the old man spoke. "Who are you?" he said. "Sea-gods or men who have had the same bad luck as we? Though we two are human beings, born and bred on land, we've turned into marine life: we swim along with this beast that envelops us, and we're not at all sure just what

we're experiencing—our guess is it's death, though we're
convinced we're alive."

"We're human beings too," I replied. "New arrivals swal-
lowed just yesterday, boat and all. We're here right now
because we wanted to find out what was going on in this
forest which looked so deep and thick. Apparently some
god led us here to lay eyes on you and discover that we're
not the only ones imprisoned in this monster. But tell us
your story. Who are you? How did you get here?" He
answered that he would neither talk about himself nor in-
quire about us until he had shared whatever hospitality
he had available. He took us into his house—a building
just big enough, furnished with beds and fitted out with
everything else necessary—put before us greens, nuts, and
fish, and poured out some wine. When we had eaten all
we wanted, he asked about our experiences. I told him all
our adventures in order: the storm, the island and what
we had found there, the voyage in air, the war, and every-
thing else up to our descent into the whale. After express-
ing amazement he, in turn, told us his story.

"Gentlemen," he said, "I am a Cypriot. I left my home-
land along with my son here and a large number of serv-
ants to go on a trading voyage. I headed for Italy with a
general cargo aboard a big ship; you perhaps noticed the
wreckage near the whale's mouth. We had a good voyage
as far as Sicily. But at that point a gale caught us and,
within three days, we were swept out into the Atlantic
Ocean. There we met up with this whale and were gulped
down, ship and all. Only we two were saved; everyone
else perished. After burying our shipmates, we erected a
shrine to Poseidon and began the life you see us living—
growing vegetables and existing on fish and nuts. The for-
est, as you can see, is extensive, but you can actually find
inside it a good many vines which produce a very sweet
wine. And you may have observed the spring; its water is
delicious and ice-cold. We have leaves for bedding, burn
all the wood we want, trap the birds that fly in, and catch

live fish by going up to the monster's gills—where we can
also bathe whenever we feel like it. What's more, not far
away is a lake two miles around, full of all sorts of fish,
and there we swim or sail in a little boat I built. It's been
twenty-seven years since we were swallowed up. We can
cope with just about everything except the people living
around us; they're wild savages, hard to get along with,
and they cause serious trouble."

"You mean to say," I broke in, "that there are others
besides us in this whale?"

"Lots," he replied. "Hostile creatures with weird fea-
tures. In the western part of the forest, that is, toward the
tail, live the Kipperites who have an eel's eyes and a lob-
ster's face; they're a bold, warlike people who eat their
food raw. As for the sides, along the starboard flank live
the Mermencats, human from the waist up and polecat
below; they, however, have a somewhat less primitive
sense of justice than the others. Along the port flank are
the Crabhands and the Tunaheads, bound to each other
by a military pact as well as emotional ties. In the central
sector are the Lobstertails and Flounderfoots, belligerent
and fast as a flash on their feet. The eastern sector, near
the mouth proper, suffers from flooding and is, conse-
quently, mostly uninhabited. In spite of this I live in it
and pay the Flounderfoots an annual levy of five hundred
oysters. That's the kind of country we're in. What you
people have to do now is figure out how to stay alive in it
and how to contend with so many enemies."

"How many are there all told?" I asked.

"Over a thousand," he said.

"How are they armed?" I asked.

"Nothing but fishbones," he replied.

"Then," I said, "since we're armed and they're unarmed,
the best plan would be to fight it out with them. If we
win, we'll live in peace for the rest of our lives."

Everybody agreed, so we went back to the ship and
started our preparations. The provocation to war was to be

a refusal to pay the tax. The due date was already at
hand and, sure enough, messengers from the Flounder-
foots arrived, demanding payment. The old man gave
them a contemptuous answer and chased them away. The
first to react were the Flounderfoots and Lobstertails; in a
rage at Scintharus—to give the old man his name—they
raised a great uproar and advanced to attack us. We had
anticipated this and were ready for them: we were armed
to the teeth, and twenty-five of our number were posted
on the road in ambush. The ambuscade's orders were to
lie low until they saw the enemy go by and then strike.
They did precisely that. While they hit the enemy from
behind and cut down his rear, the twenty-five of us—for
Scintharus and his son fought, too—advanced on the ene-
my's front and, coming to grips with them, put up a des-
perate struggle with all the strength and courage we could
command. Finally we put them to flight and chased them
to the mouths of their caves. They had 170 casualties and
we only one—our navigator, stabbed in the back with a
mullet rib. The rest of the day and that night we spent on
the battlefield. As a commemorative monument we planted
in the ground the dried-out backbone of a dolphin.

By the next day the rest of the tribes had gotten the
word and were on hand. On the right were the Kipperites
under the command of General Tunny, on the left the
Tunaheads, and in the center the Crabhands. The Mer-
mencats stayed out, preferring to remain neutral. We ad-
vanced to meet the throng and, near the shrine of Poseidon,
joined battle with a great war whoop that made the mon-
ster's insides re-echo like a cave. Since they were fighting
unarmed, we forced them to break and run and, chasing
them into the forest, made ourselves masters of the land
once and for all. Pretty soon messengers arrived to parley
about burying the dead and concluding a truce. It was not
our intention to come to terms with them, so the next day
we took the offensive and cut them down to a man—all
except the Mermencats, that is. When they saw what was

happening they made for the gills where they threw them-
selves into the sea. We advanced over the countryside,
now wiped clean of enemies, and settled down to a life of
peace from that moment on. Most of the time we spent in
sports, hunting, raising vines, and gathering fruit from the
trees—it was, in a word, like living a luxurious and un-
trammeled life in a vast prison from which there was no
escape.

For twenty months we lived like this. On the fifth day
of the twenty-first, toward the second opening of the
mouth—the monster opened its mouth once every hour,
and we used this as a way of reckoning time—toward the
second opening of the mouth, as I was saying, we sud-
denly heard a great shouting and commotion plus what
sounded like rowers at the oars and coxswains giving the
stroke. In great excitement we crept right up to the mouth
and, standing just back of the teeth, witnessed the strang-
est sight I have ever seen in my whole life: giants, three
hundred feet tall, were sailing about on vast islands the
way we do on war galleys. I know that what I'm going to
describe will sound incredible, but I shall tell it anyway.

The islands, though not very high, were long, approxi-
mately ten miles around. Aboard each were about one
hundred and twenty of these giants. Some, seated one be-
hind the other along the two long sides of each island,
were manipulating large cypress trees, leaves, branches,
and all, like oars; aft, on the part that would be the poop,
the helmsman stood atop a lofty hill, holding a bronze
steering oar a thousand yards long. On the foredeck were
about forty giants under arms to do the fighting; they re-
sembled men in every feature except their hair, which was
flaming fire, thereby doing away with the need for a hel-
met. There were no sails; instead, the wind struck the
trees which grew all over, bellied them out, and so drove
the island wherever the helmsman steered it. There was a
rowing officer on each, and they had the oarsmen moving
the islands at a smart pace just as on war galleys.

At first we saw only two or three but, after a while, about six hundred were visible. They split into two lines, clashed—and a naval battle was in full swing. Many of them met prow to prow and dashed each other to bits; many were sunk by a ram-thrust in the side; some were grappled and managed to break loose only after a long and hard struggle, for the marines on the foredecks boarded and fought gallantly, giving no quarter. Instead of grappling irons, they hurled huge octopuses tied to the end of a line; these wound their tentacles about the trees on an island and held it fast. For missiles they used, and very effectively, wagon-sized oysters and hundred-foot sponges. Fastcentaur commanded one side, Seadrink the other. The reason for the fight, apparently, was dolphin-rustling: Seadrink, it was alleged, had stolen great numbers from Fastcentaur's herds. All this we gathered from the shouting as they called to their leaders by name or hurled accusations at each other.

Finally Fastcentaur's forces won the day. They put about a hundred and fifty enemy islands out of action and captured three with crews and all; the rest backed water and fled. For a time the victors gave chase; then, since night was falling, they turned back to the disabled ships, took most of the enemy's as prizes, and salvaged all of their own—they had themselves suffered no less than eighty islands put out of action. To commemorate the naval victory they planted a monument on the whale's head, an enemy island nailed to a stake.

The victors moored their fleet for the night just off the beast, the sterns held by lines made fast to its flanks and the prows by anchors (they use big, powerful ones made of glass). The following day, after making a burnt offering on the whale's back and burying their dead there, they sailed off in the best of spirits, singing some sort of song of victory.

And so ended the battle of the islands.

PART II

Fed up with our stay in the whale and unable to bear
the life there any longer, I cast about for some way to
escape. My first thought was to get out by tunneling
through the starboard flank, and we began to hack away.
However, after penetrating over half a mile without get-
ting anywhere, we stopped digging and decided to start
a forest fire instead. This, we figured, would kill the whale
and, once that happened, a way out would be simple. So,
beginning at the tail, we set a raging fire going. For seven
days and nights the beast showed no reaction to the heat.
On the eighth and ninth we could tell it was getting sick:
it opened its mouth very slowly and each time quickly
shut it again. On the tenth and eleventh necrosis finally
set in and the body began to putrefy. On the twelfth we
realized just in time that, unless we took advantage of a
mouth-opening to prop the jaws apart so they couldn't be
closed again, we were in danger of being locked up inside
and dying along with the beast. So we braced the mouth
open with huge beams and made our vessel ready for sea,
putting aboard all the water and provisions it could carry.
Scintharus was to be our navigator and helmsman.

The next day the whale was dead. We hauled the ship
forward and worked it through a gap between the teeth.
There, by slacking off on lines made fast to the teeth, we
slowly lowered it into the sea. Then we climbed on the
whale's back and, near where the giants' monument stood,
offered up a sacrifice to Poseidon. Since there was no wind
we camped there for three days. On the fourth we set off
and en route ran into a great many corpses from the naval
battle and kept going aground on them. We took the meas-
urements of the bodies and were astonished.

A moderate wind carried us along for a few days. Then
a strong northerly began to blow, bringing bitter cold and
freezing the sea solid, not only on the surface but three

hundred fathoms deep as well, so that we were able to leave the boat and run about on the ice. When the wind persisted and we could no longer bear it, we solved the problem by following a suggestion of Scintharus': we excavated a large cave in the ice and stayed in it for a month, keeping a fire going and eating the fish we had found while digging. Eventually our food ran out, so we emerged, pulled the ship free from where it had been frozen in, and, raising sail, glided easily and smoothly over the ice just as if we were traveling over water. Four days later the weather turned warm, the ice thawed, and all was water again.

After covering somewhat over thirty miles we put in at a small deserted island. Here we replenished our water supply, which had run out, and shot down two wild bulls. These had horns, not on the head, but under the eyes, just where Momus had argued horns ought to be.[12] We sailed away and before long left salt water and entered a sea of milk. In it was visible a white, vine-covered island which proved to be, as we found out later when we ate some of it, an enormous solid piece of cheese three miles around. The vines were full of clusters; we pressed some and got milk to drink instead of wine. In the center of the island was a shrine dedicated, as its inscription indicated, to Galatea,[13] the sea nymph. During the whole of our stay there the ground furnished our bread and meat and the vine-milk our drink. We heard that Salmoneus' daughter Tyro[14] was queen of the place; Poseidon had given her the appointment after he let her go.

We spent five days on the island and then sailed away before a light breeze over a gentle sea. Two days later we were out of the milk and back in blue salt water. Here we caught sight of a great number of men running about on the surface of the sea. They were like us in body, size, and every other respect except feet: theirs were of cork, and I presume this is why they were called "Corkfoots." We were amazed at the way they traveled fearlessly over

the tops of the waves without going under. They came
toward us and, greeting us in Greek, told us they were
hurrying to their homeland, Cork. For a while they ran
alongside and kept us company; then, after wishing us bon
voyage, they turned off to head in their own direction.

Soon a great many islands came into view. Nearby, to
port, was the Cork our friends were hurrying to, a town
built on a large dome-shaped piece of cork. Farther on,
and more to starboard, five enormous islands towered up-
ward; huge flames were spurting from their summits.
Dead ahead, over fifty miles away, was a low, flat island.
When we finally came within range, we were caressed by
a marvelous offshore wind, sweetly scented like the breeze
the historian Herodotus tells us carries the perfume of
southern Araby.[15] For it was like a blend of the fragrance
of roses, narcissuses, hyacinths, lilies, and violets, plus
myrrh, laurel, and wild-grape blooms. Soon we drew near,
breathing in the aroma joyfully and looking forward to a
respite from our long succession of hardships. We could
see any number of harbors, all capacious and sheltered on
every side, crystal-clear rivers flowing placidly toward the
sea, meadows, woods, and a multitude of songbirds, some
warbling on the shore and many in the trees. An atmos-
phere rare and pure pervaded the place. Sweet, gently
blowing breezes stirred the trees, and the movement of
the leaves produced a continuous melodic whistling like
the sound from a shepherd's pipe in some deserted spot.
And we could hear the mingled noises of a crowd, not a
confused babel, but as at a banquet when some are play-
ing music, some singing, and others beating time to the
flute or lyre.

Entranced by it all, we headed for shore, moored, and
disembarked, leaving Scintharus and two others in the
boat. Advancing through a meadow filled with flowers, we
ran into the local guards and sentries who bound us with
rose garlands—the strongest fetters used there—and took us
to their ruler. On the way we learned from them that the

place was called the Isle of the Blest and that Rhadaman-
thus of Crete ruled it.[16] Sure enough, we were brought
before him, and our hearing was put fourth on his docket.
In the first case the defendant was Ajax the Greater:[17]
charged with having gone mad and committed suicide, he
was being tried to determine whether he should be allowed
to associate with the Heroes. After a good deal of debate
Rhadamanthus finally handed down his verdict: for the
present Ajax was to take a dose of hellebore[18] and be
turned over to Dr. Hippocrates; later, when he had re-
gained his sanity, he could attend the daily Heroes' ban-
quet. The second involved the eternal triangle: a wrangle
between Theseus[19] and Menelaus over which of them
Helen should live with. Rhadamanthus decided in favor
of Menelaus because of all the trouble and danger he had
gone through on behalf of his marriage, plus the fact that
Theseus had a number of other wives, the Amazon girl
and Minos' daughters. The third was an argument between
Alexander the Great and Hannibal of Carthage over pre-
cedence; judgment was in favor of Alexander, and a
throne was set up for him alongside Cyrus the Elder of
Persia.[20]

The fourth case was ours. We were brought before
Rhadamanthus; he asked us how it was we had set foot on
hallowed soil while still alive, and we gave him a complete
account of our adventures. He then had us removed and
deliberated for a long time with his associate justices—
quite a few shared the bench with him, including Athens'
Aristides the Just.[21] He closed the discussion, and they
handed down their verdict: after death we were to stand
trial for leaving home and meddling; for the present, how-
ever, we could remain a specified time on the island, at-
tend the Heroes' banquet, and then leave. Our departure
date was set at not more than seven months hence.

The next thing we knew, our fetters of flowers had fallen
from us of their own accord and we were being led toward
the city and the banquet of the blest. Now this city is all

of gold and encircled by walls of emerald. There are seven gates, each made from a solid piece of cinnamonwood. The city rests on foundations of ivory, and the entire area within the walls is paved with ivory. All the gods have temples built of beryl; inside each is an altar made of a huge single block of amethyst, on which the hecatombs are offered up. Around the city flows a river of the finest myrrh, almost two hundred feet wide and deep enough to swim in comfortably. The baths are large chambers of glass heated by cinnamonwood fires; instead of water the tubs are filled with warm dew. All clothing is made of finespun purple cobwebs.

The inhabitants are disembodied, i.e., they are without flesh or substance. They do have a discernible outline and form but no more than this. In spite of having no body, they stand and move, think and talk; in short, it's as if their naked souls were walking about clad in the semblance of their bodies. Without testing them by touch, you would never know you weren't looking at actual bodies; they're like shadows but shadows that stand erect and have color. They never grow old but remain the age they were when they arrived.

The island experiences neither night nor the full light of day. Something like the bright gray we see preceding the dawn, when the sun hasn't yet risen, illuminates the place at all times. There is only one season of the year, an eternal spring, and only one wind blows, the Zephyr. The countryside is lush with every variety of flower and of fruit and shade tree. The vines bear twelve times a year and are harvested monthly. The pomegranate, apple, and other fruit trees bear, we were told, thirteen times a year since they bear twice during Minosmonth, as it's called in the local calendar. Instead of wheat the grain stalks are tipped with loaves of bread like mushrooms. Around the city are 365 springs of water, 365 of honey, and 500 of myrrh (smaller, however, than the others), plus seven rivers of milk and eight of wine.

The Heroes' banquet is held on the outskirts of town in what is called the Elysian Field, a lovely meadow in the center of a thick stand of trees of every kind which shade the diners. The couches are mounds of flowers. The winds wait on table and serve everything except wine. There's no need to serve this—the banqueting area is surrounded by large glass trees of the finest crystal whose fruit is wine-glasses of all sizes and shapes; as each Hero takes his place at table, he harvests one or two, puts them by his setting, and they immediately fill themselves up. This takes care of the wine; for garlands the nightingales and other song-birds gather in their bills flowers from the nearby meadows and, hovering overhead and warbling sweetly, let them flutter down like snowflakes. And perfume is provided as follows: thick clouds suck up myrrh from the five hundred springs and the river, float over the banqueters, and, squeezed gently by the wind, send it down in a fine rain like the dew.

At table ample time is given over to music and singing. The songs are mostly from the epics of Homer (who is there in person, taking part in the festivities; his seat is just above Odysseus'). There's a boys' and a girls' chorus. The leaders, who also provide the musical accompaniment, are Locris' Eunomus, Lesbos' Arion, Anacreon, and Ste-sichorus (I actually saw him: since Helen had by this time forgiven him, he was one of the company).[22] When these choruses finish, a relief chorus of swans, swallows, and nightingales takes over and sings to a musical accompaniment supplied by the whole forest under the leadership of the wind. What chiefly ensures a good time for all, how-ever, is this: right beside the banquet area are two springs, one of laughter and the other of joy; inasmuch as all the guests begin the feast with a drink from each, they spend the rest of the time laughing and enjoying themselves.

I want to mention some of the celebrities I saw there. All the demigods were present, plus all the veterans of the Trojan War except Ajax the Lesser;[23] he, we were told,

was the only one from either army undergoing punishment
in the Land of the Damned. Of the non-Greeks, there were
Cyrus the Elder and Younger, Scythia's Anacharsis,
Thrace's Zamolxis, and Italy's Numa.[24] Also present were
Sparta's Lycurgus, Athens' Phocion and Tellus, and all the
Sages except Periander.[25] I saw Socrates chatting with
Nestor and Palamedes amid a circle of good-looking boys,
among whom were Hyacinth, Narcissus, and Hylas.[26] I
got the impression Hylas was the one he was in love with;
at least it was mostly Hylas he was refuting. We heard
that Rhadamanthus was annoyed with him and had
threatened a number of times to throw him off the island
if he kept on with his nonsense and refused to give up his
Socratic irony and have fun. Plato wasn't there—the only
one missing; they told us he was living in the republic he
had invented, running it with the constitution and laws he
had written. Aristippus and Epicurus were not only there
but were the island's favorites—they were such nice, pleas-
ant fellows and such good company at parties.[27] I saw
Aesop, who's assigned the role of buffoon at the banquets,
and Diogenes, so changed in his ways that he had married
Lais the courtesan[28] and gone in for drink; he was always
getting up from the table to go into a dance or other alco-
holic carryings-on. None of the Stoics was there: we were
told that Chrysippus had been denied permission to enter
the island until he had had his fourth dose of hellebore,
and all the others were still toiling up the straight and
narrow path to virtue.[29] We heard that the people of the
Academy wanted to come but were still holding off and
arguing; the one point they couldn't come to any conclu-
sion about was whether an island such as this existed. Be-
sides, I imagine they were afraid to stand judgment before
Rhadamanthus; after all, they were the ones who denied
all standards of judgment.[30] Rumor had it that a big
group of them once did follow the people who were head-
ing here but, being dawdlers and lacking the courage of

conviction, fell behind and turned back at the halfway point.

These were the chief celebrities. Of them all the most respected was Achilles and, after him, Theseus.

Their attitude on sex and making love is as follows. They have intercourse with both males and females, and in public with everybody looking on; this doesn't strike them as anything to be the least bit ashamed of. Socrates is an exception. He swore up and down that his relations with young men were of the purest—and everybody there accused him of perjuring himself; as a matter of fact, he still insisted on it even after Hyacinth and Narcissus had a number of times confessed the truth. They all share women in common ungrudgingly; on this point they're perfect Platonists. And young boys offer themselves without hesitation to whoever wants them.

I didn't let more than two or three days go by before I went to see Homer at a time when neither of us was busy and quizzed him at length.[31] I made a point of asking him where his birthplace was, explaining that it was a matter people were still trying hard to settle at this late date. He told me he was aware that some thought it was Chios, others Smyrna, and most Colophon, but actually he was a Babylonian; his real name was Tigranes and he only changed it to Homer when he was later sent as a hostage (*homeros*) to Greece. Next I asked him about the verses marked by editors as spurious: had he written them? His answer was yes, every one; this made me realize what a lot of nonsense Professors Zenodotus and Aristarchus[32] had written. Since he had satisfied me on these points, I then asked why he had started the *Iliad* with the words "Sing of the wrath."[33] For no particular reason, he replied; it had just come into his head that way. I also wanted to know whether he had written the *Odyssey* before the *Iliad* as is generally held, and the answer was no. And he's not blind, as is also generally believed; I knew that immediately—I didn't have to ask; I could see it with my own eyes. I quizzed him like this on a number of occasions later on as well, whenever I saw he had time to spare, and he answered all my questions readily—particularly after his success in the lawsuit. This was an action for criminal assault brought by Thersites[34] on the grounds that the poet had jeered at him in the *Iliad;* Homer retained Odysseus as attorney and won the case.

About this time Pythagoras arrived; having gone through his seventh metamorphosis and seventh mortal existence, he was finally finished with the transmigrations of his soul. The whole right side of his body was of gold. He was judged qualified to join the company, although even when I left there was still uncertainty under what name, whether Pythagoras or Euphorbus. Then Empedocles showed up, cooked through and through, his whole body roasted. In spite of all his begging he was denied admission.[35]

Time passed, and the date came around for the athletic contests they call the Mortuaric Games. The board of commissioners consisted of Achilles, serving his fifth consecutive term, and Theseus, serving his seventh. To go through the whole program would take too long, so I'll report on only the most important events. In wrestling Carus, one of Heracles' descendants, threw Odysseus to take the championship.[36] In boxing Areus, the Egyptian whose grave is in Corinth, was paired with Epeus, and the match ended in a draw.[37] Combined boxing and wrestling wasn't on the program; they don't go in for it. I can't remember any longer who was the winner in track. In the poets' contest Hesiod was awarded the victory, although Homer actually won by a wide margin.[38] The prizes for all events were crowns made of plaited peacock feathers.

The games had scarcely ended when word came that the condemned in the Land of the Damned had broken their chains and overpowered the guards and were advancing on the island; the ringleaders were the Sicilian dictator Phalaris, the Egyptian despot Busiris, the Thracian despot

Diomed, plus Sciron and Pityocamptes.[39] On receiving the
news, Rhadamanthus mobilized the Heroes, and they
formed up on the shore; the commanding officers were
Theseus, Achilles, and Ajax, who had by now recovered
his sanity. Battle was joined and the Heroes won, with
most of the credit going to Achilles. Socrates also distin-
guished himself in action, much more than he had at
Delium during his lifetime.[40] He was stationed on the right
wing and, when four of the enemy charged him, he didn't
retreat; he never once turned his back. For this he was
afterward awarded a lovely, spacious estate in the suburbs
where he would gather his disciples and hold dialogues
with them; he named the place Post Mortem Academy.[41]
The defeated forces were rounded up and sent back in
irons to serve even stiffer sentences. Homer wrote an epic
about the fight and, when I left, gave me the manuscript
to bring to the people on earth, but I subsequently lost it
along with everything else. The first line went:

> Sing to me this time, O Muse, of the war fought by
> ghosts of the Heroes.[42]

After the battle they declared a holiday and, as is the
custom whenever they win a war, cooked up beans for a
great victory feast. Everyone took part except Pythagoras,
who sat by himself and went hungry since he can't stand
bean food.

Six months had passed and we were in the middle of
the seventh when an unexpected situation arose. For some
time Scintharus' son Cinyras, a big, handsome boy, had
been in love with Helen, and it wasn't hard to see that she
was madly in love with him. In fact, time and again dur-
ing the banqueting they would exchange signals or drink
to each other or get up, just the two of them, and go
wandering in the forest. The boy was so much in love that
the moment came when he lost his head and made plans
to abduct her—she was perfectly agreeable—and escape to
one of the surrounding islands, either Cork or the Isle of

Cheese. Well in advance they swore in the three most reck-
less men in my crew as accomplices. To his father Cinyras
didn't mention a word; he knew the old man would have
put a stop to the whole business. When the time seemed
right they put their plan into action. After nightfall—I
wasn't there; I was still at the banquet where I happened
to have dozed off—giving everybody the slip, Cinyras
smuggled Helen aboard our ship and quickly got under
way. Toward midnight Menelaus woke up and, seeing his
wife's bed empty, raised a hue and cry, routed out his
brother,[43] and hurried to the chief authority, Rhadaman-
thus. When day dawned the lookouts reported they
could see the ship well out to sea. So Rhadamanthus or-
dered fifty Heroes to take one of their men-of-war (galleys
hewn from a single stalk of asphodel) and give chase. By
rowing hard they caught up around noon, just as the run-
aways were about to enter the sea of milk near the Isle
of Cheese; that's how close they had come to making their
escape. The ship was taken in tow with a hawser of roses,
and everybody returned. Helen was in tears and hid her
face in shame. Cinyras and his accomplices were brought
to Rhadamanthus who, before passing sentence, asked
them whether there were any more in on the scheme; when
they said no, he had them bound by the penis, flogged
with mallow, and sent off to the Land of the Damned.
The Assembly of Heroes then voted to expel us from the
island before our time was up; we could stay the next day
and no longer.

This filled me with dismay; I broke into tears at the
thought of leaving such a good life and becoming a wan-
derer again. They consoled me with the assurance that I
would be back before many years had passed, and even
pointed out my future assembly seat and banquet couch,
both in choice locations. I called on Rhadamanthus and
begged him to tell me my future and show me my route.[44]
He vouchsafed that, after a good deal of wandering and
danger, I would eventually return home, but he refused

to add how long it would take. However, he did point to
the surrounding islands—five were visible nearby and a
sixth in the distance—and say, "These five, the ones you
see spurting great flames, are where the damned are. That
sixth is the City of Dreams. Beyond it is Calypso's is-
land,[45] but you can't make it out from here. After sailing
past all these you will come to the vast continent that lies
across the sea from Europe.[46] There you will have many
adventures, pass through various lands, and live among
hostile peoples before you finally reach your own con-
tinent."

This was all he would tell. But he plucked a mal-
low root from the ground and, handing it to me, told
me to pray to it when we were in mortal danger. And
he warned me, when I did reach the land across the sea,
not to poke fires with a sword, eat beans, or make love
to boys over eighteen;[47] if I kept these rules in mind, I
could look forward to making my return to his island.

So I made the ship ready for sea and, when it was
banquet time, had my final feast with the Heroes. The fol-
lowing day I went to see Homer and asked him to compose
a two-line memorial for me. He did so, and I had it in-
scribed on a slab of beryl which I set up on the water
front. The inscription read:

Lucian, a man who is dear to the blessed immortals in
     heaven,
Witnessed the things that are here, then returned to his
     dearly loved homeland.

We stayed that day as well and the following morning,
with all the Heroes on hand to see us off, sailed away. At
the last minute, while Penelope wasn't looking, Odysseus
came up to me and handed me a letter to deliver to
Calypso in Ogygia. Rhadamanthus had Nauplius[48] the
ferryman go along with us so that, in case we stopped
off at the islands of the damned, we wouldn't be mistaken
for the usual callers and arrested.

We passed out of range of the island's breeze, and the fragrance was suddenly replaced by a stink like burning asphalt, sulphur, and pitch combined. In addition there was an unbearable odor of human flesh roasting. The air was murky and misty, and a pitchy dew dripped steadily down. We could hear the crack of whips and the screams of a great many men.

Of these islands I will describe only the one we went ashore on; we didn't go near the others. It was a parched expanse of jagged stone without a tree or spring on it, girdled by sheer rock walls. We managed to creep up along ledges and made our way inland by a path full of prickles and thorns over a revoltingly ugly countryside. We came up to the prison and punishmentarium, and the first thing to astonish us was the nature of the place. The very ground was carpeted with knife points and thorns. Three rivers ringed the area: the outer of slime, the middle of blood, and the inner of fire. This last was a vast and impassable body that flowed like water, had waves like the sea, and was full of fish, some of which looked like torches and others, a smaller variety called candlefish, like glowing coals. There was only one narrow entrance way across all three, and the man on guard at the gate was Timon of Athens.[49] With Nauplius in the lead, however, we got through and witnessed the condemned undergoing punishment. There were plenty of kings as well as ordinary people; we even recognized some faces among the latter. We also spotted Cinyras hanging by the penis and smoldering over a slow fire. Guides took us around and, for each case, filled in the biographical data and reasons for punishment. The stiffest sentences of all were being served by those who, in life, had been liars or had written books that didn't tell the truth; Ctesias, Herodotus, and a good many others were in this group. The sight of them gave me high hopes for my own future: I knew in my heart that I had never told a lie. But I couldn't take any more of the sight, so I rushed back to the ship, said good-by to Nauplius, and sailed away.

Soon we sighted, not far off, the Isle of Dreams, dim and hard to make out. It behaved very much the way dreams do: as we approached, it receded, moving further away and eluding us. Eventually we caught up and sailed into what is called Sleepy Harbor, situated near the ivory gates and the spot where the Shrine of the Holy Rooster stands. Late in the afternoon we went ashore, entered the city, and were confronted by hosts of dreams of all kinds.

I want first to describe the city itself, since no one else has ever written about it except Homer, who does little more than mention it and not very accurately at that.[50] It's completely surrounded by a forest of lofty poppy and mandrake trees where hordes of bats, the only species of bird on the island, roost. Alongside flows Nightway River, as it's named, and by the gates are two springs called Sleepytime and Allnight. The city wall is high and gaily painted the colors of the rainbow. There are four gates, not two as Homer says. One of iron and one of ceramic lead to Drowsy Meadow; we were told that nightmares and dreams of murder and violence leave by these. Then two others lead to the water front and the sea, one of horn and the one we came through, of ivory. As you enter the city, on the right is the Temple of Night—Night is one of the two chief local deities; the other is the Holy Rooster whose shrine is near the water front—and, on the left, the palace of Sleep. Sleep is king of the place along with two subordinates chosen by him, Prince A. Confusing Revery and Prince I. Dreamof Wealth. In the middle of the main square is a spring called Fount Snoreful. Nearby are the twin temples of Trick and Truth as well as the holy of holies and the local seat of prophecy. This last is in the hands of Antiphon,[51] the interpreter of dreams, who also delivers the oracles; he received his appointment from Sleep.

As for the dreams, no two are alike in either character

or appearance. Some are tall, with good figures and good looks, others short and ugly; some are golden (that was my impression, at least), others plain and cheap. There were dreams with wings, freakish dreams, and dreams which, dressed up like kings, queens, gods, and the like, looked as if they were going to a carnival. Many we recognized because we had seen them long ago. These actually came up and greeted us like old friends, then invited us to their homes and, putting us to sleep, extended us the warmest and most generous hospitality, including lavish entertainment of every sort plus a promise to make us kings and princes. Some of them even led us to our homelands, gave us a look at our families, and brought us back, all the same day. We stayed a month among them, regaling ourselves with slumber. Then a sudden clap of thunder awoke us; we sprang up, provisioned the ship, and sailed off.

Three days later we put in at Ogygia and disembarked. The first thing I did was to open Odysseus' letter and read it. Here is what it said:

Dear Calypso,

Let me tell you what happened to me. Right after I finished the raft and sailed away from you, I was shipwrecked, and Leucothea barely managed to rescue me and bring me to Phaeacia. The Phaeacians escorted me home and there I found a mob of my wife's suitors living high, wide, and handsome at my expense. I killed them all, and Telegonus, the son I had by Circe, later on killed me. Now I'm on the Isle of the Blest full of regrets at having given up my life with you and the immortality you offered me. If I ever get the chance, I'll run away and come to you.

This is how the letter read, except for a postscript about us, a request to furnish us hospitality. I went a short distance in from the beach and came upon the cave—it was just as Homer had described it—and the lady herself busy.

with her spinning. She took the letter, read it, and had a
good long cry. But then she invited us to be her guests
and, in the course of serving us a fine dinner, quizzed us
about Penelope as well as Odysseus: What did she look
like? Was she as discreet as Odysseus used to brag she
was? We gave her the answers we imagined she wanted
to hear.

Afterward we went back to the ship and camped for
the night alongside it on the beach. At dawn we set off
with a strong wind driving us on. For two days we were
buffeted about and then, on the third, ran into the Pump-
kinpirates. These are savages from the neighboring islands
who prey upon all passing traffic. Their ships are enor-
mous pumpkins, ninety feet long, which they make into
boats by removing the pulp to leave just a hollow shell,
drying thoroughly, and stepping a reed mast with a pump-
kin leaf for a sail instead of a piece of canvas. They at-
tacked with two detachments of marines who, by firing
pumpkin seeds instead of stones, wounded quite a few of
us. The battle went on with neither side gaining until,
about noon, we noticed the Sailingnuts coming up on the
Pumpkinpirates' rear. The next moment made clear that
the two were enemies. For, as soon as our opponents real-
ized who were heading their way, they forgot all about
us, put about, and engaged the new foe. We seized the
occasion to raise sail and flee, leaving the two of them to
fight it out. The Sailingnuts were sure to win since there
were more of them—they had five detachments of marines
—and they were fighting from stronger ships. These, made
from the shells of nuts cracked in half and scooped out,
were each thirty yards long.

As soon as they were out of sight we attended to our
wounded. From that moment on we generally kept our-
selves fully armed in the constant expectation of attack—
and not for nothing; just before sunset, from the shore of
a barren island a second band of pirates dashed out at
us, this time twenty or so men riding big dolphins. The

dolphins, rearing and neighing just like horses, carried them in perfect safety. When they came within range they divided their forces and, from both sides at once, peppered us with dried cuttlefish and crabs' eyes. We replied with a volley of arrows and javelins which they couldn't stand up to; they fled back to their island, most of them nursing wounds.

About midnight, in a calm sea, before we realized what was happening we ran aground on an immense kingfisher's nest, no less than seven miles around.[52] The kingfisher, not much smaller than the nest, was sailing along on it, hatching her eggs. She flew away in fright with a mournful cry, and the stream from her wings as she took off nearly capsized our ship. When day dawned we climbed into the nest and saw that it was constructed of huge logs, very much like a raft. There were five hundred eggs, each larger than a seven-gallon jug. The chicks inside were already alive and croaking away. As a matter of fact, we hacked one of the eggs open with axes and hatched out a chick that, even without feathers, was twenty times as big as a buzzard.

We had sailed a little over twenty miles from the nest when a series of tremendous miracles left their mark on us. The figurehead of the goose on our stern suddenly flapped its wings and honked; our helmsman Scintharus, who had been bald for years, grew a shock of hair; and, strangest of all, the mast burst into bloom, sprouting branches at its sides and bearing fruit at its tip, figs and a cluster of dark grapes not quite ripe. The sight naturally left us in consternation; we prayed to the gods at these singular apparitions.

A little over fifty miles further on we sighted a vast and thick forest of pine and cypress. We figured it was land, but it turned out to be a bottomless sea overgrown with rootless trees. In spite of this the trees stood firm and erect, as if floating upright. When we drew near and sized up the situation, we were in a quandary as to what to do: to sail

through the trees was impossible—they were too thickly
massed—nor did it seem any easier to go back the way we
had come. I climbed to the top of the tallest tree and took
a look at what lay beyond. I could see that the forest
stretched for only five miles or a bit more, and after that
was more ocean. So we decided to set the ship on the
solidly matted foliage of the treetops and see if we couldn't
transport it that way to the water on the other side. And
so we did: we made a heavy cable fast to the vessel,
heaved and hauled until we had swayed it up, set it on
the treetops, and, hoisting sail, were drawn along by the
force of the wind just as on water. At this point I was
minded of a line by Antimachus;[53] somewhere he writes of

> Those who arrived after setting a course through the
> shadowy forest.

Having forced our way through the forest, we arrived
at open water and, using the same technique, lowered the
ship into it. We sailed on over a crystal-clear sea until
we came to a point where the water had parted to form a
vast chasm like the fissures, caused by earthquake, that
we so often see on land. We doused sail and the ship lost
way just inches short of going over the brink. Leaning
over, we peered down to a depth of more than a hundred
miles. It was a weird and frightening sight—the sea stood
fixed on each side as if split apart. We then looked about
us and noticed that, not too far off on the right, the chasm
was spanned by a bridge of water which, joining the sur-
face of the sea on either side, flowed from the one into the
other. So we ran out the oars, drove the ship over the
bridge, and, after a grueling struggle, completed a cross-
ing we had never expected to make.

On the other side we were met by a calm sea and an
island of no great size, inhabited and easy to approach.
The natives, a race of savages called Bullheads, had horns
and looked like the mental image we have of the Minotaur.
We disembarked and headed inland to see if we could se-

cure water and provisions somewhere, for we had run out of both. We found water nearby but nothing else. However, we did hear not far off a great bellowing. Thinking it was a herd of bulls, we inched forward and came upon the Bullheads. The minute they saw us they charged and managed to snatch three of my men; the rest of us made it back to the sea. We armed ourselves—we had no intention of leaving our comrades go unavenged—and then fell on the Bullheads as they were dividing up the flesh of the men they had killed. They scattered in fear, and we went after them. After cutting down about fifty and taking two alive, we returned to the shore with our prisoners.

We still hadn't found any food. All my shipmates were in favor of slaughtering the two captives, but I didn't approve. Instead, I tied the pair up and kept them under guard until a delegation arrived from the Bullheads bringing an offer of ransom. We could make out what they were after from the way they nodded their heads and bellowed mournfully, as if pleading. The ransom consisted of a big batch of cheeses, dried fish, onions, and four deer of a species which had only three feet—two in back but in front, where the forelegs had fused, only one. We accepted these terms, surrendered our prisoners, and, after spending a day on the island, sailed off.

By now we were seeing fish, birds were flying by, and many other signs that we were nearing land kept appearing. A little farther along we saw men using a novel method to travel over water, one in which they were boat and passenger at one and the same time. This is the way it was done: a man would lie on his back in the water, induce an erection, hoist a sail on it (their penises were enormous), and, holding the sheets in his hands, bowl along before the wind. Behind these came others sitting on pieces of cork and driving, reins in hand, teams of dolphins; these plunged ahead, pulling the corks behind them. None of these people harmed us or fled from us; they continued fearlessly and peaceably on their way after looking our ship over from all sides and registering astonishment at its shape.

Toward evening we arrived at an island of middling size. It was inhabited by women—at least so we thought. They spoke Greek, as we discovered when they came up to greet us and bid us welcome. They were all beautiful and young, heavily made up the way courtesans are, and dressed in flowing gowns that swept the ground. The place was called Nag Island and the city Waterburg. Each of the women paired off with one of my men and, leading him to her house, made him her guest. I held back a bit—I had a premonition all was not well. Looking about me more closely, I caught sight of piles of human bones and skulls lying about. But to raise an alarm, gather my men, and make a rush for our arms didn't seem the thing to do. Instead I took out my mallow and prayed to it long and hard to rescue us from the tight spot we were in. A little while later, as my hostess was serving me, I got a glimpse of her legs—and they weren't a woman's limbs but a donkey's shanks. Drawing my sword, I seized her and tied her up. Then I interrogated her thoroughly. Very reluctantly she admitted to me that she and the others were women of the sea called Asslegs and that their food was the strangers who came to the island. "We get them drunk," she explained, "go to bed with them, and then attack them in their sleep." The minute I heard this I left her there trussed up and, climbing on the roof, summoned my shipmates with a shout. When I had gotten them together, I told them the whole story, pointed out the bones, and led them inside to my prisoner. She dissolved into water on the spot and disappeared. However, just as a test, I thrust my sword into it—and it turned into blood.

We rushed back to the ship and sailed off. When day dawned we sighted a continent that we took to be the one across the ocean from Europe. After falling on our knees and praying, we held a council about the future. Some of us felt we should merely step ashore and then turn right around and sail back; others held we should leave the ship and proceed into the interior to see what the natives were like. In the midst of the discussion a violent storm broke which dashed our ship on the beach and smashed it to pieces. We barely managed to swim to safety, each of us clutching his weapons and anything else he could carry.

You now know our story up to the moment we reached this new continent: our adventures on the sea, during our trip around the islands, in the air, and, after that, inside the whale; then, after escaping from there, our further adventures among the Heroes, the dreams, and, finally, the Bullheads and Asslegs. What happened to us on the new continent I will tell in the subsequent volumes.[54]

NOTES

[1] *Odyssey*, Books 9–12.

[2] A crack at Plato's Myth of Er told in Book 10 of *The Republic*.

[3] The Greeks drank their wine mixed with water; only alcoholics took it straight.

[4] Daphne was a nymph who resisted Apollo's advances and was changed into a laurel tree to be kept safe from him.

[5] Selene, goddess of the moon, seeing the beautiful youth Endymion asleep, fell passionately in love with him.

[6] Son of Apollo who was god of the sun.

[7] Mallow juice was used to *heal* wounds.

[8] *Iliad* 16.459. Sarpedon, Zeus's son by a mortal mother, was slain by Patroclus.

[9] A crack at the Athenian Assembly which did just this on at least one historic occasion during the famous Peloponnesian War.

[10] The Greek word for comet literally means "long-haired."

[11] In his *Birds*, Aristophanes has the birds create an empire in the air and build there a fully equipped capital named Cloudcuckooland.

[12] Momus (see p. 98) had criticized Poseidon, the creator of bulls, for not putting the horns where the animal could see what it was doing with them.

[13] A pun: *gala* is the Greek word for "milk." For Galatea, see p. 121.

[14] Another pun: *tyros* is the Greek word for "cheese." For Tyro, see p. 206, n. 1.

[15] Herodotus 3.113.

[16] For Rhadamanthus and other post-mortem officials, see p. 173.

[17] The Trojan War hero who, when the dead Achilles' arms were given to Odysseus, was so outraged he went mad and killed himself.

[18] The standard ancient remedy for mental disorders.

[19] Cf. p. 120, n. 9. Helen came early in Theseus' career. His later conquests included the Amazon Hippolyta and Minos' daughters Phaedra and Ariadne.

[20] See p. 210, n. 4.

[21] See p. 169, n. 48.

[22] Eunomus and Arion were semihistorical renowned minstrels, Anacreon and Stesichorus famous early lyric poets. There was a legend that Stesichorus wrote a lampoon against Helen which her brothers, Castor and Pollux, forced him to retract.

[23] Wrecked and drowned by Poseidon for his insolence.

[24] Cyrus the Younger, a brilliant and engaging Persian prince, started the expedition (401 B.C.) immortalized in Xenophon's *Anabasis*. Anacharsis, an enterprising South Russian princeling (6th century B.C.) interested in broadening his horizons, visited Athens and studied under Solon. Zamolxis was a slave of Pythagoras; returning to his native Thrace, he taught his former master's doctrines there and became a local god after death. Numa was a semihistorical king of Rome to whom the Romans ascribed their laws and religion.

[25] Lycurgus was the founder of Sparta's constitution. For Phocion, see p. 169, n. 48; for Tellus, p. 224, and for the Sages, p. 210, n. 8. Periander was often left out of the list.

[26] For Nestor and Palamedes, see p. 211, n. 12; for Narcissus and Hyacinth, p. 206, n. 1. Hylas was the young beauty whom Heracles took with him on the celebrated voyage of the *Argo*.

[27] See p. 211, n. 13.

[28] The notorious Lais had in real life numbered Aristippus among her lovers.

[29] Chrysippus (280–207 B.C.) was the chief figure of the

Stoic school, so called because its founder lectured under the Poecile Stoa (see p. 168, n. 17). Stoicism was an earnest, extremely demanding, moral philosophy which, in Lucian's day at least, made extravagant claims about what it could do for faithful adherents. It taught that all things beyond a man's power to choose—level of birth, physical abilities, and the like —were to be regarded as "indifferent." It held that reason was the guide of life and, consequently, paid great attention to logic and went in for thorny, hair-splitting technical terms. In Lucian's time Stoicism enjoyed a great vogue and numbered many more followers than any of the other schools.

30 I.e., the New Academy whose members were complete skeptics.

31 There was as much wrangling among the ancients about Homer's life and works as there is among us about Shakespeare's. Lucian touches on three key controversies: the poet's birthplace, the genuineness of certain verses, and the relation between the *Iliad* and *Odyssey*.

32 Famous editors (3rd and 2nd centuries B.C.) of Homer's works.

33 A crack at the pedants who insisted on scrutinizing every word of the poems.

34 Thersites was the only buck private Homer mentions—and not very sympathetically (*Iliad* 2.212–20).

35 For Pythagoras and Empedocles, see p. 210, n. 7 and p. 211, n. 9.

36 Carus isn't otherwise known. Odysseus, among his other accomplishments, was a champion wrestler (*Iliad* 23.700–37).

37 Areus was a philosopher at the court of Augustus and presumably a scrawny specimen. Epeus won the boxing crown at the funeral games for Patroclus (*Iliad* 23.664–99).

38 There was an apocryphal popular story to the effect that Hesiod had once won an unfair decision over Homer.

39 Mythical rulers, all masters at particularly gruesome ways of killing people; cf. p. 148 and p. 168, n. 22.

40 At the Battle of Delium (424 B.C.) during the Peloponnesian War the Athenians suffered a signal defeat. Every man in the ranks broke and ran for the nearest exit from battle except Socrates—he walked.

41 The counterpart, presumably, of the famous Academy patronized by the living that his disciple Plato had founded.

42 A parody of the opening line of the *Odyssey*.

43 Agamemnon.

44 What follows is a telescoped parody of Circe's instructions to Odysseus (*Odyssey* 12.37–141).

[45] The goddess with whom Odysseus had a lengthy affair (*Odyssey* 5.1–268).

[46] Stories, many of them tall, were current among the ancients about such a continent. It was vaguely known as the Island of Atlantis.

[47] A parody of the mystic injunctions Pythagoras, who ran a sort of secret society, laid down for his disciples.

[48] The name means "ship-sailer."

[49] See pp. 239–66.

[50] *Odyssey* 19.562–67. Homer mentions little more than the two gates, one of horn for true dreams and one of ivory for false.

[51] The name means "answerer."

[52] It was popularly believed that the kingfisher (*halcyon*) built its nest on the water and that during the days the eggs were hatching—the "halcyon days"—the sea remained perfectly calm.

[53] An epic poet who lived about 400 B.C. None of his works has survived.

[54] The biggest lie of all, as a disappointed ancient scribe noted in the margin of his copy.

LUCIUS, THE ASS

The tale of the man who turned into a donkey occurs in the folklore of a number of nations. Ancient Greece had a version, which supplied the inspiration for this piece as well as for its longer, more elaborate Latin cousin, Apuleius' Golden Ass.

Just as A True Story *was the tall story to end all tall stories,* Lucius, the Ass *is the folk tale to end all folk tales. The traditional elements are here but simply to be mocked. Lucius becomes a donkey through a sort of clerical error; in his new form he distinguishes himself as a combination of Escoffier and Don Juan; the bandits he meets are comic-supplement desperadoes whose views on punishment outdo even those of W. S. Gilbert's* Mikado; *and our hero regains his shape thanks to the public's relish for sophisticated debauchery. Moreover, as so often in Lucian, the mockery rubs shoulders with a deadly seriousness. The episode of the mendicant brethren of the Syrian goddess (pp. 80–83) is cut from the same cloth as* Alexander the Quack Prophet *(see p. 267), and there are telling pictures of human inhumanity to dumb beast that can hardly be paralleled anywhere else in literature before the nineteenth century, when civilization first achieved such things as societies for the prevention of cruelty to animals.*

In the past few centuries many critics have challenged the long-standing tradition that ascribes this work to Lucian. A bitter wrangle has gone on which is still not settled. For our purposes it need never be: the story of Lucius is a celebrated tale; it has Lucian's spirit, and it is good enough to have come from his pen.

I once made a trip to Thessaly to settle with someone there a money matter involved in my father's estate. With a horse to carry me and the bags, and one servant walking behind, I set out along the main route.

As luck would have it, I met up with some fellow travelers headed for Hypata in Thessaly, their home town. Joining forces, we hit it off together, which helped to get us through the long, hard trip. As we neared the town, I inquired whether they knew a man living there by the name of Hipparchus; I had a letter for him from home asking him to put me up. They knew who he was and where he lived, they told me, and then they added that, though he had plenty of money, the only people living with him were his wife and one serving girl, since he was one of the stingiest men alive.

By now we were in the outskirts, and we came upon a very modest cottage surrounded by a garden; it was Hipparchus' house. My companions waved good-by and went off, and I walked up to the door and knocked. It took some time and trouble, but finally the wife heard me and came out.

"Is Hipparchus in?" I asked.

"Yes," she replied. "But who are you? And what do you want with him?"

"I have a letter for him from Professor Decrianus in Patras," I said.

"Wait here," she said, and she closed the door and went back inside. A little later she came out again and invited us in. I entered, greeted Hipparchus, and handed him the letter. He happened to be just starting dinner and was seated on a narrow bench, his wife alongside, in front of a bare table.

"Well," he said, after reading the letter, "I'm glad to see that Decrianus isn't shy about sending his friends to me; he's my own best friend and the finest fellow in all Greece. Lucius, as you see, my cottage is very small, but it's happy to have people under its roof. If you're willing to put up with it and stay, you'll make it feel like a mansion." Then, calling the maid, he said, "Palaestra,[1] fix up a bedroom for my friend here. Bring in any baggage he has, and send him off to the public bath; he's had quite a trip today." The words were hardly out of his mouth when Palaestra led us away and showed us to a most charming little room.

"You sleep on this couch," she said, "and I'll lay out a mat and pillow alongside for your servant." Giving her money to buy feed for the horse, we went off to take our bath. While we were away, she carried in all our gear and left it in the room.

As soon as we had finished at the baths, we came back. Hipparchus welcomed me warmly and invited me to join him at table. We were served a meal that was far from frugal plus a fine old wine, and afterward we had drinks and chatted. Things were no different than at any good dinner party. We spent the evening over the bottle and then went to bed.

Next morning Hipparchus asked me what my travel plans were and whether I would spend the rest of my stay with him. "I'm headed for Larissa," I explained, "but it looks as if I'll be here for three or four days." I was just making this up. I had my heart set on staying in town until I ran down one of the women I had heard about who were experts in witchcraft[2] and got a look at some of their marvels, a man flying, say, or a man turned to stone.

Yielding completely to the passion for a spectacle of this sort, I tramped about the whole town. I had no idea where to begin looking, but I kept walking anyway. Then, at one point in my wanderings, I noticed that a woman was coming toward me. She was still on the young side and, so far as one could tell in the street, well off: she was wearing an embroidered coat, was loaded with gold jewelry, and had a flock of servants at her heels. As she drew near she greeted me. I returned the greeting.

"I'm Abroea," she said, "a friend of your mother's; you may have heard her mention my name. I'm as fond of you

and all her children as I am of my own. Why don't you
come and stay with me, my boy?"

"That's very kind of you," I said, "but I hate to run out
on a friend for no cause. But my thoughts will stay with
you!"

"Where are you staying, anyway?" she asked.

"With Hipparchus."

"The miser?"

"My dear lady, don't say that," I replied. "He's been
so lavish and openhanded with me, a person could accuse
him of extravagance."

She smiled and then, taking me by the hand, led me
off to one side and said into my ear, "Do everything you
can to be on your guard against Hipparchus' wife. She's
not only a terrible witch, she's oversexed; she's always
making eyes at the young men. And, if they don't do what
she says, she uses her magic to get even with them. She's
turned lots of them into animals and even done away with
a few. You're not only young, my boy, you're also good-
looking, the kind women go for on sight. Besides, you're a
stranger in town, and who ever bothers about a missing
stranger?"

When I heard that what I had been searching for all
this time was living under the same roof with me, I had no
more interest in Abroea. The minute I could get away
from her I headed for home, mumbling to myself as I
went, "All right, you're always talking about wanting to
see one of these marvels; now get a move on and figure
out some smart trick to fulfill this passion of yours. Go
after that maid Palaestra—not the wife; keep your dis-
tance from the wife of a friend and host. Take your
clothes off, tumble the girl on the mat, have a preliminary
workout, then grapple a while with her, and, believe me,
you'll find out everything with no trouble at all; servants
know all about their masters, the good things as well as
the bad."

Muttering like this, I made my way to the house. When

I got there I found neither Hipparchus nor his wife at home but only Palaestra, who was standing by the fire, cooking our dinner. I seized the opportunity and said, "Palaestra, my dear, you give your rump and your pot such a nice rhythm as you walk around and bend over. My hips are catching the motion. I envy the man who's had a chance to dip into *that*."

There was nothing backward about this little charmer. "Mister," she answered, "if you've got any sense and want to stay alive, you'll keep away from it. It's steaming hot. You just touch it and you'll get a burn that'll keep you right alongside me forever. You know why? Because no one, not even the god of doctors himself, will be able to cure you; only I, the one who burned you. And the strangest thing of all is, I'll make you want even more. You can be on fire with the pain of the treatment, yet you'll never give it up; stoning won't keep you away from that delicious hurt. What are you laughing for? You're looking at a cook who makes the best roast loin of man there is. I don't use only the common, everyday cuts of meat. I go for the biggest and best—man. I know how to butcher and skin and mince him. My favorite recipe, though, is hot innards and heart."

"It's absolutely true, every word," I said. "Take my case. I was standing over here, nowhere near you, and, so help me, you've not just burned me, you've got me all on fire. You've sent those invisible flames of yours through my eyes deep into me, and my innards are frying. But I never did you any harm, so, for god's sake, use that bittersweet treatment I heard about from your own lips and cure me. I'm already butchered; now take me and skin me; do what you want with me."

This evoked a hearty and most encouraging laugh, and from that moment on she was mine. We arranged that, as soon as she had seen her master and mistress into bed, she would come to my room and spend the night with me.

Eventually Hipparchus returned, and we washed up,

ate, and then had a lot to drink during the after-dinner conversation. Finally I pretended I was sleepy and got up and actually did go to my room. There the preparations were complete: my servant's mat had been spread outside the door; a table with glasses stood by the bed; the wine was ready, and so was the hot and cold water. Palaestra had seen to everything. The bedspread was covered with roses—petals, whole blossoms, garlands. Now that my party was all set, I sat down to wait for my partner. As soon as she had put her mistress to bed she hurried to me, and, what with the kissing and the toasts, we had a gay time. When the drinks had us in the proper mood for the night, Palaestra said, "Don't you forget one thing, mister: this is Palaestra you're dealing with. So now you've got to show me you were one of the tough boys in your gym class and learned lots of wrestling holds."

"You won't catch me running away from a test like that," I replied. "Take your clothes off and let's wrestle."

"You'll put on the exhibition the way I want it," she asserted. "I'll be coach and referee and call for the holds I'm after, and you be ready to follow orders and do whatever I say."

"Order away," I said, "and you'll see a wrestling technique as slick, smooth, and strong as they come."

She got out of her clothes and, standing there stark naked, began to issue orders. "Strip. Rub yourself down with this perfume. Take hold of your opponent. Grab her by both thighs and force her down. Get on top and pin her to the mat. Go between her thighs. Give her a spread-eagle. Lift her legs up, way up. Now let them down a bit and put them in place. Now grapple! Go on in, push, push hard, shove till it hurts. Put your back into it! Now pull out. Now nip in, level, between the thighs; shove in, all the way to the back wall, and flog away. Watch out—she's beginning to weaken. Lean over her, clamp a waist-lock on her, and hold her tight. Try not to hurry—don't be impatient; hold back and wait for her to catch up. All right, now break."

After I had carried out all these instructions without any trouble and we had finished our bout, I said with a laugh, "Well, coach, did you see how obedient and expert a wrestler I was? But watch out—don't start mixing up the holds you ask for; you were calling for all different kinds one after the other."

She slapped my cheek and said, "What a stupid trainee I've got here! *You* watch out that you give me only the holds I ask for or you'll have a lot more slaps coming to you." With this admonition she got to her feet, fixed herself up a bit, and said, "Now show me if you know how to grapple and work on your knees." Then she knelt down on the bed and said, "All right, my champion, you've got your opponent by the middle. The trick is to give her a good shake, drill in, and go deep. Look at her—she's bare and open for attack. Use your chance! Make the standard opening move and clamp a lock on her. Now force her back and go into her. Hold her tight—don't leave an inch of space between you. She's beginning to weaken, so hurry, pick her up and change your position. Bend over and keep banging away—watch out! Don't break till you're told to!—keep her scrunched up till she's moved around. Now lay her out flat, stay in there, and keep pumping. All right, break—your opponent's got her shoulders to the mat; she's gone limp; she's turned to water."

At this I laughed out loud and said, "Coach, now *I* want to call a few holds, and you obey orders. Get off your back. Sit up. Put some oil on your hands and rub the rest of me down. Wipe me off. Now, for god's sake, give me a hug and put me to bed."

So, night after night, we held pleasant wrestling games like this—and both of us kept winning championships. I was having so much fun I forgot all about my trip to Larissa. But then I suddenly remembered to ask the question which had started me on these athletics. "Sweetheart,"

I said to her, "please let me get a look at your mistress practicing her magic and changing her shape. For years I've had my heart set on seeing a marvel like this. Or, if you know how to do these transformations yourself, so much the better; you work the magic and show me all kinds. I have a feeling you're as expert as she is. I haven't heard this from anybody, but my instinct tells me it's so. Look what you did to me: I was always Mr. Ironman, as the girls used to call me; so far as sex was concerned I never gave a woman a second look, and yet you had the witchcraft to lay hands on me, to take my soul prisoner in the battle of love."

"Don't make jokes," she answered. "Magic charms can't produce love. Love is the master charm itself. I swear to you, Lucius darling, by your life and by the happiness we've had on this bed, I don't know a thing about magic. How could I? I never even learned to read or write. Besides, my mistress guards her secrets like any witch. But, if I ever get the chance, I'll try to let you watch her while she goes through one of her magic changes of shape." With this understanding we went to sleep.

A few days later Palaestra reported to me that her mistress was planning to turn herself into a bird in order to fly to her lover. "Palaestra," I said, "here's your chance to do me that favor I've been pleading and begging for and to satisfy this lifelong yearning of mine."

"Don't worry," she replied.

That night she took me by the hand and led me to the room where Hipparchus and his wife were sleeping. She told me to go up to the door and watch through a tiny hole what went on inside. I peeked in and saw Hipparchus' wife taking her clothes off. When she was naked, she walked over to the lamp, took two grains of incense, dropped them into the flame, and, standing in front of it, went through some long mumbo-jumbo. Next she opened a little strongbox which held a lot of small jars, selected one, and took it out. I couldn't tell what was inside, but from the looks of it I imagined it was olive oil. Pouring some out, she smeared her whole body from the tips of her toes up. The next moment wings sprouted from her shoulders, her nose turned into a beak, and she developed all the other characteristics of a bird—she had made herself into an owl. As soon as she was aware that she had wings, with a hair-raising hoot just like an owl's she took off and flew out the window.

I thought I must be dreaming. I kept digging my fingers into my eyes—they were my own eyes but I didn't believe what they saw; I didn't even believe they had been open. It took some doing, but I eventually convinced myself that I wasn't asleep. Then I began to beg Palaestra to let me rub the same magic mixture on myself so I, too, could grow wings and fly. I wanted to experiment and find out whether, if I changed in form from man to bird, my mind would change into a bird's too. So she sneaked into the room and came out with the jar. I stripped in a hurry and smeared myself all over.

Poor me! I didn't turn into a bird at all! My rear sprouted a tail. My fingers and toes vanished somewhere or other; all ten extremities became four, each exactly like a hoof in shape—my hands and feet had turned into an animal's hoofs. My ears grew long. My face grew big. I looked around at myself and saw what I had become—an ass.

I wanted to give Palaestra a tongue-lashing but I couldn't—I no longer had a voice. So I stretched my lip outward and downward and looked upward, the way donkeys do; this was all I could manage to let her know what I thought of her for turning me into an ass instead of a bird. "What have I done?" she moaned. "This is terrible! The jars all looked alike and, in my hurry, I made a mistake—I took some other instead of the one that grows wings! But, sweetheart, don't worry. It's the easiest thing in the world to fix up. All you have to do is eat roses, and the next moment you'll shuck off this animal shape

and I'll have my darling back again. Just put up with
being an ass for this one night, sweetheart, and first thing
in the morning I'll run out and pick you some roses, and
you'll eat them and be all better." As she talked, she fon-
dled my ears and stroked my hide all over.

Though I was an ass in everything else, in mind and
brain I was still a human being—the old Lucius, though a
Lucius without a voice. Cursing Palaestra silently for her
blunder, and biting my lip in chagrin, I went off to where
I knew my horse was stabled along with an ass—a real one
—that belonged to Hipparchus. When they saw me come
in they got worried that I was there to share their feed,
so they laid their ears back and were all set to defend
their bellies with their hoofs. As soon as I realized what
was on their minds, I moved away from the manger and
stood laughing—but no laugh came out, just a bray.

"What a time to go sticking my nose into other people's
business! Suppose a wolf or some other wild animal
should get in here? I've never broken the law in my life—
and I'm in danger of being torn to pieces!"[3] These were
the thoughts that ran through my head. Poor me! When
I had them, I had no idea of all the trouble that was still
to come.

It was now the dead of night. The whole town was
sleeping peacefully, and there wasn't a sound to be heard.
Then, from outside, came a noise as if someone was break-
ing through the garden wall. As a matter of fact, someone
was, and before long there was a hole in it big enough for
a man. A second later a man came through, and then an-
other and another. In no time at all a whole gang was in-
side, all carrying swords. They trussed up Hipparchus,
Palaestra, and my servant in their rooms and leisurely ran-
sacked the house, making off with all the money, clothes,
and furnishings. When there was nothing left inside, they
led us out—me, the horse, and the other ass—put packsad-
dles on us, and tied all their loot on our backs. Then they
headed for the mountains and, clobbering us with sticks,

drove us, loaded down as we were, up a rough, unused path they had chosen for their getaway. I can't tell you how the other two found it, but for me, a beginner at walking barefoot, forced to clamber over those sharp rocks with all that weight on my back, it was a living death. Time and again I stumbled, but I wasn't allowed to fall—someone behind would immediately whack me on the buttocks. Time and again I wanted to cry in desperation, "Oh, lord!" but all that happened was a bray. I managed to get the "Oh" out, and very clearly at that, but I just couldn't follow through with the "lord." Even for this they beat me since my braying advertised their whereabouts. When I realized that all my noise was getting me nowhere, I decided to walk in silence and profit at least by less of the stick.

By now it was daylight, and we had made our way deep into the mountains. They muzzled the three of us so we wouldn't waste any time grazing for breakfast along the roadside. Daybreak had come and gone, and I was still an ass. Around noon they halted at a farmhouse which, to judge by what soon went on, belonged to friends of theirs. For the people from the farm greeted them with handshakes and kisses, invited them to stay, served them lunch, and poured out some barley for us animals. My companions munched away, but I stood there famished: I had never had raw barley before, and I was looking around for something I could eat. Back of the farmhouse I spotted a truck garden full of fine-looking vegetables and, beyond, I could make out rose blossoms. Everybody was busy inside with lunch, so I was able to sneak off and make for the garden without being seen. Not only did I want to fill up on raw vegetables; I wanted to get at the roses as well: I figured that, by swallowing some of the blooms, I could become a man again. Stepping inside, I gorged myself on lettuce, radishes, and celery, the sort of things humans can eat raw. The roses, however, weren't really roses; they were the blossoms of the wild laurel—rhododendron, as we call it—the worst possible food for horse or ass, since people say that eating it means instant death.

At this point the owner heard me and, grabbing a stick, ran into the garden. Catching sight simultaneously of the enemy and the ruin of his vegetables, he put that stick to me with the energy of some rich squire who has caught one of the hated poor stealing; he had no mercy for either my ribs or buttocks, and he even bashed my ears and clobbered my face. Finally I could take no more of it, so I let go a kick with both legs that laid him out flat among those vegetables of his and headed for the mountains. Seeing me running off, he shouted out to let the dogs loose after me. They were a pack of big hounds, strong enough to take on a bear. I was fully aware that, if they ever caught me, they would tear me limb from limb so, after wandering aimlessly for a while, I came to the well-known conclusion that "prudence is the better part of virtue," turned around, and went back to the farmhouse. When the dogs came tearing in after me, the men caught them and tied them up. Then all hands turned to beating me and kept at it until the pain made me puke up all the vegetables I had put down.

When it was time to take to the road again, they piled the biggest and heaviest part of the loot on me, and off we went. By now I was at the end of my rope: I had been thrashed, I was carrying that backbreaking load, and my hoofs were all cut up from the road. I made up my mind to collapse and never get up again even if they beat me to death. I had high hopes for this scheme. I imagined they would admit defeat and, splitting my load between the horse and the other donkey, would leave me lying there for the wolves. But some demon got wind of my plan and turned things completely around. The other ass, perhaps with the same idea in mind, fell down in the road. First the men clobbered the poor thing with sticks and ordered him to get up. When he failed to respond to the beating, one group took him by the ears and another by

the tail, and together they tried to heave him to his feet.
Since this got them nowhere, and he just lay there ex-
hausted in the road, like a stone, they talked it over and
decided that bothering this way with a dead donkey was
a waste not only of energy but of time better spent cover-
ing ground. So, after dividing all the gear he had on his
back between the horse and me, they took this partner of
my bondage and burdens, hacked off his legs with their
swords, and shoved him, still breathing, over a cliff. Down
to his death he spun.

When I saw how my scheme had turned out in my
comrade's case, I decided to be a hero about my aching
hoofs and walk with a will. I had every hope that sooner
or later I would come across some roses and, through
them, my salvation.

I overheard from the bandits' talk that we didn't have
much further to go and that our next stop would be the
last. So, load and all, we proceeded at a trot and just be-
fore evening came to the camp. Inside, by a blazing fire,
an old crone was seated. They brought in all the loot we
had been carrying and then said to her, "What are you
sitting around for? Why aren't you getting dinner ready?"

"It's all ready," she answered. "Plenty of bread, jugs of
good wine, and some game I cooked for you."

"Good work," they replied. Then they undressed and
rubbed themselves down with oil in front of the fire and
gave themselves a makeshift bath by scooping warm water
from the caldron inside and splashing it over themselves.
A little later a crowd of young fellows arrived, loaded
down with gold, silver, clothing, and women's and men's
jewelry. They were also part of the gang. After stowing
their loot away inside, they, too, took the same kind of
bath. Finally the whole crew of these cutthroats sat down
to a big meal, followed by a long session of talk over
drinks. The horse and I were given barley by the old
woman. The horse rushed to bolt it down—he was afraid,
naturally, that he would have to share with me—but I

helped myself to some of the bread inside every time
the crone stepped out.

The next day they all went off to work except one young
fellow who was left behind with the old woman. I groaned
inwardly at having an alert guard like this around; the old
woman was nothing to worry about—I could give her the
slip easily—but the young fellow was husky, had a mean
look, carried a sword wherever he went, and never left
the door open. Three days later, just about midnight, the
gang came back. They had no gold or silver, nothing ex-
cept one young and beautiful girl bathed in tears, with her
hair disheveled and her dress in tatters. Telling her to cheer
up, they threw her down on a mat inside and ordered the
old woman to mount guard and not leave under any cir-
cumstances. The girl refused to eat or drink a thing; all
she did was sob and tear her hair. Soon I, who was stand-
ing beside my manger nearby, joined in with the poor
little beauty and shed tears too.

The bandits in the meantime had settled down in the
courtyard for dinner. At daybreak one of the guards as-
signed to watch the road rushed in to report that a traveler,
loaded with rich pickings, would be passing by soon.
Jumping up, without further ado they grabbed their weap-
ons, threw packsaddles on the horse and me, and drove
us off. I was unfortunately aware that we were marching
into action, so I proceeded most reluctantly; as a result
they quickened my pace by clobbering me with sticks. We
came to the spot on the road where the traveler was to
pass. The bandits leaped on to his carriage, slaughtered
him and his servants, took the most valuable things and
piled them on me and the horse, and hid the rest of the
haul in the woods. Then they headed back. What with
the rush and the constant beating I was taking, I banged
a hoof on a sharp rock; the blow left a very painful sore,
and I began to limp on the way home. This evoked such
comments as "Why waste feed on a donkey that's always
falling? He's a jinx. Let's push him over a cliff," or "Right.

Let's do that. Sacrifice him to atone for our crimes." They
were ready to go for me, but I, overhearing it all, stepped
along the rest of the way as if someone else had the hurt;
fear of death kept me from feeling the slightest pain.

Finally we arrived at where we were staying. They un-
loaded both of us and carefully stowed their haul away.
Then they sat down to dinner. When night fell they set out
again to pick up what they had left. "Why take this mis-
erable donkey?" one of them remarked. "He's useless be-
cause of that hoof. We can carry some of the load our-
selves and put everything else on the horse." So they
went off with only the horse.

It was a brilliantly moonlit night. "You poor devil," I
said to myself, "you'd better not hang around here any
longer. You'll be feeding every available vulture plus its
family. Didn't you hear the plans they have for you? Do
you want to go over a cliff? It's nighttime now and there's
a full moon. They've all gone off. Take to your heels and
save yourself from those cutthroat masters of yours." While
this was passing through my head, I happened to notice
that I wasn't tied up: the strap they used for dragging me
along the road was hanging loose. That brought my
thoughts of escape to fever pitch, and I started for the gate
on the run. But the old woman caught sight of me just as
I was on the point of taking off and, grabbing me by the
tail, held me tight. Telling myself that capture by an old
crone fully deserved the cliff or any other kind of death,
I dragged her along. She began shrieking to the captive
girl inside. The girl ran out and, seeing the old woman
being pulled, like a latter-day Dirce,[4] by a donkey, acted
with magnificent daring; no hero with his back to the wall
could have done better. She leaped up, took her seat on
me, and drove me off. Between my own burning desire to
get away and my concern for the girl, I galloped as fast
as a horse, and we left the old woman far behind.

First the girl prayed to heaven to help us make our es-
cape, and then she said into my ear, "Darling donkey, if

you get me back to my father, you'll never have to do a
bit of work again, and you'll have a bushel of barley to
eat every day." Since I was running away from my own
murderers and, moreover, anticipated all kinds of help and
favors if I saved the girl, I rushed along, oblivious to my
sore hoof.

But when we reached the point where the road forked,
we ran into our enemies on their way back. In the moon-
light they were able to recognize their miserable captives
on sight from a long way off and, racing up, they grabbed
me. "Little lady," they said to the girl, "where are you go-
ing at this time of night? You poor thing! Aren't you
afraid of the bad witch? Now you just come along with
us; we'll take you back to your family." All this with much
sarcastic guffawing.

They turned me around and started dragging me back.
Suddenly I was conscious of my bad hoof again and be-
gan to limp. "So," they said to me, "now that you've been
caught running away, you're limping, eh? But when you
made up your mind to escape you were perfectly sound,
you were faster than any horse, you practically had wings."
The words were followed by the stick, and soon I had a
sore on my buttocks as a reminder.

When we got back, we came upon the old woman dan-
gling at the end of a cord from a rock; obviously she had
been so terrified of what her masters would do to her for
letting the girl get away that she hung herself and strangled
to death. The bandits, admiring the crone's consideration
for their feelings, cut her down and heaved her over a
cliff, cord and all. Then they tied the girl up, left her in-
side, and sat down to dinner and a long session with the
bottle.

At one point the conversation turned about the girl.
"What are we going to do with our young runaway?" asked
one of them.

"There's only one thing to do," another answered.
"Heave her on top of the old woman. That girl nearly did

us out of a fat ransom and almost gave away our whole gang. Believe me, fellows, if she had made it safely home, not one of us would be left alive. The police would have been all ready for us; they'd have jumped on us, and not a man here would have gotten away. She's against us, and we should get even with her. I say death; but being dropped from a cliff is too mild. Let's find a really lingering, painful death for her, one that'll keep her alive a long while in agony before she's finished off."

They racked their brains for something appropriate, and then one of them said, "Here's an idea that's a masterpiece; I know it'll appeal to you. The donkey has to go: he's always been a slacker and now he's faking lameness; besides, he gave aid and assistance to the girl in making her escape. First thing in the morning let's slit his throat. Then we'll cut open his belly, pull his guts out, and stuff our charming guest in. We'll fix it so she can stick her head out and not die right away of suffocation, but all the rest of her body will be out of sight inside. Then we'll sew her up tight in there and heave the both of them out for the vultures, who should find the combination an interesting new dish. See what a terrific torture it will make, fellows? In the first place she'll be living inside a dead donkey. Next, since it's summer now and the sun is scorching hot, she'll broil inside that beast. Third, she'll slowly starve to death with no chance to end it all by strangling herself. I'll skip what she'll suffer from the stink of the rotting carcass or the worms crawling all over her. And, lastly, when the vultures make their way inside to tear the flesh from her bones after finishing with the donkey's, they might even get her still alive."

Everyone applauded this monstrous idea as if it were something wonderful. I groaned at my fate: I was going to be slaughtered, and my corpse, instead of being left to lie in peace, was to accommodate this poor creature, was to become a coffin for an innocent girl.

Then, just before daybreak, suddenly a troop of soldiers

appeared on the scene and fell on the whole godforsaken
gang. In short order they had them all in irons and were
hustling them off to the local authority. The girl's fiancé,
it so happened, had come with the men; in fact, it was
he who had shown them to the bandits' hideaway. Taking
the girl under his wing, he seated her on me and led us
home.

The townspeople spotted us when we were still far off
and ran up to greet us and escort us into town; they knew
all had gone well since I was broadcasting the good news
with brays of joy. The girl made a great fuss over me, but
it was no more than I deserved. I had been, after all, her
fellow captive, fellow runaway, and fellow victim-to-be of
that common gruesome death. My new mistress then had
me served a bushel of barley and enough hay to feed a
camel. This was the moment when I really cursed Palaestra
for having transformed me into a donkey instead of a dog:
I could see the dogs go into the kitchen and gorge them-
selves on the rich pickings from the wedding banquet of a
wealthy bride.

My mistress had told her father how grateful she was
to me and how anxious she was to see this donkey given
his due. So, a few days after the wedding, he gave orders
to turn me out to graze in the open fields along with a
herd of mares. "Your donkey's to have no duties," he said.
"Let him live a life of pleasure mounting the mares." It
seemed at the time an eminently fitting reward—looking
at it, of course, from a donkey's point of view. Her father
called in one of his grooms and handed me over to him,
and I went off, rejoicing at the thought of no more loads
to lug. When we got to the ranch he put me in with a
herd of mares and led us all out to pasture.

At this point, like Candaules, I, too, was "sentenced by
fate to suffer."[5] The man in charge of the ranch took to
leaving me home with his wife, Megapole,[6] who harnessed
me to the mill wheel to grind the wheat and barley. Now
it was no great hardship for a grateful donkey to do some

grinding for the people in charge of him. But this charming specimen of womanhood hired out my poor neck to grind for all the neighbors—and there were plenty of them —taking a cut of the flour as pay. She even used to commandeer my ration of barley, roast it, add it to all I had to grind, and then bake it into cakes which she promptly gobbled up. I got the husks to eat.

Whenever the groom drove me out with the mares, the stallions all but did me in with kicks and nips; they forever suspected me of carrying on affairs with their wives and would come after me, hitting hard with both legs. I found it impossible to put up with this equine jealousy. It didn't take long before I got scrawny and ugly: indoors it was no joy to turn that mill wheel, and, grazing out of doors, I was always at war with my pasture mates.

Then, too, I was often sent into the mountains to bring down loads of wood. This was the worst of my troubles. For one thing, I had to climb far up by a path that was terribly steep. For another, I was barefoot, and the slope was nothing but rock. On top of all this, they sent along as driver a fiendish slave boy who devised a new torture for me each trip. To begin with, even when I ran he beat me, and not with an ordinary stick but with a branch studded with pointed twigs; he would always aim for the same spot on my buttocks until the flesh split open—and then he always aimed for the wound. Next, he used to put a load on me that an elephant would have trouble carrying. The descent was precipitous, but he would still beat me. If he saw that the wood had shifted and was leaning to one side, he would never do the right thing and take part of it off to put on the lighter side and so balance the load; his solution was to pick up some heavy rocks from the slope and add these to the lighter side. And I, poor devil, would have to go down lugging useless rocks in addition to the wood. A stream that never ran dry crossed the road at one spot. Since he didn't want to wet his shoes, he used to get over by riding on my rump behind the load.

There were times when I was so tired and worn-out I would drop in my tracks. Then my ordeal really became unbearable. He would never dismount and lend me a hand to get me to my feet or, if necessary, take off some of the load. No helping hands from him—he would sit there, take his stick, and, starting with my ears and face, clobber me until the beating forced me up.

Then he had another dirty trick I could barely endure. He would collect a load of the sharpest thorns he could find, bind them into a bundle, and tie them to my tail so that they hung down behind. Naturally, every step I took, these dangling thorns bounced off me and dug into my rear, making it sore all over. I had no possible way of protecting myself: hanging there as they did, they forever followed me and forever cut into me. What's more, if I walked slowly to avoid attack from the thorns, I got drubbed by the stick, and if I hurried to avoid the stick, there was that excruciating needling from behind. In a word, my driver had taken it on himself to do away with me.

Once, when things got so bad I couldn't stand it any longer, I delivered a kick in his direction. He never forgot it. So, when he happened to be given orders to transport tow from one place to another, he brought me out, piled on an enormous bundle he had collected, and then lashed the load to me so tightly it hurt; he was cooking up something particularly nasty. When it was time to leave, he sneaked a faggot still hot from the fire, waited until we were well beyond the gate, and then buried it in the tow. Only one thing could happen, and it did: the tow immediately started to smolder. Soon what I had on my back was no load but a bonfire, and I knew that in a matter of minutes I would be roasted alive. Luckily I came upon a deep pond by the road. I threw myself into the middle of it, rolled over onto the tow, and, by squirming in the mud, managed to quench that blazing burden I was carrying. The rest of the trip was less dangerous: since the tow was now saturated with wet mud, my driver could no longer set me on fire. At that he had the nerve to lie about me when we got back: he reported that, as I passed by the fireplace, I had deliberately thrown myself into it.

So, much to my surprise, I survived the incident of the tow. But then the filthy liar thought up something far worse. He took me up the mountain and piled a huge load of wood on me. He then went and sold it all to a farmer living nearby and, leading me home without a stick on my back, accused me in front of his master of the most vicious possible practices. "Sir," he said, "I don't know why we waste feed on this donkey. He's always been lazy and slow, but now he's trying a new kind of funny business. Whenever he sees a pretty woman or girl, or even a good-looking boy, he kicks up his heels and starts running after them. He gets aroused just the way men do for the women they're passionate about. If he catches a girl, he bites her—that's his way of kissing—and then rapes her. He's attacking and violating every woman in town. He'll get you into lawsuits and lots of other trouble with all this. Why, just now he was carrying a load of wood and he happened to see a woman walking across the fields. So with one shake he dumped the wood all over the ground, laid her out flat on the road, and had every intention of playing husband to her when people ran up on all sides and saved the woman from being split in two by her handsome beau."

"Well," the others answered on hearing this, "if he won't walk or carry loads and makes love to humans and has this uncontrollable itch to go after women and boys, you'd better do away with him. Give the guts to the dogs and save the meat for the workmen. If anyone asks how he died, say a wolf got him."

The little fiend was overjoyed at this and wanted to kill me then and there. But one of the farmers who lived in the neighborhood happened to come along at just that moment and he saved me from death—by suggesting a fate worse than death. "Never kill a donkey who's still able to turn a mill wheel or carry a load," he said. "Besides, the problem's simple. If he's got such a passionate itch to go after humans, take him and castrate him. The minute he's released from this sexual drive he'll become tame and fat and carry big loads with no trouble at all. If you haven't had any experience with the treatment, I'm coming back this way in three or four days, and I'll do the operation. Make him meeker than a lamb for you."

"Good idea," everyone chorused approvingly at this advice. I, however, was in tears at the prospect of my donkeyhood costing me my manhood; if I was to be a eunuch I didn't want to go on living. So I made up my mind to starve myself to death or throw myself over a cliff. Though I tumbled down to a piteous end, my corpse would at least be intact and with all its parts.

Then, at midnight, a messenger from the village rushed all over the estate and to the ranch, announcing that the newlyweds—the girl who had been held by the bandits along with me and her young husband—were dead: they were walking along the beach at twilight when a sudden tidal wave carried them out of sight. Such was the death that brought an end to all their troubles.

Now that the estate had lost both its young master and young mistress, everybody thought that the time had come to stop being slaves. So, taking whatever was in the house, they ran for their lives. My groom added me to his share, grabbed all he could lay his hands on, and piled it on me and the horses. I was unhappy at carrying loads again like an ordinary donkey, but I was overjoyed at having had the plans for my castration interrupted.

We followed a difficult road all night long. Three days later we had covered it and were at Beroea in Macedonia, an important, well-populated town. Our drivers decided to settle down here permanently. So they held an auction of all us animals, and a fast-talking auctioneer stood up in the middle of the main square and went into his patter.

The prospective customers all wanted to open our mouths and look in so they could see how old we were by our teeth. The horses went to various buyers, but at the end I was still left, and the auctioneer told me to go back to the camp. "Look at that," he commented. "The only one that couldn't find a buyer."

But Fate, who spins all destinies around and who is forever making changes, led an owner even to me—although hardly the kind I would have asked for. There was an old man in the crowd, one of those homosexual priests who carry around an image of the Goddess of Syria[7] to all the villages and farms and make their deity beg for a living. He bought me for a stiff price—sixty dollars—and off I went, heartsick, at the heels of my new master.

The minute we came to where he lived, Philebus[8]—to give my buyer his name—standing in front of the door, shouted at the top of his lungs, "Oh, girls! I've bought you a lovely, big slave. One of the ones from Cappadocia."[9] The "girls" were a troop of Philebus' fellow priests, all homosexuals. At the news they clapped their hands—they thought he had really bought some man. When they saw that "he" was a donkey, they began to pass caustic comments at Philebus' expense: "Why, that's no slave; that's the man you're going to marry. Just think—you'll have him all to yourself! Where did you get him? What a lovely couple! We wish you every happiness! May you have children right away—and may the little foals take after their father!" All this with much giggling.

The next day we set ourselves up for "work," as they called it. Decking the image of the goddess out in her finery, they loaded it on my back, and we left the city to make the rounds of the countryside. Whenever we came to a village I, with my divinity, would stand stock-still, our flute band would tootle like wild men, and the rest would roll their heads down and around from the neck and slash their forearms with swords. They would even stick out their tongues and nick the tip. In a few seconds the place would be dripping with nice, girlish blood. The first few times the sight made me stand shivering at the thought the goddess might demand donkey's blood too. After carving themselves up this way they would take up a collection from the onlookers. This brought in gold as well as silver and coppers, plus food: people would give them a string of dried figs, or a cheese, or a jug of wine, or a bushel of wheat and barley for the donkey. The collections took care not only of their upkeep but the costs of maintaining the goddess I carried.

In a certain village we once came to, the bunch of them snared some village lummox and, leading him off to where they were staying, went to work on him, doing to him the sort of thing these godforsaken perverts always enjoy doing. At this moment I found my change in form a torment. "O God of Woe, I have borne my sorrows till now!" I wanted to cry aloud. My own voice didn't come out, however; from my donkey's vocal chords I emitted an ear-splitting bray. Some villagers who happened to have lost a donkey and were hunting for it heard my cry to heaven and thought it came from their own beast. They walked in without announcing themselves and, coming upon the perverts in the midst of their unspeakable carryings-on, broke into roars of laughter. The next minute they were out the door to spread the story of the ungodly doings of these priests through the whole village.

My masters, dying with embarrassment at having been shown up this way, left the town at nightfall and, as soon as we got to a lonely spot on the road, tore into me in a rage for revealing their "mysteries."[10] Being called names I could put up with, but what they did next I couldn't: they took the image from my back and put it on the ground, stripped off all my saddle blankets till I hadn't a thing on, lashed me to a big tree, and then, taking that scourge made of pieces of bone that they use on themselves, beat me to within an inch of my life, explaining in the process that hereafter I was to bear my divinity in silence. They even had plans to slit my throat after the scourging for the terrible insult I had caused them and for making them leave the village before they had gotten their "work" in, but the sight of the goddess with no means of transportation shamed them so, they spared my life.

My punishment over, I shouldered her ladyship again and we started off. Toward evening we halted at the estate of some rich squire. The owner was at home, and he cordially invited the goddess into his house and made offerings to her. Here I suddenly became aware that I was in great danger. One of the squire's friends had sent him a loin of wild donkey as a gift; it was handed over to the cook to prepare. He was careless enough to let a pack of dogs sneak into the kitchen, and that was the end of the loin. Terrified at being flogged and tortured for losing the meat, he decided to hang himself. But his wife, a bane to my existence, said to him, "Don't kill yourself, dear. Don't be so downhearted. Listen to me, and you'll set everything to rights. Here's the donkey that belongs to those homosexuals. Take him to some deserted place and slaughter him. Then chop off the exact same cut of loin, bring it back here, cook it, and serve it. You can shove the rest of the carcass over a cliff. Everyone will think he ran off somewhere and disappeared. Besides, look how fat he is. Much tenderer than that wild donkey."

The husband approved of his wife's idea heartily. "Wonderful!" he said. "The only way I can avoid the whips. Consider it done."

That fiend of a cook was standing right beside me as he hatched this plot with his wife. Foreseeing my future, I decided that the very first thing to do was to rescue myself from the cleaver, so, snapping my halter strap, I made a dash for the hall where my perverts were having dinner with the squire. Coming in on the gallop, with one leap I upset lamps, tables, everything. I thought I had hit on a smart idea for saving my life. I figured the squire would immediately order a nervy donkey like me to be locked

up and kept under strict guard. But my smartness landed
me in the worst peril possible. Everyone, thinking I had
gone mad, pulled out swords or grabbed spears and long
poles and, so armed, were all set to kill me. Realizing how
serious the situation was, I made for the room assigned
to my masters to sleep in; when they saw this, they
slammed the door shut behind me and bolted it.

At dawn I shouldered the image again and off we went,
I and my band of beggars. When we came to the next
village, a populous and prosperous one, they pulled some-
thing new: they gave the locals a cock-and-bull story to
convince them that our image ought stay in the temple
of the local goddess, a highly revered deity, instead of in
someone's home. The villagers very hospitably let the visi-
tor share their own goddess's quarters and assigned us the
house of some poor family. After a long stay here my
masters finally felt the urge to move on to the next town;
putting in a request to the villagers for the return of the
goddess, they went themselves into the sanctuary, brought
the image out, loaded it on my back, and drove me off.
It developed, however, that while the godforsaken bunch
of them were in the temple they had helped themselves
to a gold dish, somebody's thank offering, and had smug-
gled it out under the goddess's garments. The minute the
locals discovered the loss they galloped after us and
quickly caught up. Leaping from their mounts and block-
ing the road, they cursed us for being damned temple
robbers and demanded the stolen dish back. After search-
ing everywhere they finally located it tucked in the god-
dess's bosom. So they tied up the whole girlish crew, es-
corted them back to town, and threw them in jail. They
removed the image I was carrying and set it up in a tem-
ple of its own, and the gold dish they returned to their
goddess.

The following day they decided to sell off the prisoners'
possessions, including me. I went to someone from the
next village, a baker by trade. He took me and, piling on

my back ten bushels of wheat he had also bought, led
me by a grueling route to his house. When we arrived
he brought me straight to the mill. Inside I saw a herd
of my fellow slaves plus a lot of mill wheels, each being
turned by a donkey. The whole place was covered with
flour dust. Since I was a newcomer and had just carried
an enormous load over a hard road, I was given the rest
of the day off in my stall.

When morning came the millers blindfolded me with a
piece of cloth, yoked me to the bar of a wheel, and started
me going. I knew very well how to do grinding—I had
had my dose plenty of times—but I pretended I didn't.
What a vain hope! A lot of the men took stations in a
circle, each with a stick in his hand, and, when I least
expected it—I couldn't see a thing, after all—started whack-
ing me, one after the other. In a second those sticks had
me spinning that wheel like a top. Through sad experience
I've learned that a slave must not wait for his master's
hand to remind him to do his duty.

I grew so skinny and feeble that my owner decided to
sell me. I was bought by a truck farmer, that is, a peasant
who had a patch of vegetable garden to till. The routine
we carried on together was this: he got up at dawn and
loaded me with vegetables, which we brought to the mar-
ket; after handing these over to the vegetable vendors we
went back to the farm; then he dug and planted and
watered while I stood around, doing nothing. Yet the
life was terribly hard on me. For one thing, winter had
already begun, and he didn't have the money to buy a
blanket for himself, let alone me. For another, I had to go
barefoot over mud that was either clammy or frozen stiff
into sharp ruts. Besides, the only food we had was bitter,
stringy lettuce leaves.

One day on our way into town we passed somebody,
obviously a gentleman, wearing a soldier's uniform. Speak-
ing in Latin, he asked my master where he was taking
the donkey—meaning me. My master made no answer: he

probably didn't speak the language. The other, thinking
he was being snubbed, lost his temper and brought his
stick down on my master, who promptly made a dive for
him, yanked his feet out from under him to lay him flat
on his back in the road, and then, pinning him there,
proceeded to kick, punch, and pound him with rocks. At
first the soldier fought back, swearing that, if he could
only get to his feet, he would draw his sword and run
him through. My master, having been as good as given a
lesson by his opponent in how to fight without running
any risks, pulled out the sword and tossed it away—and
then resumed the pummeling. The soldier, realizing he
couldn't take much more of such punishment, played dead.
This threw my master into a panic. Leaving the man ly-
ing there, he picked up the sword and drove me at a
gallop into town.

As soon as we arrived he arranged to turn the garden
over to a neighbor to work and then, scared stiff of serious
repercussions from his contretemps on the road, took me
and went off to the house of some friend in town to lie
low. The next day, after a council of war, the following
precautions were taken: my master was stowed away in
a chest, and I was hauled up a ladder by the legs to a
garret and locked up there.

In the meantime the soldier painfully picked himself up
from the ground—so it was reported to us later—and, his
head throbbing from the beating he had taken, made his
way into town, where he met up with the rest of his unit
and told them about the insane peasant he had run across.
They joined the search and, finding out our hiding place,
brought the police, who sent in a flunky with orders for
everyone inside to come out. Everyone did—but no peas-
ant was to be seen. The soldiers insisted that there was
not only a peasant in there but also his donkey. The others
claimed there was neither peasant nor donkey nor any-
thing else left inside. With both sides hollering lustily a
tumult arose in the narrow street, and I, a nervy busybody,

had to know who was doing all the shouting. So I stuck my head out the window and took a look. The soldiers, spotting me, immediately began to yell; the others, caught in a barefaced lie, stood speechless. The police ran in, searched the place from top to bottom, found my master lying in his chest, and promptly packed him off to jail to stand trial for trying to commit mayhem. Me they hauled down and handed over to the soldiers. The whole town couldn't stop laughing at how I had managed to give away my master and do him in from an upper story. As a matter of fact, this escapade of mine is the origin of our expression "to make an ass of someone."

I have no idea what happened to my master, for the next day the soldiers decided to sell me, and sold I was for fifty dollars to the servant of a millionaire whose main residence was in Thessalonica, the biggest city of Macedonia. My new owner was a cook by trade. He prepared the entrees and main dishes for his owner while his brother, a fellow slave, was the expert at baking bread and making pastries. The two were inseparable. They ate together, shared the same quarters, and used each other's cooking utensils. Once I had been purchased, they shared me, too, and moved me in with them.

Every night after their master had finished dinner they would bring home a load of leftovers, one brother meat and fish, the other bread and pastries. They would then lock me up with these goodies and leave me to stand guard over them while they went off for their bath. How I loved that guard duty! "Good-by forever," I said to the barley in my box and, giving myself over to the products of my masters' art and skill, loaded up on the real food I had been away from so long. Because they had so much on the table and I was still stealing so sparingly, they had no idea, the first few times they came back, that I was eating like a gourmet at their expense. When I realized how completely unaware they were of what I was doing, I began gobbling up the choicest cuts and lots else. Eventually they tumbled to the fact that embezzling was going on. Their reaction was to throw suspicious looks at each other, and such words as "thief" and "dirty share-snatcher" were bandied back and forth. From that moment on they started to watch like hawks and counted every morsel.

I, of course, was living off the fat of the land. Now that I was again eating the food I was used to, I got my figure back and my coat became sleek and glossy. Those two geniuses, seeing me grow big and fat without any consumption of barley—the level in my feedbox always stayed the same—finally suspected what I was up to. One day they left the house ostensibly to go for their bath. Instead they put their eyes to a hole in the door and watched what went on inside. Blissfully ignorant of the trap, I went up to the table and helped myself to dinner. The first thing they did at the sight of this feat of feeding was hoot with laughter. Then they rounded up all their fellow servants for a look at the show, and the roars became so loud their master heard them—there was a full-scale hullabaloo by now in front of my door—and asked what all the laughing was about outside. On hearing the answer he ran out in the middle of the dinner party he was giving and, peeking through the hole, spotted me in the act of putting away a cut of wild boar. He burst out laughing and charged into the room. I felt utterly humiliated. There I was, caught red-handed in thievery and gluttony combined, by the head of the household. But he just guffawed and gave orders to have me brought into his dinner party, where he had a table set before me with a complete spread of all the things no other donkey could possibly eat: meats, oysters, soups, fish, all done in sauce or oil or swimming in mustard. I saw that fortune was now smiling sweetly on me—but I also saw that only by playing court jester this way could I save my life. So, even though I was stuffed to the ears, I went up to the table and packed in a meal. The party was convulsed. Then someone said, "I bet this donkey will drink wine if you offer it to him."

So the master issued orders to serve me a glass, and I downed it.

The master, of course, could see that I would make an extraordinary thing to own. So he had one of his clerks count out to the cook who had bought me the price he paid plus a 100 per cent bonus and then handed me over to a young fellow, a retainer of his, with orders to teach me whatever tricks I could do that would amuse him the most. My trainer had a sinecure; I carried out all instructions instantly. First he had me lie on a couch, leaning on my elbow just like a man, then wrestle a fall with him, then dance standing upright on my hind legs, then nod or shake my head in answer to questions. I didn't have to be taught; I was able to do everything.

It became the talk of the town: the master had a donkey that could tipple, wrestle, or dance. My most impressive feat was giving the right answers to questions with a nod or a shake of the head. The next was the way I had of signaling to the wine steward with my eyes whenever I wanted my glass filled. Everyone there, having no idea of the human intelligence buried in this donkey, thought they were seeing something miraculous, and I capitalized on their ignorance to live like a king. I also let myself be taught to walk and carry the master on my back and to trot so that my rider felt none of the motion and sat completely undisturbed. They fitted me out in gorgeous style: I had red silk saddle blankets, my reins were studded with silver and gold, and the bells they hung on me tinkled a most engaging tune.

Menecles, the master, came from Thessalonica, as I mentioned before. His reason for being in the town where we were was a promise he had given his fellow citizens to put on for them a gladiatorial show featuring experts in single combat. By now his fighters were all ready, and it was time to start the march to the city. We set out at dawn, and I took the master on my back whenever we came to a bad stretch of road that was too rough for a carriage. When we arrived at Thessalonica, everyone there was in a fever of excitement not only to see the fights but to get a look at me; my reputation had raced on ahead, particularly the reports of the humanlike quality and wide range of my ballet performances and the professional skill of my wrestling.

My first showing, however, was limited to the important people in town at a party Menecles gave for them. The dinner program included my repertory of amazing tricks. At the same time my trainer, discovering a way to make a pretty penny out of me, opened up the stall where he kept me shut in for anyone who wanted to see me and my marvelous feats—and was willing to pay the price. My customers would bring with them all kinds of food, especially things they were sure would ruin a donkey's stomach. Whatever it was, I downed it. What with eating for my master and eating for everybody in town, within a few days I was unbelievably big and fat.

One day some foreign lady, well-to-do and quite good-looking, came to see me eat and fell madly in love. Partly the sight of such a handsome donkey, partly the extraordinary nature of my accomplishments aroused in her the desire to have sexual relations with me. She spoke to my trainer and offered him a huge bribe if he would allow her to spend the night with me. Without bothering his head about how much satisfaction, if any, she would get out of me, he grabbed at the money. In the late evening, after Menecles had sent us off from the nightly dinner party, we came back to our quarters and found the woman there; she had arrived hours in advance for her tryst. A bed was ready, made up with sheets and soft pillows; she had seen to it all. Her maids were spending the night within call just outside the room. Inside a lamp was blazing brightly. She took off her clothes and, standing stark naked in front of the light, poured out some perfume from a little flask and rubbed it on herself. She did the same to me, taking particular care to apply it liberally about

my nose. Then she kissed me and, whispering the things a
woman will to the man she's in love with, drew me by the
halter down to the bed. I needed no urging. I was already
tipsy from a lot of good wine, the perfume on our skins
had me wild with desire, and I could see she was a little
beauty. I lay down—but I had no idea how to mount her.
I hadn't made love once since my transformation and I
had no experience in doing it donkey fashion—I had never
even mounted a female ass, to say nothing of a woman.
What's more, I was terribly afraid my partner would prove
too small and I would split her in half—and serve a nice
sentence for manslaughter as a result. I didn't realize that
all my fears were groundless. First she led me on by
kissing me again and again—love kisses, no less. Then, when
she saw I could no longer contain myself, she lay down
beside me just as if I were a man, put her arms about me,
and, raising herself up, took all I had. I, poor fool, was
still worried, so I pulled back a bit, but she held on to
my rump tightly to keep me from drawing away; *I* did
the fleeing and she the chasing. When I was finally con-
vinced that she needed me for her pleasure and enjoyment,
I put myself completely at her service without any qualms;
if Pasiphaë's lover[11] could do it I could, too, I told my-
self. The woman was so passionate, and her appetite for
the joys of love-making so insatiable, that she spent the
whole night in my arms.

Next morning she got up and went off, after arranging
with my trainer to pay him the same fee for the same
privilege that evening. *He* was willing—on top of making
more money out of me he had plans to show the master
a new trick of mine—and shut us up together, but me she
wore to a frazzle. At one point he ran off to Menecles and
reported my latest feat, letting on that it was something
he had taught me. Since it was now dark, he sneaked
Menecles to my quarters without my knowing a thing
about it and, through a hole in the door, let him get a
look at me in the arms of my sweetheart. Menecles en-

joyed it so, he was taken with the idea of having me demonstrate this particular stunt in public. "Don't say a word to a soul," he told my trainer, "and, on the day of the show, we'll take him to the theater along with some woman who's been sentenced to death, and he can mount her in front of the whole audience." Then they brought to my room a woman who had been condemned to die in the arena and instructed her to go up to me and fondle me.

Finally the day arrived that Menecles had set for his grand spectacle. When they decided it was the moment to escort me to the theater, here's how it was done. They had prepared an oversize bed made out of tortoise shell imported from India and fitted with gold hardware. They laid me out on it and had the woman lie down beside me. Then they loaded us, bed and all, on a sort of float, hauled us into the middle of the theater, and set us down there. I was greeted by a great shout and a burst of applause from every person present. A table was put before us, covered with the special delicacies served only at gourmet banquets. The wine stewards, who stood on either side of us, were handsome young boys, and they poured the wine from a gold carafe. My trainer, from his station behind me, told me to begin my dinner, but I couldn't: it was not only embarrassment at lying there in the middle of an arena— the thought that any second a bear or a lion would be springing out at us had me petrified.

At that moment a boy passed by carrying a bouquet, and, mixed in with all the other flowers, I caught sight of a mass of fresh-cut roses. Without a second's hesitation I jumped up and sprang out of the bed. The crowd thought I had gotten up to dance. Instead, I went over the flowers one by one, picked out the roses, and gobbled them up. While everybody was still wondering what I was about, the animal exterior fell away from me and crumpled up into nothing. The donkey I had been for so long disappeared; the Lucius that had been inside stood there in the flesh—naked.

Everyone gasped at this miraculous and unexpected sight. Then a terrible furor broke out. The crowd was split into two camps: one demanded I be burned then and there as an evil sorcerer who mixed magic drugs and could change his shape; the other was for waiting and hearing what I had to say for myself and then passing judgment. I raced over to where the governor of the province, who happened to be in the audience, was sitting and, shouting up to him, explained that some girl from Thessaly, the maid of a woman who was also from Thessaly, had turned me into an ass by smearing me with a magic ointment, and I begged him to take me and keep me safely under guard until I could convince him I wasn't lying, that it had all happened this way.

"State your name, father's name, mother's name, names of near relatives if you have any, and place of birth," he replied.

"My father's name is so-and-so," I said. "Mine is Lucius, and I have a brother named Gaius. We both have the same middle and last names. I write history and other kinds of prose, and my brother is a poet, specializing in elegiac verses. He's also a very good prophet. We were both born at Patras in Greece."

At these words the governor cried out, "Your parents are my dearest friends! They've entertained me in your house, and I've been proud to receive gifts from them. I know very well, if you're a son of theirs, you can't be lying." And, jumping from his seat, he embraced me and kissed me again and again and then carried me off to his home.

Pretty soon my brother arrived with money and lots of other things I needed. At the same time the governor, at a full hearing, publicly dismissed the charges against me. My brother and I then went down to the water front, booked passage on a ship, and loaded all our baggage aboard.

At this point I decided that I simply had to pay a visit

to the woman who had been so much in love with me
when I was a donkey. She'll find me, I told myself, so
much more attractive now that I'm a man. She was very
glad to see me—I imagine she was intrigued by the novelty
of what had happened to me—and begged me to have
dinner with her and stay the night. I let her persuade me.
I felt it would be downright indecent if the donkey she
loved so passionately, now that he had become a man,
were to be high and mighty with his old mistress and
snoot her.

We had dinner together. I had perfumed myself all
over and was wearing a garland of roses, the flower I
loved best, the one that had restored me to the company
of men. When it grew late and it was time to go to bed,
I got up and, certain I had a wonderful treat in store for
her, took off my clothes and stood there naked, awaiting
her joyous reaction to the improvement over the donkey.
But at the sight of me with all human parts she practically
spit in my face. "Get the devil away from me and out of
this house!" she shrieked. "You do your sleeping some-
where else, the further the better!"

"What have I done wrong that's so terrible?" I asked.

"I wasn't in love with *you*. I was in love with the don-
key you were. I slept with *it* those times, not you. I
thought you might have saved at least one thing and still
have that nice big emblem of your donkeyhood trailing
between your legs. You've gone and turned yourself from
a lovely, precious beast into an ape, that's what you've
done." Whereupon she called her servants and ordered
them to carry me out of the house bodily. So, stark naked,
with my lovely garland and my aroma of perfume, out
the door I went to embrace bare Mother Earth and spend
the night with her.

At daybreak, still naked, I legged it for the ship and
gave my brother a laugh with the story of my adventure.
A fair wind sprang up; we sailed off from the city, and a
few days later I was back in Patras. Here I offered heaven

fervent prayers of thanksgiving for bringing me home after so long an absence and so many hardships and for saving me not from a dog's ass, as the saying goes, but from a donkey's, where my curiosity had taken me.

NOTES

[1] This common female name is identical with the Greek word for "wrestling school," and the allusions to wrestling, which shortly come thick and fast, are punning references to it.

[2] According to ancient popular belief, witches were a specialty of Thessaly.

[3] Being thrown to wild beasts was one form of capital punishment.

[4] A mythological villainess who was dragged to her death by a bull as punishment.

[5] An allusion to a line (1.8) in Herodotus' account of Candaules, the Lydian king so proud of his wife's beauty that he insisted his favorite officer, Gyges, see her in the nude—with unfortunate results.

[6] This looks like an ordinary Greek name but is not. It's a made-up name meaning "mighty hard turner."

[7] The famous Semitic mother-goddess, called Atargatis by the Greeks. Her priests were often eunuchs and mendicants.

[8] The name is aptly chosen: it means "lover of boys."

[9] A province of eastern Asia Minor that supplied large numbers of slaves.

[10] Cf. p. 169, n. 32.

[11] A bull. The product of the union was that celebrated monster of Greek mythology, the Minotaur.

ZEUS'S WORLD

Dialogues of the Gods

Dialogues of the Sea-Gods

Prometheus

Zeus the Opera Star

ZEUS'S WORLD

Lucian's gods come not from Greek religion but from Greek literature and art. The actions and mental attitudes they reveal in his pages are based on the verses of Homer and Hesiod and their physical appearance on the celebrated statues turned out by Greek sculptors in the fifth and fourth centuries B.C.

From the cloud-capped summit of Mt. Olympus the gods exercised their unending and unlimited control. They had not always been the world's rulers—they had to wrest the scepter from the grasp of Cronus and his Titans, who had reigned from earliest times, and imprison them in the underworld for eternity. But ever since the Olympians' rule had been virtually unchallenged; they lived a life of ease, enjoying daily banquets of nectar and ambrosia and relishing to the full the rich savor that rose to their nostrils from the burnt offerings sacrificed by men to gain their good will.

The chief figures in Lucian's celestial dramatis personae are:

ZEUS: *The majestic, all-powerful, impressively bearded king of the gods, who ruled heaven and earth, wielded the mighty thunderbolt—and couldn't resist a pretty mortal face. Since his appearance was too awesome for human eyes to behold, he carried on his love affairs in a variety of disguises.*

HERA: *Zeus's statuesque, handsome wife, who took a dim view of her husband's extramarital activities and didn't hesitate to tell him so.*

POSEIDON: *Zeus's brother, who caused earthquakes and ruled the sea, wielding the trident as his symbol of power.*

HERMES: *Zeus's son by the goddess Maia, an agile and athletic young god, far and away the busiest deity on Olympus. He was patron god of thievery, trade, un-*

expected windfalls or lucky discoveries, public speaking, and gymnastic sports. He was personal messenger to Zeus. He waited on table at the celestial banquets. And every night he left heaven to escort the shades of the dead to the underworld; his winged feet carried him down, and he shepherded his ghostly flocks with the caduceus, a staff entwined with serpents. And somehow he found time to invent the lyre.

APHRODITE: *The seductively beautiful goddess of love. Her illicit love affair with Ares, god of war, was the talk of Olympus. She had a child by him—Eros, the winged cherub who mischievously shot his love-producing arrows at immortals and mortals alike. According to some legends, however, the little fellow, despite his looks and size, was really the offspring of ancient Titans.*

APOLLO: *The slim, boyish, delicately handsome god of music and learning, who maintained a famous seat of prophecy at Delphi. He was a skilled archer and went about armed with a silver bow.*

ATHENA: *The radiantly handsome, masterful, virgin daughter of Zeus, who, as goddess of power and statecraft, wore a suit of armor over her robes.*

HEPHAESTUS: *The lame god of fire who ran Olympus' blacksmith shop.*

HERACLES: *The celebrated strong man, son of Zeus by a mortal mother, Alcmena. Armed with a mighty club and a magic bow that never missed, he performed the benefactions to mankind known as the Twelve Labors. After his death he was immortalized and brought to heaven.*

DIONYSUS: *Another son of Zeus by a mortal mother, Semele. Dionysus was god of wine; he was pretty rather than good-looking, dressed effeminately, and appealed particularly to female worshipers.*

To these must be added Momus, god of criticism, an obscure and insignificant deity whom the satirist, for obvious reasons, elevates to prime rank.

7

Hephaestus and Apollo

HEPHAESTUS. Apollo, have you seen the new baby? Maia's little tot, Hermes? He's beautiful. And he smiles so sweetly at everybody. It looks as if he'll grow up to be a fine young god.

APOLLO. That tot a fine young god? When it comes to making trouble, he acts as if he's been at it a lifetime.

HEPHAESTUS. How could he do anything wrong? He's just been born.

APOLLO. Ask Poseidon—the tot stole his trident. Or ask Ares—he sneaked the sword right out of his scabbard. Or ask *me*. I'm disarmed—he stole my bow and arrows.

HEPHAESTUS. That baby? He can hardly stand up. He's still in diapers.

APOLLO. Just wait until he gets near you, Hephaestus. You'll find out.

HEPHAESTUS. But he already has.

APOLLO. Well? Do you have all your tools? None missing?

HEPHAESTUS. Everything's here.

APOLLO. No, take a good look.

HEPHAESTUS. My god! I don't see my tongs!

APOLLO. You'll see them, all right—somewhere in his crib.

HEPHAESTUS. So light-fingered! What did he do? Learn to pick pockets in the womb?

APOLLO. You haven't heard him talk. He can chatter a mile a minute. And he wants to be our serving boy. And yesterday he challenged Eros to a wrestling match and somehow or other had him on his back in a second. Everybody applauded. Aphrodite bent down to give him a hug for winning—and he stole her girdle. Zeus was doubled up with laughter at the quick fall—and he made off with his scepter. He'd have taken the thunderbolt, too, if it wasn't so heavy and hot.

HEPHAESTUS. Sounds as if the boy has real spirit.

APOLLO. That's not all. He's a musical prodigy too.

HEPHAESTUS. How can you tell?

APOLLO. He found the shell of a tortoise somewhere and made an instrument out of it. He attached a pair of arms and a crossbar to the upper edge, stuck in pegs, stretched seven strings over a bridge, and played such a lovely, sweet tune that even I was jealous—and I've been practicing on the cithara for years. Maia says he won't spend the night in heaven; he has to go down and poke his nose even in the underworld—probably to try his hand at a bit of burglary there too. He has wings on his feet and he's made himself a sort of magic staff that he uses to herd the shades of the dead and lead them below.

HEPHAESTUS. I gave him that. It was supposed to be a toy.

APOLLO. He's paid you for it, all right. Turned around and stole——

HEPHAESTUS. My tongs! Glad you reminded me. I'm going to get them this minute—if you're right about finding them in his crib.

24

Hermes and Maia

HERMES. Mother, there isn't a god in heaven worse off than I am.

MAIA. Hermes! Don't say such things.

HERMES. Why shouldn't I? Who else has so much to do? I'm exhausted. I have so many jobs I can't keep them straight. I have to get up at the crack of dawn, clean up the banquet hall, straighten the cushions, put everything in order; then I have to go on duty with Zeus and play dispatch rider, delivering messages up here and down below. The minute I'm back, before I can wash the dust off, I'm serving the ambrosia. Until that new cupbearer[1] came I even had to take care of the nectar. Worst of all, I'm the only one who doesn't go to bed at night. That's when I have to be shade leader and herd the dead for Pluto and act as court clerk at the judgment seat. It isn't enough that I work all day long in the gymnasiums, the political assemblies, and the public speaking classes; no, I've got to split my time and help out with the dead too. Each of Leda's twin boys[2] spends one day in heaven and the next in the underworld, but *I* have to do jobs in both every day. The sons of Alcmena and Semele[3]—miserable mortal women —sit at our banquets without a worry in the world, and who waits on them? I—the son of Maia, the grandson of Atlas! Here I am, just back from Sidon where he sent me to see how Europa was getting along, and, without giving me time to catch my breath, he's sending me off to Argos to look Danaë over. "On your way back," he adds, "go by Boeotia and see Antiope." I tell you, I'm fed up. I wish I could be sold like those poor slaves on earth; I'd be glad to see it happen.

MAIA. Enough of this, my son. You're still a young boy— you must mind your father. Now then, do as you're told. Off with you to Argos and Boeotia; he'll give you a whipping if you waste time. These anxious lovers have quick tempers!

NOTES

1 Ganymede; see pp. 103–7.

2 Pollux and Castor were the twin sons of Leda, queen of Sparta. One of them, Pollux, was immortal. When Castor died, the two were allowed to share Pollux's immortality: they shuttled back and forth, each spending alternate days on earth and in the underworld.

3 Hermes manages to make mention of five of Zeus's more notorious amours. Semele mothered Dionysus and Alcmena Heracles. The other three Zeus wooed in celebrated disguises: he came to Europa as a bull, to Danaë as a shower of gold, to Antiope as a satyr.

2

Eros and Zeus

EROS. But, Zeus, even if I've done something wrong, you've got to forgive me. I'm still just a thoughtless little boy.

ZEUS. Little boy? You? You're older than Father Time! You've spent a lifetime making trouble but, just because you don't have gray hairs and a beard, you've got the idea that everyone should treat you like an infant.

EROS. Well, what's the "old man" done to you that's so terrible it's making you talk about locking me up?

ZEUS. Damn you, do you think it's nothing to play around with me the way you do? There isn't a thing you haven't made me turn into—satyr, bull, gold, swan, eagle. . . . What's more, you've never made any girls fall in love with me, and I don't recall one single time that you've made me attractive to women. No, I've always got to use magic on them and hide my looks. It's the bull or the swan *they* make love to; if they catch sight of me they're scared to death.

EROS. Of course. They're only mortal. They set eyes on Zeus? Impossible!

ZEUS. Then how is it Branchus[1] and Hyacinth can make love to Apollo?

EROS. Yes, but Daphne[2] ran away from him. That fancy hair-do and boyish look didn't do him much good with her. Zeus, if you want women to fall in love with you, stop waving your shield around and put down that thunderbolt. Spruce yourself up a bit. Let your hair grow. Have it curled, and wear a headband. Get yourself some purple robes and gold-embroidered shoes. Get a flutist and drummer and step along to the music. You'll see. You'll have more girls running after you than Dionysus has Maenads.[3]

ZEUS. Oh no. I'm not interested in having women fall in love with me if I have to do things like that.

EROS. Then forget about having love affairs. Matter of fact, that's the easier thing to do.

ZEUS. No. I like having love affairs. I just want to have them with less fuss. If you promise me this, I'll let you go.

NOTES

[1] Two exceptionally good-looking young boys with whom Apollo had had love affairs.
[2] See p. 54, n. 4.
[3] The fanatical female devotees of Dionysus.

4

Zeus and Ganymede

Ganymede was a strikingly good-looking Trojan boy who tended flocks on Mt. Ida. One day Zeus took the form

of an eagle, swooped down, picked the boy up in his
talons, and flew him off to heaven to be cupbearer for the
gods.

ZEUS. Well, Ganymede, now that we've reached our des-
tination, give me a kiss. I want you to see I no longer
have a curved beak, claws, and wings the way I did
when you thought I was a bird.

GANYMEDE. You're a man! But weren't you a bird a little
while ago? Didn't you swoop down and snatch me from
the middle of my flock? How did those wings fall off
you? How were you able to change your appearance
just now?

ZEUS. My boy, what you're looking at is neither man nor
eagle. I'm king of the gods, that's who I am, and I
change into whatever shape the occasion calls for.

GANYMEDE. What? Oh, then you must be Pan.[1] But how
come you don't have a pipe, horns, and shaggy legs?

ZEUS. Is he the only god you think there is?

GANYMEDE. Yes. We sacrifice a goat to him. We bring it
to the cave where his statue is. You a god? You look
like a kidnaper to me.

ZEUS. Tell me, haven't you ever heard the name Zeus?
Haven't you seen his altar on Gargara?[2] The god of
thunder, lightning, and rain?

GANYMEDE. Oh, sir, you mean you're the one who poured
all the hail on us the other day? The one they say lives
in heaven and makes all that noise? The one my father
sacrificed the ram to? Oh, King of the Gods, why did
you carry me off? What did I do wrong? Now my sheep
are all alone and the wolves will probably come down
on them and ruin the flock.

ZEUS. You're immortal now. You're going to live with us.
What are you still worrying about your sheep for?

GANYMEDE. What's that you say? You mean you're not going to take me back to Mt. Ida today?

ZEUS. I should say not. And waste all the effort it took to turn myself from a god into an eagle?

GANYMEDE. But my father will be looking for me and he'll get angry if he doesn't find me. And afterward he'll give me a whipping for leaving the flock.

ZEUS. Where's he going to find you?

GANYMEDE. No, no, I want to go home to my father right now. If you take me back, I promise he'll pay you for it. He'll sacrifice another ram. We have a three-year-old, the big one that leads the flock to pasture.

ZEUS. How simple and ingenuous the boy is! When you come right down to it, he's still just a child. Ganymede, put all that out of your mind. Forget about your flock, Mt. Ida, and the rest. Why, you're in heaven now, and from here you'll be able to do a world of good for your father and your fatherland. And instead of cheese and milk you'll eat ambrosia and drink nectar. What's more, you'll even pour the nectar and serve it to the rest of us. Best of all, you won't be mortal any longer; you'll be immortal, and I'll make your star shine the brightest in the heavens. Oh, you'll be perfectly happy.

GANYMEDE. But if I want to play, who'll play with me? There were lots of boys my age on Mt. Ida.

ZEUS. You'll have a playmate here, too—Eros over there. And we have plenty of checkers for you. So cheer up, let's have a smile, and no more sighs for what you left down there.

GANYMEDE. But what use can I be to you? Do you need shepherds here too?

ZEUS. No, but you can pour for us. You can be in charge of the nectar and serve when we're having drinks.

GANYMEDE. That's not hard. I know how to pour milk and hand the mug around.

[4.4–5]

ZEUS. Listen to that! He's back to milk again! He thinks it's mortals he's going to serve. Ganymede, this is heaven. I told you we drink nectar here.

GANYMEDE. Is nectar sweeter than milk?

ZEUS. You'll see for yourself in a little while. Once you've tasted it you'll never want milk again.

GANYMEDE. Where will I sleep at night? With my play-mate Eros?

ZEUS. No. I brought you here so we could sleep together.

GANYMEDE. Can't you sleep alone? You mean it's nicer for you to sleep with me?

ZEUS. With someone as beautiful as you are, Ganymede? Oh yes.

GANYMEDE. How can my being beautiful help your sleeping?

ZEUS. Your looks have a lovely magic; they'll make my sleep all the sweeter.

GANYMEDE. But my father used to get angry at me when I slept with him. When dawn came he used to say that, with my twisting and turning and kicking and talking in my sleep, I didn't let him close his eyes for a minute. So he used to send me to bed with my mother most of the time. If *that's* the reason you carried me off, you'd better take me right back to earth or you'll be in trouble. I'll get on your nerves, too, with all my twisting and turning. You'll be lying awake all night.

ZEUS. If I can lie awake with you, kissing you and hold-ing you in my arms, that's the nicest thing you can do for me.

GANYMEDE. You'd know about that. But I'll be asleep, even while you're kissing me.

ZEUS. We'll see to what has to be done when the time comes. Hermes! Take this boy and give him a drink of the immortal nectar. Then teach him how to serve drinks and bring him to wait on us.

NOTES

[1] As the patron deity of shepherds, Pan was presumably the god Ganymede knew best. In ancient art he is represented as goat from the waist down and man from the waist up save for goat's ears and horns, and he carries the shepherd's pipe which, legend has it, he invented.

[2] One of the peaks of Mt. Ida.

6

Hera and Zeus

Ixion was a king who, admitted by Zeus to the banquets of the gods, took advantage of the situation to make advances to the lady of the house. He was tricked into making love to a dummy made from a cloud and, for his presumption, received a unique and renowned punishment: he was lashed for eternity to a perpetually spinning wheel.

HERA. Zeus, what kind of person do you think this Ixion is?

ZEUS. I think he's a fine fellow, Hera, and very good company. He wouldn't be here drinking with us if he didn't deserve to.

HERA. But he doesn't deserve to. He's a disgrace. He's not to stay here any longer.

ZEUS. A disgrace? How? I think I should know about this.

HERA. You certainly should. But I'm ashamed to talk about it. What that man had the nerve to do!

ZEUS. All the more reason for you to tell me, if he tried to do something insulting. You don't mean he made advances to anyone? I gather this is what the insult's about if you're so reluctant to mention it.

HERA. To anyone? To *me*, that's who. And it's been go-
ing on for a long time. At first I didn't know what it
was all about, why he was staring at me. But then he'd
sigh and wipe his eyes, and whenever I was drinking
and I'd hand the cup back to Ganymede, he'd insist on
having a drink out of it and he'd take it and kiss it and
raise it to his eyes and look my way. It finally dawned
on me that all this meant he had love on his mind. For
a long time I was ashamed to mention it to you; I
thought the man would stop this madness. But when
he had the cheek to make me a proposal, I covered
my ears so I wouldn't hear the disgraceful things he
was begging for, and I left him groveling in tears and
came to tell you. It's up to you now to do something
about punishing him.

ZEUS. So the damned rascal was out to take my place,
was he? Was after my own wife, eh? Did he guzzle
that much nectar? Well, it's our own fault. We're too
nice to these mortals—inviting them to our parties this
way. Once they've had the same drinks we're served
and seen the beauties we have here in heaven, the likes
of which they've never seen on earth, you can't blame
them if they fall in love and go wild with desire. Love
is a very powerful thing. It can take possession not only
of mortals but even of us sometimes.

HERA. It's lord and master of you, all right. It leads you
by the nose, as the saying goes, and you follow right
after it and meekly change your shape into whatever it
tells you to. It owns you; you're its toy, you are. I
know what you're going to do now. You're going to let
that Ixion off because you once had an affair with his
wife, the time she gave birth to Pirithoüs.

ZEUS. I go down to earth to have a little fun, and you
never forget it! But about Ixion—you know what my
idea is? Not to punish him or send him packing from
our parties. That's so crude. No, since you tell me he's

in love with you and is weeping and suffering simply unbearably——

HERA. What's that, what's that? Now I'm worried. Are *you* going to insult me too?

ZEUS. No, no. I was going to suggest we make an exact likeness of you from a cloud and, when the party breaks up and he's lying wide-awake in bed, as he presumably will be because he's so madly in love, we bring it in and lay it down beside him. You see, if he thinks he's gotten his heart's desire, he'll stop making himself miserable over you.

HERA. We will do nothing of the sort! I hope he chokes. Getting ideas like that about his betters!

ZEUS. Don't say no, Hera. It's just a trick. What harm will it do you if Ixion makes love to a bit of cloud?

HERA. But the bit of cloud will look like me. The resemblance will make him do it and he'll be disgracing *me*.

ZEUS. Nonsense! You can't be a cloud and a cloud can't be you. We'll fool Ixion, that's all.

HERA. But men are so vulgar. When he gets back he'll probably brag and give everybody a long story of how he made love to Hera and cuckolded Zeus. He might even tell them I'm in love with him. And they'll believe it. They won't know it was a cloud he made love to.

ZEUS. Well, if he does anything of the kind, we'll send him to the underworld and lash the poor devil to a wheel that'll spin him around for eternity. He'll suffer forever, not for falling in love—there's nothing so terrible about that—but for bragging.

9

Poseidon and Hermes

As lord of the gods, Zeus had a number of extraordinary powers. On at least two occasions, for example, he took over the business of childbirth: his daughter Athena came out of his head (a grown girl and in full armor, to boot), and his son Dionysus from his thigh.

POSEIDON. Hermes, may I see Zeus?

HERMES. Impossible, Poseidon.

POSEIDON. Impossible? You go in and announce me!

HERMES. Now please don't make trouble. You can't see him right now. It's a bad time.

POSEIDON. Don't tell me he's with Hera.

HERMES. No, no. This is something different.

POSEIDON. I get it. Ganymede's in there, eh?

HERMES. Not that either. He's not feeling well, that's why.

POSEIDON. What's the matter? This sounds very queer, Hermes.

HERMES. It *is* queer. I'm ashamed to tell you about it.

POSEIDON. Ashamed to tell me? Your own uncle? No reason for that, my boy.

HERMES. Poseidon, he's just had a baby!

POSEIDON. You don't say! A baby? He? Who with? You mean he's bisexual and he's kept it a secret from us? But his belly didn't shown a sign of bulging!

HERMES. That's right. He didn't carry the child there.

POSEIDON. I understand—he gave birth from the head again, the way he did with Athena. A regular womb, that head of his.

HERMES. No, he was pregnant in the thigh. He had Semele's infant there.

POSEIDON. What a genius! Gets pregnant all over, any place in his body he wants. Who is this Semele, anyway?

HERMES. She's from Thebes. One of Cadmus' daughters. He had an affair with her and she became pregnant.

POSEIDON. And then *he* had the child instead of her?

HERMES. It may sound queer to you, but that's exactly what happened. You see, Hera—you know how jealous she is—worked her way into Semele's good graces and talked the girl into asking Zeus to bring his thunder and lightning the next time he came to visit. He agreed and brought the thunderbolt. Well, the roof caught on fire and Semele went up in smoke. So he ordered me to cut open her belly and bring him the fetus; it wasn't fully grown, only in its sixth month. I did, and he split open his thigh and put it in there to finish its time. Three months have passed, he's just given birth, and he doesn't feel well because of the labor pains.

POSEIDON. Where's the infant now?

HERMES. I brought him to Nysa and gave him to the nymphs there to nurse. His name is Dionysus.

POSEIDON. So my brother is mother and father all in one of this Dionysus, eh?

HERMES. It looks that way. Well, I'm off now. Have to bring him water for his incision and do whatever else you generally do for someone who's just had a baby.

20

THE JUDGMENT OF PARIS

Zeus, Hermes, Aphrodite, Hera, Athena, Paris

At a particularly well-attended wedding Eris, the god-dess of discord, tossed into the midst of the guests a golden apple inscribed "For the fairest." Three goddesses claimed it: Hera, Aphrodite, and Athena. Zeus entrusted the deci-sion to Paris, a strikingly good-looking Trojan prince. Paris awarded the prize to Aphrodite, seduced by her promise to give him Greece's great beauty, Helen, as wife. This led to the famous war that ended so disastrously for the Trojans.

ZEUS. Hermes, take this apple to Troy and give it to Priam's son, the one that's a cowherd; he keeps his herd up at Gargara[1] on Mt. Ida. Tell him you have orders from me that, since he's so good-looking himself and knows his way around women so well, he's to be judge in a beauty contest for goddesses and that the winner gets this apple as prize. Well, you three had better leave now to meet with your judge. You see, I refuse to make the decision myself because I love you all equally and, if it were possible, I'd gladly see all three of you win. What's more, I can't give the prize to one of you without becoming the sworn enemy of two of you. That's why I can't serve as judge. Now, this young Trojan you're going to is a prince and a relative of Ganymede here. Besides, he's a simple country boy. He's a perfectly proper person to set eyes on you.

APHRODITE. So far as I'm concerned, Zeus, you can ap-point Momus himself, our worst critic, as judge. I'd be glad to show myself to him. What could he find to criticize in me? But your man has to be agreeable to these two also.

HERA. My dear Aphrodite, *we* wouldn't be afraid even if the verdict was in the hands of that Ares of yours. We're willing to take this Paris, whoever he is.

ZEUS. Athena, my child, what about you? Are you satisfied? What's that? Turning away and blushing? That's the way all you virgins are—always embarrassed by this sort of thing. Ah, you're nodding yes. All right, off you go, and remember—if you lose, don't get angry at the judge and cause that boy any trouble. You can't all be equally beautiful, you know.

HERMES. Let's go straight to Troy. I'll lead, and please follow right behind. Don't be nervous. I know Paris. He's a fine-looking young fellow and, besides, he knows his way around women; just the person to settle a matter like this. There's no chance of a wrong decision from him.

APHRODITE. If you tell me our judge is impartial that's all to the good, and fine for my side. But, Hermes, is he a bachelor? Does he have a wife?

HERMES. Well, he's not exactly a bachelor.

APHRODITE. What do you mean?

HERMES. I think he's living with some girl from the neighborhood.[2] Very nice girl, but the country type, terribly unsophisticated. He doesn't seem to be too attached to her, though. Why do you ask?

APHRODITE. Oh, nothing. I just asked.

ATHENA. Hermes! You're not being fair. What do you mean by holding private conversations with *her*?

HERMES. No harm done, Athena. It was nothing against you two. She just asked me if Paris was a bachelor.

ATHENA. The busybody! Why?

HERMES. I don't know. For no reason in particular, she says; she just asked.

ATHENA. Well? Is he?

HERMES. He doesn't seem to be.

ATHENA. Tell me, is he interested in a military career? Is he ambitious? Or is he just a cowherd at heart?

HERMES. I can't say for certain. My guess is that, since he's young, he probably is interested and would like to be a war hero.

APHRODITE. You see, Hermes? *I* don't complain or scold you for holding a private conversation with *her*. Only chronic complainers do such things. It's not *my* way.

HERMES. She asked me practically the same thing you did. So don't get angry or think your chances are being hurt if I simply answered a question for her too. Well, during all this talk we've been moving along. We've left the stars behind and we're almost at Troy. I see Mt. Ida and all of Gargara plainly and, if I'm not mistaken, there's your judge.

HERA. Where? I don't see him.

HERMES. Look off to the left, Hera. Not at the peak but at the slope, by the cave where you see the herd.

HERA. Herd? I don't see any.

HERMES. You don't? Here, look where I'm pointing. Don't you see calves coming out from among the rocks and someone with a crook running down the slope and keeping them together so they don't go every which way?

HERA. Oh, you mean that one. Yes, I see him.

HERMES. That's Paris. Since we're near now, if you don't mind, let's land and walk the rest of the way so we don't startle the man by suddenly swooping down on him.

HERA. Good idea. Let's do that. Aphrodite, now that we've landed, why don't you take the lead and show us the way? You must certainly be at home around here after all those visits we hear you made to Anchises.[3]

APHRODITE. Your catty remarks don't disturb me in the least, Hera.

HERMES. I'll lead the way. When Zeus fell in love with that youngster from Troy,[4] I spent a lot of time on Mt. Ida. He used to send me here all the time to keep an eye on the boy, and then, when he turned himself into an eagle, I flew alongside and helped carry the little beauty. If I remember correctly, he snatched him up from this rock right here. The boy happened to be piping away to his flock at the time and Zeus flew down from behind, put his claws around him very gently, held the youngster's turban in his beak, and carried him off. The poor boy was terribly upset and kept craning his neck to see who it was. He was so scared he dropped his pipe and I picked it up—ah, here's our judge, so let's go right up to him. Morning, cowherd.

PARIS. Morning to you, mister. Who are you and what are you here for? And who are these women? They're not the mountain-climbing type, not women that good-looking.

HERMES. Ah, but they're not women. Paris, you're looking at Hera, Athena, and Aphrodite. And I'm Hermes, here on orders from Zeus. What are you trembling for? Why so pale? Don't be afraid. There's nothing to worry about. He just wants you to judge a beauty contest for them. He told me to tell you that, since you're so good-looking yourself and know your way around women so well,[5] he's putting the matter in your hands. You'll know what the prize is as soon as you read the inscription on this apple.

PARIS. Let me see it. I want to find out what this is all about. "For the fairest," it says. Lord Hermes, I'm just a mortal and a country boy at that. How could I possibly judge such rare beauty? The very sight's too much

for a cowherd. A thing like this is for some city so-
phisticate to decide. Me, I could probably tell which is
the better of a pair of goats or a pair of cows—it's my
business. But these goddesses! All three are equally
beautiful, and I don't know how a person could even
drag his eyes away from one of them to look at the
other two. It's not easy to do. Once your eyes fall on
one, they're held fast and marvel at what's before them.
Then, when they move to the next, that one seems just
as beautiful and there they stay—and all the time are
distracted by what's on either side. I tell you, I'm over-
whelmed by such beauty; I'm swallowed up by it. My
only regret is that I can't have eyes all over my body
like Argus![6] If you ask me, the best verdict would be to
give the apple to all three of them. And let's not forget
that this one happens to be Zeus's sister and wife and
these two his daughters. What a situation to be called
in to judge!

HERMES. I wouldn't know. But I know this: you can't dis-
obey orders from Zeus.

PARIS. Hermes, please get them to agree to one thing: the
losers aren't to hold any grudge against me; they're to
understand my eyesight's to blame, not me.

HERMES. They promise. Now it's time for you to con-
sider your verdict.

PARIS. I'll try. What else can I do? I'd like to know this
first, though: will it be enough to look them over as
they are or must they strip so I can make a careful ex-
amination?

HERMES. You're the judge—it's up to you. Whichever way
you want. Just give the orders.

PARIS. Whichever way I want? Nude!

HERMES. Will all of you please strip? Examine them, Paris.
I'll look the other way.

HERA. All right, Paris, I'll strip first. I want you to see
that I have more than just white arms and that being

ox-eyed is not the only feature I'm proud of.[7] I'm beautiful all over.

PARIS. Now you, Aphrodite.

ATHENA. Paris, don't let her strip yet. First make her take off that girdle. It's magic—don't let her put a spell on you. Besides, she shouldn't come before you with all that paint and powder on; she looks just like a whore. She should show you only her natural beauty.

PARIS. They're right about the girdle. Please take it off, Aphrodite.

APHRODITE. Then why don't you take that helmet off, Athena, and show yourself with your head bare, instead of waving that plume around and frightening the judge? What are you worried about? That those gray eyes of yours[8] won't look so good without that scary thing over them?

ATHENA. See? The helmet's off.

APHRODITE. So's the girdle.

HERA. Let's all strip now.

PARIS. God of wonders! What a sight! They're so beautiful, so lovely! Oh, that virgin! And this queen—she's dazzling, superb. She deserves to be the wife of the king of the gods. And how sweet this lady's look is, what a charming and seductive smile! But enough of this bliss. Ladies, if there are no objections, I'd like to look each one of you over individually. Right now I'm confused. I don't know where to look—my eyes are drawn every which way.

APHRODITE. Let's let him.

PARIS. Hera, will you please stay? And you two step aside?

HERA. With pleasure. And after you've looked me over carefully, there's something else I want you to give thought to—whether you'd like the gifts I can offer in return for your vote. You see, Paris, if you decide in my favor, I'll make you lord of all Asia.

PARIS. Sorry, I'm not selling my verdict for gifts. You may go now. I'll vote as I think best. Athena, will you please step forward?

ATHENA. Here I am. Now, Paris, if you vote in my favor, you'll never lose a battle. You'll always be victorious. I'll make you a conquering hero.

PARIS. War and battles don't interest me, Athena. As you can see, Troy and Lydia are at peace; no one's challenging my father's rule. But don't worry—your chances won't be hurt even if I'm not letting gifts influence my decision. You may get dressed and put on your helmet. I've seen enough. Aphrodite's turn now.

APHRODITE. Standing right by you. Look me all over, every detail. Don't skip a thing. Spend all the time you want on every part of my body. Now, my handsome young man, if you don't mind, I'd like to tell you something. I noticed a long time ago how young and handsome you are; I don't think there's another to match you in all of Troy. I congratulate you on your good looks—but I don't at all approve of your living here among these cliffs and rocks instead of in the city and ruining your good looks in this desert. What good do these mountains do you? What good do your looks do these cows of yours? You should have been married by now—not to one of the country girls you have around here, but to a Greek girl, someone from Argos or Corinth or Sparta. Like Helen, for example. She's young, every bit as beautiful as I am, and—what's most important—the amorous type. One look at you and I know she'd give up everything, surrender herself to you completely, follow you home, and live with you. I'm sure you've heard all about her.

PARIS. Not a word, Aphrodite. And I'd be very happy to hear all you can tell me.

APHRODITE. She's the daughter of Leda, that beauty Zeus flew down to in the form of a swan.

PARIS. What does she look like?

APHRODITE. Very fair, as you'd expect in the child of a swan; has lovely, soft skin, since she was born from an egg; is athletic and goes in for sports; and is so irresistible there's already been a war fought over her, the time Theseus[9] carried her off when she was still a child. On top of all this, when she reached the bloom of youth the most eligible men in Greece came to sue for her hand. The choice fell on Menelaus, one of Pelops' descendants. If you want, I'll arrange to have her marry you.

PARIS. What? Me? But she's already married!

APHRODITE. You're so naïve, my little cowherd. I know how these things are done.

PARIS. How? I'd like to know too.

APHRODITE. You'll leave here and tell everyone you're going on a tour of Greece. When you get to Sparta, Helen will see you. The rest—to make her fall in love and follow you home—will be up to me.

PARIS. You mean she'd be willing to leave her husband and run off with some foreigner she's never met? I can't believe it.

APHRODITE. Don't worry your head about that. I have two beautiful children, Desire and Love. You can have them as guides. Love will come upon her with all his force and make her fall in love with you, while Desire will suffuse you and make you like himself, infinitely desirable. I'll go too. And I'll ask the Graces to come along with me so we can all use our influence on her together.

PARIS. I have no idea how all this will turn out, Aphrodite. One thing I do know—I'm already in love with your Helen. Somehow I seem to be seeing her before my very eyes . . . I'm sailing off to Greece . . . I'm in Sparta . . . I'm coming back with her in my arms—and I'm miserable because I'm not actually doing all these things this minute.

APHRODITE. Don't fall in love yet, Paris. First, in exchange
for my services as matchmaker and go-between, you
have to give me your vote. Because, if I help you, it's
only fitting I do so as Queen of Beauty and celebrate
your marriage and my victory at the same time. So you
see, Paris, you can buy everything—love, beauty, mar-
riage—with that apple you're holding.

PARIS. I'm worried that you'll forget all about me once the
contest is over.

APHRODITE. Do you want me to swear?

PARIS. Oh no. Just give me your promise again.

APHRODITE. I promise that I shall make Helen your wife,
that she will follow you and come to you in Troy, and
that I will be on hand and do all I can to help.

PARIS. And you'll bring Desire and Love and the Graces?

APHRODITE. Don't worry. I'll even bring Passion and the
god of marriage too.

PARIS. Then, with this promise in mind, I give you this
apple. Take it—but remember your promise!

NOTES

1 One of the peaks of Mt. Ida.

2 Oenone, who, when jilted, bitterly foretold all the trouble
in store for Paris.

3 A Trojan prince with whom Aphrodite had had an affair.
Aeneas, hero of Vergil's famous poem, was the product of the
union.

4 Ganymede; see pp. 103–7.

5 Lucian is mimicking Homer's practice of repeating mes-
sages verbatim.

6 A special guard who had one hundred eyes.

7 "White-armed" and "ox-eyed" (i.e., with large, lovely
eyes) are Homer's standard epithets for Hera.

8 "Gray-eyed" was Homer's standard epithet for Athena.

9 King of Athens and a notorious philanderer.

1

Doris and Galatea

Polyphemus was a Cyclops, one of the brood of one-eyed giants that Poseidon had fathered. He and his brothers lived a simple shepherd's existence on the slopes of Mt. Etna in Sicily. One day he caught sight of the sea nymph Galatea "milk-white" playing with her sisters and fell in love with her.

DORIS. That swain of yours, the shepherd from Sicily they tell me is so mad about you, is certainly no beauty, Galatea.

GALATEA. Don't you make fun of him, Doris. Never mind, I'll have you know he's a son of Poseidon.

DORIS. He is, is he? And what has that got to do with his looks? He could be the son of Zeus himself and it wouldn't help. So wild and hairy and—the worst of all —that one eye!

GALATEA. He may be wild and hairy, but that doesn't make him ugly. It's very masculine. And his eye looks very nice in his forehead and it sees just as well as two would.

DORIS. The way you sing his praises, anyone would think you were the one in love, not he.

GALATEA. I'm not in love with him, but I just can't stand listening to all of you run him down. If you ask me, you do it because you're jealous. When we were playing on the shore at the foot of Mt. Etna, where there's that long strip of beach between the sea and the slope, and he came by with his flock and looked down from the cliff and saw us, I was the one he thought was the best-looking of all; I was the only one who caught his eye. That's why you're all so mad at me. It proved I'm better than you, that I've got sex appeal. He didn't give one of you a second look.

DORIS. You think I'm jealous because some half-blind shepherd thought you were good-looking? Anyway, the only nice thing he was able to say about you was that you had a white skin—and, if you ask me, that's because he's always handling milk and cheese; anything that looks like these he thinks is beautiful. If you're interested in finding out what the rest of you happens to be like, climb on a rock some day when the sea is calm, bend over, and take a good look at yourself in the water —white skin, that's all you've got. And there's nothing to brag about in a white skin, not unless there's some color to set it off.

GALATEA. Well, I may be all just white skin, but I have a lover, even if he's not so perfect. But no one—shepherd or sailor or ferryman—has a nice word to say about any of you. Besides, Polyphemus is very musical.

DORIS. Oh, come off it, Galatea. We heard him sing the other day when he was serenading you. My god! You'd think it was a donkey braying. And that lyre! The skull of a deer with the antlers for arms, a crossbar stuck between them, and strings without any tuning pegs. And his singing! Simply awful, and all off-key. He howled one tune; the lyre played another—what a love song! We couldn't keep from laughing. Even Echo, who's always so ready to open her mouth, refused to answer that bellowing. She was ashamed to be caught mimicking anything so horrible. And that cute little present your handsome beau brought in his arms for you—a bear cub as shaggy as he is. Believe me, Galatea, nobody envies you a lover like that.

GALATEA. And just where is *your* lover, Doris? The one who's handsomer and knows how to sing and play the lyre so much better?

DORIS. I don't have any—and I don't go around bragging how irresistible I am to men. But someone like that Cyclops—why, he smells like a goat, and they tell me he eats raw meat and gobbles up any strangers that come his way. He's all yours, dear, and you can be all his.

6

Triton, Poseidon, Amymone

The fifty daughters of King Danaüs of Egypt were demanded in marriage by the fifty sons of his brother, Aegyptus. Danaüs fled with his daughters to Argos in Greece where they all pitched in to help combat a drought Poseidon had brought on the land.

TRITON. Poseidon, every day an absolute beauty comes to Lerna for water. I think she's the best-looking girl I've ever seen.

POSEIDON. Is she from a good family, Triton, or just some domestic assigned to carry water?

TRITON. Domestic? I should say not. She's Amymone, one of the fifty daughters of that Egyptian king. I made a point of finding out her name and family. Danaüs doesn't coddle those girls. He teaches them to do things for themselves. He has them fetch water, and he's trained them not to turn up their noses at any chores.

POSEIDON. She comes all the way from Argos to Lerna by herself?

TRITON. By herself. Argos is a pretty thirsty place, you know. So she has to keep hauling water all the time.

POSEIDON. Triton, what you tell me about this girl has me all excited. Let's go see her.

TRITON. Let's. As a matter of fact, it's just about time now for her to be on her way. She must be about halfway to Lerna.

POSEIDON. Then bring out the chariot. Wait—it takes such a long time to harness the horses and get the thing ready. Give me one of those fast dolphins of yours instead. I'll ride it; that'll be quickest.

TRITON. Here you are. The fastest I've got.

POSEIDON. Good. Let's go. You swim alongside. Ah, here we are in Lerna. I'll go into ambush somewhere and you keep a lookout. The minute you see her coming——

TRITON. There she is!

POSEIDON. Triton, that girl *is* a beauty! She's lovely! We've got to get her.

AMYMONE. Please! Where are you taking me? You're a kidnaper! I know—you were sent by Uncle Aegyptus! I'm going to call my father!

TRITON. Quiet, Amymone. It's Poseidon.

AMYMONE. Poseidon? What are you talking about? Hey, stop pulling me! You're dragging me into the water! Help! I'll sink! I'll drown!

POSEIDON. Don't worry. Nothing bad is going to happen to you. I'm going to strike the rock near the beach with my trident, make a fountain spring up right here, and name it after you. You'll be very happy. And when you die you'll be the only one of the family who won't have to haul water.[1]

NOTES

[1] The fifty sisters slew their unwanted lovers and, as punishment, after death had to haul water in a leaky container for the rest of time.

PROMETHEUS

Hermes, Hephaestus, Prometheus

Prometheus, son of the Titans Iapetus and Clymene, created mankind by molding figures out of clay and persuading Athena to breathe life into them. He then did men two great favors: he stole fire from heaven for them, and he tricked Zeus into letting them give the gods the poorer part of a burnt offering (he divided an animal into two portions, one of bones wrapped in fat and the other of meat, and inveigled Zeus into choosing the bones for his share). Zeus punished him for all this by shackling him to a cliff and sending an eagle to tear at his liver. Heracles, another of mankind's benefactors, shot down the eagle, and Zeus ultimately freed Prometheus in exchange for important information his prophetic powers enabled him to have.

HERMES. Here's the Caucasus, Hephaestus, where we're supposed to shackle this poor Titan. Let's look around for just the right crag. Some place with no snow. We can drive the spikes home there, and he'll hang in full view.

HEPHAESTUS. Let's do that, Hermes. We can't put him too low down near the flat because men—after all, he made them himself—will come to his rescue, and, if we put him up by the peak, they won't be able to see him from below. How about halfway up, over this cleft here? We'll spread his arms and shackle one hand to this rock and the other to the one opposite.

HERMES. Good idea. The cliffs all around are sheer and even overhang a little; they can't be scaled. And the foothold here on the crag is so narrow you can barely stand on tiptoe. All in all, it should make a perfect spot for the crucifixion. All right, Prometheus, no hanging back. Come on up here and let us shackle you to this cliff.

PROMETHEUS. Hephaestus! Hermes! You at least ought have pity on me. I don't deserve this fate.

HERMES. Have pity on you? You mean get promptly nailed up instead of you for disobeying orders! What do you think—the Caucasus isn't big enough to hold two more crucifixions? Stretch out your right arm. Hephaestus, put on the shackles and make them fast. Spike them down hard. The other arm now, Prometheus. Make it good and tight, Hephaestus. Fine. Pretty soon the eagle will be flying down to tear at your liver. Then you'll have payment in full for your virtuosity at modeling clay.

PROMETHEUS. Cronus! Iapetus! Mother! I'm innocent and look how I'm made to suffer!

HERMES. Innocent, Prometheus? In the first place, when you were put in charge of serving the meat course, you were so tricky and unfair that you sneaked all the best cuts for yourself and fobbed off on Zeus some bones

covered with fat, white and greasy;[1]

so help me Zeus, I remember Hesiod's exact words. In the second place, you invented human beings, the worst creatures in existence, particularly the females. And, to top it all, you stole fire, the most valuable thing the gods own, and gave it to mankind. After acts like these you mean to say you're being crucified for doing no wrong?

PROMETHEUS. It seems to me that even you, to use the poet's words, are

branding as guilty the guiltless.[2]

For such charges, if justice were to be done, I'd have suggested a sentence of lifelong support at public expense.[3] As a matter of fact, if you have the time, I'd

4–6]

be happy to plead my case against them and prove to you that Zeus's sentence was a gross miscarriage of justice. And, since you're an expert pleader before the bar,[4] you defend him—prove he was just in sentencing me to crucifixion near the Caspian Gates here in the Caucasus to wring pity out of every Scyth in the land.

HERMES. You're filing an appeal after the legal time limit has elapsed; it's useless. No matter, speak your piece. We have to wait around, anyway, until the eagle flies along to take care of your liver. Not a bad idea at all to use the time to listen to some expert sophistry. You're a damned clever rascal when it comes to making a speech, Prometheus.

PROMETHEUS. You present your side first, Hermes. Make the worst accusations you can against me. Don't leave out a single thing to justify that father of yours. Hephaestus, I'm appointing you judge.

HEPHAESTUS. Not me. You'll have a prosecuting attorney instead of a judge. When you stole that fire you left my forge stone-cold.

PROMETHEUS. Then divide the prosecution. You lead off with the theft, and you, Hermes, follow with the meat serving and the man making. Both of you look to me like expert trial lawyers.

HEPHAESTUS. Hermes will do the talking for me. I don't go in for this courtroom stuff; I'm mostly around the forge. He's the lawyer. He's really studied this sort of thing.

PROMETHEUS. I'd have thought Hermes wouldn't be particularly anxious to discuss the theft or throw anything of that kind up at me—considering he's in the same line of work himself. However, my dear Hermes, if you'll take over this charge, too, then the time has come to get on with the prosecution.

HERMES. I hardly think we require a lengthy brief or long-winded speeches for what you've committed. All I need do is cite the chief offenses: when entrusted with serving the meat you kept the best parts for yourself and cheated our king; you invented men although there was no need for them; and you stole fire from us and gave it to them. You don't appreciate, my dear Prometheus, how very humane you've found Zeus to be, considering the magnitude of your offenses. Now then, if you deny having perpetrated these acts, I'll have to refute you and deliver a long-drawn-out speech as I try my best to bring out the truth. But if you admit them—that you served the meat in the manner stated, invented men, and stole fire—then the prosecution rests; I need say no more. To do so would be sheer nonsense.

PROMETHEUS. Maybe what you've already said is sheer nonsense too. But we'll find out about that later. Since you claim to have stated the prosecution's case as fully as need be, I'll now do the best I can to disprove the charges.

First I'll take up the meat. So help me heaven, merely talking about it makes me blush for Zeus! Can he be that niggling a faultfinder? Just because he found a little bone in his share, to send off a god of my ancient standing to be crucified, to forget all about the time I fought as his ally? Never to realize how petty is his reason for getting angry—how childish it is for him to lose his temper and carry on so, simply because he doesn't get the best portion for himself? In my opinion, Hermes, a person shouldn't remember from one day to the next the sort of tricks played at dinner parties. If some *faux pas* is made while everybody is having a good time, you should consider it just a joke and leave your bad temper behind when you leave the party. But to save up your hatred until the following day, to bear a grudge, to nurse a stale anger—believe me, that's not worthy of a god, let alone a king of gods. As a matter of fact, if you take away the diversions from a banquet, the tricks and the jokes, the smiles and the kidding, all that's left is drunkenness, full bellies, and silence—a dull and gloomy state of affairs that won't do at all for a party. That's why I had no idea Zeus would remember even one day later what had happened—to say nothing of his getting all het up and thinking he'd been made to suffer horribly because someone who was serving the meat just in fun tried to see whether his highness, when he had the choice, could tell the better portion.

Hermes, let's make the case even stronger. Let's say that, instead of giving Zeus just a poorer serving, I made off with his whole portion. How about it? Is that a good reason for him to turn heaven and earth upside down, as the saying goes, dream up shackles and crucifixions and the Caucasian mountain range, send down eagles, and have my liver pecked out? Be careful that all this doesn't turn into a serious indictment of the aggrieved party on the grounds of meanness, pettiness, and a nasty tendency to lose his temper. If this is the way he carries on over a few scraps of meat, what would he have done if he'd lost a whole cow? You'd expect mortals to have much worse tempers than gods, yet in matters like these how much more sensible they are! If a cook dips his fingers in a stew he's preparing and licks them off, or gulps down a piece of a roast on the sly, there isn't a mortal alive who'd condemn him to crucifixion; they overlook things like that. Of course, if they're very angry, they'll box his ear or slap his face, but they've never yet crucified anyone for something so petty. But enough about the meat. It's a shame for me to have to answer such a charge but much more so for him to have brought it.

It's time now to take up my clay modeling and my creation of men. The charge as stated has two interpretations, and I don't know which you're accusing me of. Do you mean I shouldn't have created men at all, that leaving them to lie still as so much clay would have

been preferable? Or do you mean that it was all right
to have created them, but I should have used some other
form and not the one I did? No matter, I'll speak to
both. First I'll try to prove that bringing man to life
has done the gods no harm at all and, second, that
they're actually far better off this way than if the earth
had remained an unpopulated desert.

Now then, long ago—this approach is the easier way
to show whether I did wrong in rearranging things by
introducing men—long ago there existed only the immor-
tal gods up in heaven. The earth was wild and ugly,
bristling all over with trees, impenetrable forests of them.
There were no altars or temples to the gods—after all,
who was there to put them up?—no statues of wood or
stone or any of the multitude of things you see wor-
shiped with such reverence everywhere today. Now, the
common good is always on my mind; I'm always look-
ing for ways not merely to improve things for the gods
but to enhance the beauty and order of everything. So it
occurred to me that it wouldn't be a bad idea to take a
little bit of clay and mold some living beings out of it,
making their shape like ours. You see, I felt that being a
god lacked something in not having a counterpart to set
it off, something which, when used as a standard of com-
parison, would show what a very good thing divinity
is. I further felt that this counterpart, although mortal,
should be highly ingenious and intelligent and aware of
the better things in life.

Well, as the poet put it, I

mixed water with earth,[5]

worked it into a soft mass, and created men—along with
Athena, whom I called in to lend a hand. This is the
great wrong I've done the gods. Look at all the damage
I've caused by making some living beings out of clay
and quickening into life what had been lifeless up to
then. Apparently ever since, just because there are some

mortal beings on earth, the gods haven't been the same. Zeus is so angry now you'd think they had been taken down a notch by the creation of men. Or maybe he's afraid men will plot a revolution against him and make war on heaven the way the Giants did.[6]

It's perfectly clear, Hermes, that you gods haven't been wronged by me or by what I did. If you can prove even the slightest wrong, I'll shut up and admit I'm getting my just deserts. But what I've done has actually benefited the gods. Look down at the earth; you'll see what I mean. None of it's barren and ugly any longer. It's all adorned with cities and fields and domesticated plants; ships sail the seas; islands are inhabited; everywhere there are altars and sacrifices and temples and processions—

> All cities teem with men,
> And their streets are full of god.[7]

If I had made men just to keep as my private property, perhaps I could be accused of self-interest. But I didn't; I put them at the disposal of all of you for the common good. What's more, everywhere you look there are temples to Zeus, to Apollo, to Hera, and to you, too, Hermes. But temples to Prometheus? Nowhere. See how I look after only my own interests at the expense of the common good? See what a blackhearted traitor to it I am?

Then there's another point you ought keep in mind, Hermes. Do you think a thing of beauty that is never seen, something a person has bought or made that no one ever sets eyes on or admires, can give its owner the full measure of joy and satisfaction? Why do I ask this question? Simply because, if there were no men, there would be nobody to see the beauty of all things. We'd be rich—but no one else would ever marvel at our wealth, and we ourselves wouldn't think as much of it as we do. Why? Because we'd have no standard against

which to measure it. Similarly, without the constant
sight of those who have no share in our good things we
wouldn't realize how well off we are. It's by being
measured against something small that big things appear
big. You gods should have given me a medal as a
benefactor to the state. But no—crucifixion is the reward
I get for my idea.

But, you'll argue, some men are scoundrels: they se-
duce women, make war, marry their sisters, scheme
against their fathers. Isn't there plenty of this sort of
thing in heaven? Yet that's no reason why anyone should
be up in arms against Uranus and Ge for having created
us. Then, again, you might argue that taking care of
men necessarily involves us in a lot of trouble. By that
line of reasoning a herdsman should be annoyed at hav-
ing a flock because he has to take care of it. As a mat-
ter of fact, although it's a lot of trouble, he enjoys it. A
job is never a hardship inasmuch as it gives a man
something to do. What would we be doing if we didn't
have men to take care of? Lazing around, guzzling
nectar, stuffing ourselves on ambrosia, and accomplish-
ing nothing. But what really gets my gorge up is the
way all of you blame me for having made human be-
ings, particularly females, and yet you fall in love with
them, you never stop going down after them. You turn
yourselves into bulls, into satyrs, into swans to do it.[8]
You even consider it perfectly proper to have them
mother gods.

Perhaps you'll agree that the creation of men was
necessary but will argue that I should have given them
a different form, one not like ours. What should I have
chosen instead? What better pattern was there than this,
the one I knew to be the most beautiful? Should I have
made creatures that were wild brutes with no intelli-
gence? Yet, if I had, how could they sacrifice to gods or
offer you all the other honors men do? Whenever they
lead out the hecatombs for you, you're all sure to be on

hand—even if you have to go across the ocean "to the blameless Ethiopians."⁹ And what have you done with the one responsible for all these honors and sacrifices you get? Crucified him.

Enough about men. If you don't mind, I'll now take up that theft of fire which has been the target of so much criticism. In the name of heaven, will you please speak up and answer me one question: have we actually lost any fire since men have had it? You can't say we have. You see, fire, by its very nature, is the sort of possession which doesn't diminish even though someone else takes part of it. After all, if someone lights another fire from it, it doesn't go out. So it's downright selfishness on your part to prevent people who need fire from having any, when sharing it doesn't hurt you one bit. And yet gods should be noble, the

bestowers of blessings;¹⁰

they should be above selfishness of any sort. Why, even if I had sneaked off with every bit of fire in heaven and brought it all to earth without leaving a spark behind, I'd have done none of you any great harm. After all, you don't need it. You don't shiver with cold or boil your ambrosia or use artificial light. But men have to use fire for these and other things—particularly for sacrifices so that they can roast the fatty thighbones on the altars, burn the incense, and fill the streets with savory smoke. I've noticed that, whenever the aroma rises to heaven

with smoke intermingled,¹¹

all of you are delirious with joy and consider it your favorite treat. To find fault with what I did, therefore, runs directly counter to your own tastes. I'm amazed you don't order the sun to stop giving men light. After all, he's fire, too, and a good deal more sacred and fiery at that. Are you going to file charges against him for squandering your private property?

I've had my say. It's up to you two now. If anything has been improperly stated, correct it or refute it. Then I'll present my rebuttal.

HERMES. Prometheus, it's not easy to cross swords with a master at the art like yourself. But it's a lucky thing for you that Zeus didn't hear all this. Believe me, he'd have sent a dozen vultures to tear out your innards. It looked as if you were defending yourself, but you were actually making terribly serious accusations against him. There's one thing that amazes me, though. How could a prophet like yourself not have foreseen you'd be punished this way?

PROMETHEUS. I knew I would. But I also know I'll be set free. Before long some Theban, a half brother of yours, incidentally, will pass this way to shoot down that eagle you said was coming to attack me.

HERMES. I hope so, Prometheus. And I hope to see you set free and back at our banquets—but not serving the meat!

PROMETHEUS. Don't worry, I'll be at the table. Zeus is going to set me free after I do him a certain very special favor.

HERMES. What favor? Come on, tell us.

PROMETHEUS. You know Thetis, don't you? Well—but I shouldn't talk about it. I'm better off keeping my secret —so I can use it to buy my way out of this sentence.

HERMES. Keep your secret if that's the best thing to do. Let's go, Hephaestus; the eagle's coming now. Be brave, Prometheus. I hope your Theban makes his appearance with his bow soon and keeps that bird from dissecting you.

NOTES

[1] Hesiod, *Theogony* 541.

[2] *Iliad* 13.775.

[3] This is the famous offer Socrates made at his trial.

[4] For Hermes' specialties, see p. 97.

[5] Hesiod, *Works and Days* 61.

[6] The Giants, a race sprung from the earth, aided the Olympians in putting down the Titans but then revolted and had to be brought under control.

[7] From a poem (*Phaenomena*, 2–3) by Aratus, a contemporary of Lucian.

[8] See p. 102, n. 3.

[9] Cf. *Iliad* 1.423.

[10] *Odyssey* 8.325.

[11] *Iliad* 1.317.

ZEUS THE OPERA STAR

*Hermes, Athena, Zeus, Hera, Poseidon,
Aphrodite, Colossus of Rhodes, Momus,
Apollo, Heracles, Hermagoras, Timocles, Damis*

*The basic ingredients of this elaborate satire, furnishing
the action of what plot there is, are the divergent views of
the Stoic and Epicurean schools of philosophy on the na-
ture and function of the gods. The Stoics believed in a su-
preme deity to whom they ascribed the total direction of
the universe. The Epicureans held that gods either don't
exist or, if they do, exercise no control or authority what-
soever.*

*Another ingredient is the one so familiar in Lucian's
pages, Homer's treatment of the Olympian deities, the all-
too-human activities and emotions the poet assigns them
and his conception of them as deriving their sustenance
from the savory smoke wafted heavenward from burnt
offerings.*

*Still another is Greek art. Lucian pictures the gods here
as a collection of masterpieces of Greek sculpture: each is
represented by his or her most celebrated statue. Aphrodite
is the Aphrodite of Cnidus, a famous marble of which a
number of copies are extant today; Poseidon is a bronze,
one of the chefs-d'oeuvres of the great Lysippus; the sun-
god is the renowned Colossus of Rhodes, and so on.*

*This piece gets its name from the opening scene in
which Zeus and the others declaim like actors in Greek
tragedy, a form of drama which, with its highly charged
emotional content and use of music, is nearest to our grand
opera.*

HERMES.

        O Zeus, what means this furrowed brow, these
        words

[1–2]

Addressed unto yourself, this pacing back
And forth? You're white, you're pale as a professor!
Confide in me, and let me counsel to
Your woes. Scorn not a servant's simple words.

ATHENA.

Hear me, O Father, O dread son of Cronus, O ruler almighty!

Owl-eyed Athena, your daughter, the Tritogeneia, implores you:

Speak to us, tell us your secret, cease hugging it close to your bosom.

What is the care that is gnawing away at your heart and your spirit?

Why do you heave such deep sighs, Father? Why do your cheeks have this pallor?[1]

ZEUS.

There is no hurt that one may put in words,
No sadness that the tragic stage portrays,
Whose pain the godly essence does not feel.[2]

ATHENA.

Ah me, how somberly begins his speech![3]

ZEUS.

O earth, accursed is the race you've bred!
Prometheus! What woes you've brought on me![4]

ATHENA.

Yet speak. For we, the chorus, are your kin.

ZEUS.

Thunderbolt mighty and loud-crashing—now can you serve me no longer!

HERA. Enough hysterics, my dear Zeus. I don't have the flair for comedy or grand opera that these two have, and I've not swallowed Euripides whole, so I can't play a part in your histrionics. You think I don't know the reason for all this despair?

ZEUS. Of course you don't. Otherwise you'd be shrieking your head off.

HERA. I know what the chief reason is—a love affair. I don't shriek my head off because I'm used to it; you've humiliated me this way enough times by now. It certainly looks as if you've found yourself some Danaë or Semele or Europa and are madly in love. You've probably got plans all laid to turn into a bull or a satyr or gold and make your way through the roof into the arms of your inamorata.[5] All the signs—the groans, the tears, the pale cheeks—point to a love affair and nothing else but.

ZEUS. So it's your idea my troubles are just love affairs and that sort of foolishness, eh? I envy you!

HERA. Zeus all upset and not because of a love affair? How is that possible?

ZEUS. Hera, the gods' situation is desperate. We're on the razor's edge, as the saying goes. It's anybody's guess whether we'll continue to be worshiped and respected on earth or be considered nobodies and be completely ignored.

HERA. You don't mean to tell me the earth is producing Giants again? Or that the Titans have broken their chains, overpowered the guards, and are at war with us again?[6]

ZEUS.

Cheer up. Our hold on Hades is secure.[7]

HERA. Then what's happened that's so terrible? If it isn't Titans or Giants that's troubling you, I don't see why you have to come before us as Polus or Aristodemus[8] instead of Zeus.

ZEUS. Listen, Hera. Yesterday somehow or other Timocles the Stoic and Damis the Epicurean got involved in a discussion of providence. It took place in front of a large group of important people, which particularly made me unhappy. Damis insisted that gods don't exist and therefore exercise absolutely no supervision or control over what happens. Timocles—a very fine fellow—tried to defend us. A big crowd collected and the discussion went on and on and on. Finally they broke off after agreeing to continue it some other time. So now everybody is on tenterhooks until the next session begins and they can find out which will present the stronger case and win. Can't you see what a tight spot we're in? How our fate lies in the hands of one man? There are two alternatives: either Damis convinces them we're just an empty concept and we end up consigned to oblivion, or Timocles wins the debate and we go on being worshiped as always.

HERA. This is terrible! No wonder you went in for grand opera!

ZEUS. And you thought I had some Danaë or Antiope on my mind instead of this! Well, what should we do? Pitch in and help me think of something.

HERMES. I say we should call a meeting and bring the matter before the whole divine electorate.

HERA. And I agree with that.

ATHENA. Father, my idea is exactly the opposite. Don't get all heaven upset by showing how disturbed you are at what's happened. Just arrange things on your own so that Timocles wins and Damis gets hooted down and gives up.

HERMES. Zeus, we won't get away with it. Not if those philosophers are debating in public. Besides, if you don't act democratically in a matter that concerns everybody and is so important, you'll get a reputation for being a dictator.

ZEUS. You're right. Call a meeting. Have everybody come.

HERMES. Hear ye, hear ye, a celestial meeting has been called! All gods are to convene at once without delay. Important issues to be discussed.

ZEUS. What a bare, simple, unvarnished announcement, Hermes! Particularly for such a momentous meeting.

HERMES. How do you think I should make it?

ZEUS. How? I say you should dignify the announcement with some meter and poetic grandiloquence. That way there's a better chance of their coming.

HERMES. True. But that's a job for an epic poet or an elocutionist. I'm terrible at poetry. I'll put in a foot too many or leave one out and ruin the announcement. Everybody'll get a laugh at how bad my verses are. As a matter of fact, I've noticed that Apollo himself has raised a snicker with some of his oracles, even though his prophesying is generally so ambiguous the hearers don't have much time to spend on checking the meter.[9]

ZEUS. Then mix in with your announcement a lot of the verbiage Homer uses when he calls us for a meeting. You must remember.

HERMES. Not offhand, and not very clearly. But I'll try.

> Let not a god here in heaven, dee dum dee dee, let not a goddess,
> Let not a nymph or a river-god (save for the River of Ocean)
> Linger at home. Let them *all* make their way to the court of their ruler,
> All who have ever been given a share of the hecatomb's glories,
> All who have ever been given a seat by the savory altars,
> All of you, even the middle gods, lowest gods, gods who are nameless.

ZEUS. Bravo, Hermes! A perfect announcement. They're streaming in already. Take charge and seat each one according to material and workmanship: gold in the first row, silver next, then ivory, then bronze or stone; arrange the last two so that work by Pheidias, Alcamenes, Myron, Euphranor, and the like gets precedence, and jam these inartistic run-of-the-mine pieces some

place in the back where they can swell the attendance
without being heard from.

HERMES. I'll do that; they'll be seated accordingly. But
here's something I'd better know: suppose one is all gold,
weighing a ton, but is crudely made, some amateurish
job all out of proportion. Should it take precedence
over the bronzes of Myron and Polycleitus and the
marbles of Pheidias and Alcamenes? Or should work-
manship come first?

ZEUS. Workmanship should, of course. But we'll have to
give precedence to gold.

HERMES. I understand. My orders are to treat them by
value and not quality and seat them according to cost
of material. All right, gold up front here! Zeus, if you
ask me, the whole first row will go to foreigners. You
can see for yourself what the Greeks are like: they have
beautiful features; they're lovely; they're artistically
done—but they're stone or bronze. The most expensive
are ivory and gold, but the gold is just a touch of plate
here and there to give them a shine and some color,
while inside there's nothing but a wooden frame where
whole herds of mice have squatters' rights. On the other
hand, Bendis over here and Anubis over there and
Attis next to him and Mithras and Men are all heavy
solid gold worth a fortune.[10]

POSEIDON. Hermes, it's downright unfair to seat this dog-
faced Egyptian in front of me. Don't forget, *I'm*
Poseidon.

HERMES. No, it isn't. You see, Earth-Shaker, you're just
a bronze pauper. At the time Lysippus made you, the
Corinthians had no gold. It would take a gold mine to
make you as rich as dogface here. So you'll just have
to take a back seat and like it and keep your temper
even if the owner of an oversize golden snout takes
precedence over you.

APHRODITE. Then you can put *me* in the front row, Hermes.
I'm gold, you know.

HERMES. Not that I can see. Unless my eyes have gone
back on me, you're white marble, probably quarried
from Mt. Pentelicus.[11] It was Praxiteles' idea to carve an
Aphrodite, and when you were done you were given to
the people of Cnidus.

APHRODITE. But I have a reliable witness—Homer. All
through his poems he calls me "golden Aphrodite."

HERMES. Sure. He's the same one who said that Apollo was
"rich in gold" and "wealthy." But where will you find
Apollo now? Burglars relieved him of his crown and
pulled out the pegs of his lyre,[12] so he's somewhere in
the seats assigned to the middle tax bracket. Just be
thankful *you're* not sitting with the lowest tax bracket.

COLOSSUS OF RHODES. No one will dare challenge *my* rights.
I'm the colossal Helius. Why, if Rhodes hadn't decided
to make me on this enormous overblown scale, for the
same price they could have had sixteen gold gods. So
my value should be reckoned accordingly. Besides, in
spite of my size I'm very well done; I have artistic
quality.

HERMES. Zeus, what do we do? This is too hard for me to
decide. If I go by his material, he's just bronze. But if
I figure how much it cost to cast him, he belongs in
front of even the top tax bracket.

ZEUS. Now, why did he have to come and show all the
others how puny they are and overcrowd the meeting?
Listen, my Rhodian champion, even if we all agree you
should get precedence over gold, how can we possibly
give you a front-row seat? Just one of those buttocks of
yours would fill the whole auditorium; if we made room
for you to sit, everybody else would have to stand.
You'd better spend the session on your feet and stoop
over during the discussion.

HERMES. Zeus, here's another tough one. Both of bronze,

workmanship identical—two pieces by Lysippus—, and, most important, social standing the same—both sons of yours. I mean Dionysus here and Heracles. Which gets the better seat? See? They're arguing about it.

ZEUS. Hermes, we're wasting time. We should have called the meeting to order long ago. Let them sit any which place they want this time. Some other day we'll hold a special meeting on the point and then I'll know where to put them.

HERMES. So help me Heracles, what a hullabaloo they're all raising! They're hollering the way they always do: "We want our share! Where's the nectar? What, no more ambrosia? Where are the hecatombs? Equal shares in all sacrifices!"

ZEUS. Call for silence, Hermes, so they'll stop this nonsense and find out why we called this meeting.

HERMES. But they don't all speak Greek. And, since I'm no linguist, I can't make myself understood by Scyths, Persians, Thracians, and Celts. Maybe I'd better use my hand and signal for silence.

ZEUS. Do that.

HERMES. Fine. They're as quiet as a bunch of professors. Time now for you to address the meeting. See? Everybody has been looking at you all this time, waiting to hear what you're going to say.

ZEUS. Hermes, something's happened to me, and I don't mind confessing it to you; you're my own son, after all. You know how confident and effective I am when I speak in public——

HERMES. I certainly do. I used to be scared stiff when I listened to you address a meeting. Particularly the time you threatened to let down that golden cord of yours and overturn land and sea from the bottom up, gods and all.[13]

ZEUS. My boy, I don't know whether it's the seriousness of

this terrible situation we face or the size of the audience
—look at this full celestial house we have!—but right now
I can't collect my thoughts. I'm nervous. I feel as if my
tongue's tied. And the most amazing thing of all is that
I've clean forgotten the opening remarks I had care-
fully prepared so I could make a fine first impression.

HERMES. Zeus! You're ruining everything! This silence of
yours is making them suspicious. Because you're hesitat-
ing this way, they think they're going to hear something
horrible.

ZEUS. How about my reciting that famous opening I use
in Homer?

HERMES. Which?

ZEUS.

> Hear me each one of you, hear me each god and each
> goddess.[14]

HERMES. Oh no. We had enough of that nonsense out of
you earlier. If you don't mind, forget the hackneyed
metrical stuff. Pick one of those speeches Demosthenes
delivered against Philip,[15] any one you want. Change a
few phrases and give them that. As a matter of fact,
that's what most public speakers do nowadays.

ZEUS. Good idea. A nice short cut to speechmaking that,
and an easy way out when a man doesn't know what
to say.

HERMES. Get on with it then.

ZEUS. Gentlemen of heaven, I am convinced you would
sooner know the reason for being summoned to this
meeting than have a fortune in gold. And since this is
so, my words merit your undivided attention. Fellow
gods, our present situation all but tells us with a voice
of its own that we must be stern and resolute in coming
to grips with what confronts us. Yet, if you ask me, we
seem to be utterly indifferent to it.[16] And now, since I
can't remember any more Demosthenes, I'll tell you

what so upset me that I called this meeting. As you all
know, yesterday Mnesitheus[16a] the importer made a
thank offering for the ship he almost lost off Caphereus.
Those of us he invited had a feast down at the Piraeus.
After the drink offerings had been served, you others all
went your ways. However, since it was still early, I went
up to town to take an evening stroll in the Potter's
Quarter and think over how stingy that Mnesitheus was.
He invites sixteen gods to a banquet, and all he puts
on the altar is one cock, a wheezy ancient one at that,
and four pieces of incense so mildewed that a minute
after they were put on the coals they fizzled out with-
out giving off enough smoke for even one little sniff.
And this was the man who was promising us whole
hecatombs earlier, when his ship was being blown
through the reefs towards the cliffs!

Well, while I was thinking all this over, I came to
the Painted Arcade[17] and I noticed a whole crowd of
men. Some were standing under the arcade and a lot
out in the square, while a few were seated on the
benches hollering at the top of their lungs. I guessed
what was happening—a wrangle between some of those
philosophers who are always ready for an argument—
and I decided to stop and listen to what they were say-
ing. It so happened I was wrapped in a cloud, one of
my thick ones, so I switched into their kind of clothes,
pulled my beard further down from my chin, and made
myself into a pretty good facsimile of a philosopher.
Then I elbowed my way through the crowd and got to
the center without anyone recognizing who I was.
There I found that damned scoundrel, Damis the Epi-
curean, and that very fine fellow, Timocles the Stoic,
having a hot and heavy argument. As a matter of fact,
Timocles was all in a sweat and had been shouting so
much he had no voice left, and Damis, with a sneering
grin on his face, was needling him.

The whole discussion, it seems, was about us. That

damned Damis was insisting that we take no thought
for men and exercise no supervision over what happens
to them. In effect, he was saying we don't exist; this
was clearly the point of his argument. And there were
some in the crowd who were applauding him. Timocles,
on the other hand, was on our side. He was standing
up for us, fighting as hard as he could and losing his
temper with Damis. He praised our thoughtfulness and
pointed out how our rule and direction were marked in
every respect by just the proper system and order. And
some in the crowd were applauding him too. But by
this time he had gotten tired and wasn't speaking well,
and the majority were turning toward Damis. I realized
the danger and ordered night to close in on the meeting
and break it up. Everyone went off after agreeing to
hear the argument through to the end the next day.
I moved along with the crowd and eavesdropped on
people as they walked home. They were for Damis;
sentiment was already running strong in favor of his
stand, although there were some who were against con-
demning the opposition in advance and in favor of
waiting to hear what Timocles would say the next day.

Fellow gods, this is why I have called you together—
no small reason when you consider that our honor, our
prestige, and our revenues all depend upon men. If
they're convinced that gods don't exist or that, if we do,
we take no thought for them, it means the end of sacri-
fices, gifts, and honors for us from down below. We'll
sit around uselessly in heaven and starve, since our
traditional holidays, celebrations, games, sacrifices, festi-
vals, and parades will be taken away from us. Therefore,
in view of the gravity of the situation, I say it's the duty
of everyone here to rack his brains for some way to save
us in this crisis, some way to give Timocles the stronger
case and a victory and to get the audience to hoot
Damis down. Unless we do something for Timocles, I
don't have much confidence in his winning on his own.

All right, Hermes, make the formal announcement that
the floor is now open for debate.

HERMES. Order, please! Silence! Your attention, please.
Does any senior god wish to exercise his prerogative and
address the meeting? No one asking for the floor?
What's the matter? Struck dumb and helpless at the
seriousness of what you've just heard?

MOMUS.

You may have all to a man been transformed into
earth and mere water[18]

but I have not. And, Zeus, if you'd care to grant me
full freedom of expression, there are quite a few things
I could say.

ZEUS. Speak up, Momus. Don't be afraid. It's perfectly clear
you'll use your freedom of expression for the common
good.

MOMUS. Then, fellow gods, I'll speak to you from the heart,
as the saying goes. I fully expected we'd come to this
impasse, that we'd harvest a whole crop of these phi-
losophers. It's we ourselves who are responsible for their
presumption. So help me Lady Justice, we have no right
to get angry at Epicurus or his pupils or followers for
holding such ideas about us. What can you expect them
to think? They see how mixed up life is, how the good
are ignored and waste away in poverty and disease and
slavery while filthy scoundrels collect honors and grow
rich and order their betters around. They see men who
stoop to robbing temples get away with it and escape
scot-free while innocent people suffer torture and execu-
tion. With such things before their eyes naturally they
come to the conclusion we don't exist. Particularly when
they hear us handing out such oracles as "The man who
crosses the river Halys will destroy a great kingdom"
without revealing whether we mean the man's or his
enemy's.[19] Or take this example:

> O sacred Salamis, many a mother's dear son will
> you slaughter.[20]

It's my impression that the Persians as well as the
Greeks were sons of mothers. And another point. Men
hear from the epic poets about our love affairs, our
wounds in battle, our imprisonments, enslavements, po-
litical squabbles, and the thousand other troubles we
have—we who claim to be blessed immortals. Why
shouldn't they ridicule us and assume we're nothing at
all? Here we are, losing our tempers because some men
who are not exactly stupid expose all this and reject the
notion that we take thought for mankind. Why, we
ought to be thankful that there are people who still go
on sacrificing to us in spite of all our faults.

Zeus, here's a simple question to which I want an
honest answer—after all, there aren't any mortals present
at this discussion except the four who managed to
wangle celestial citizenship, Heracles, Dionysus, Gany-
mede, and Asclepius.[21] Have you ever had enough inter-
est in affairs on earth to find out which men are good
and which bad? You can't say you have. Why, if
Theseus hadn't taken time out on his way from Troezon
to Athens to cut down the rascals he found there, so far
as you and your thought for mankind are concerned,
nothing would have prevented Sciron, Pityocamptes,
Cercyon, and the others from going on living like kings
off the murder of travelers.[22] Eurystheus, a man of the
old school who knew what the words "taking thought"
meant, out of sheer love for humanity looked into con-
ditions everywhere and sent out Heracles here as trou-
ble shooter, a hard-working fellow with a taste for tough
assignments. If he hadn't done so, you, my dear Zeus,
wouldn't have given a second thought to the Hydra, the
Stymphalian birds, the Thracian horses, and the Cen-
taurs' drunken insults.[23]

To tell the honest truth, we sit around keeping an eye

on only one thing: are people sacrificing? Is smoke com-
ing up from the altars? Everything else gets swept along
wherever the current happens to carry it. So I say what
we're getting now should come as no surprise—and
there'll be more of it as men, little by little, open their
eyes and discover that the sacrifices they burn and the
processions they hold don't help them one bit. Pretty
soon you'll see the Epicuruses and the Metrodoruses[24]
and the Damises ridiculing us, beating down our de-
fenders, and stopping their mouths. *You* have pushed
things to this state; it's *your* job to call a halt and to
work a cure. I'm just Momus; there's no great danger of
my losing any honors—I was dropped from the honor roll
long ago—but all of you are still riding high and en-
joying your exclusive right to burnt offerings.

ZEUS. Fellow gods, let him drivel on. He's always been a
nasty faultfinder. As the great Demosthenes put it, it's
easy to accuse and blame and criticize, and anyone can
who wants to, but to advise how to improve a situation,
that's the mark of the true counselor.[25] And I know that's
what the rest of you will do. *He* can keep his mouth shut.

POSEIDON. As you all know, I spend most of my time un-
der water. I run things my own way down in the depths,
where I arrange as best I can for the rescuing of sailors,
the moving of ships, and the calming of winds. How-
ever, I take an interest in affairs up here as well. Now,
I say that before Damis can return to the debate we
must get rid of him—the thunderbolt or some other de-
vice will do the trick—or else he might win; after all,
Zeus, you tell us he's a very convincing fellow. At the
same time we'll be showing everybody how we go after
people who say such things about us.

ZEUS. Poseidon, either you're joking or you've clean forgot-
ten we have no such power. The Fates weave all life
spans; they decide who dies by the thunderbolt, the
sword, fever, disease. If I had the say, do you think

I'd have let those temple robbers get away from Olympia the other day unthunderbolted? They cut off two six-pound curls of mine! Take your own case. Would you have let that fisherman from Oreus make off with your trident at Geraestus?[26] Besides, even if we could do what you suggest, everybody would think we were angry and upset by what was happening and afraid of what Damis was going to say; they'd think that was why we did away with him without waiting for Timocles to refute him. Winning that way would look just like winning by default.

POSEIDON. Well, I only thought I had figured out a quick way to get a victory.

ZEUS. Poseidon, you have the brains of a fish. How thick can you be? Knock off an opponent in advance? Then he dies before he's beaten and leaves the whole argument undecided and still in doubt.

POSEIDON. Well, if I have the brains of a fish, the rest of you think of something better.

APOLLO. Too bad we juniors without beards don't have the right to address the meeting. I probably could have made a useful contribution to the discussion.

MOMUS. Apollo, the issues under discussion are so important that the floor is open to anyone, not just senior members. A fine thing if we have to split hairs about parliamentary procedure when we're on the brink of disaster! Anyway, you're already fully qualified to address the meeting. You came of legal age eons ago; you're an officially registered member of the Twelve Gods, and your membership in the Upper Chamber practically goes back to Cronus.[27] So don't put on the boy act with us. Step up and give us your ideas. Don't be bashful about addressing this body without any hair on your chin—not someone who's father of a son as long-bushed as that Asclepius of yours. Besides, this is the perfect occasion for a display of your wisdom—unless all that sitting

around on Mt. Helicon talking philosophy with the
Muses has been a sheer waste of time.[28]

APOLLO. You're not chairman of this meeting, Momus. Zeus
is. And if he recognizes me, I'll probably make a learned
speech that'll do Mt. Helicon education full justice.

ZEUS. So ordered. You have the floor, my boy.

APOLLO. This Timocles is a fine, god-fearing man who's
an expert on the ins and outs of Stoicism. That's why
a lot of young men take advanced courses with him—he
picks up quite a bit in tuition fees this way—and he's
extremely convincing when he's holding individual dis-
cussions with his students. But he's frightened to death
of talking to crowds; he's had no voice training, and he
speaks Greek like a foreigner. The result is that people
laugh at him when he debates in public. Instead of go-
ing along smoothly, he stammers and gets rattled, par-
ticularly when, in spite of his shortcomings, he tries to go
in for fancy oratory. So far as intellect goes, those who
know their Stoicism say he's exceptionally keen and sub-
tle. But his weakness in putting things in words ruins all
this. He's confusing and doesn't make his meaning clear,
he advances propositions that are like riddles, and his
answers to questions leave things more in the dark than
before. His hearers don't understand, and so they laugh
at him. I feel myself that it's every speaker's duty to be
clear; the one thing he must be most careful about is to
make sense to his audience.

MOMUS. You're absolutely right, Apollo, to preach clarity
in public speaking, even though you practice precious
little of it yourself. Those prophecies of yours are so
ambiguous and enigmatic and are generally placed so
safely on the fence that the audience needs a second
prophet to explain what they mean. Well, what do you
advise as the next step? How do we cure Timocles' in-
ability to debate?

APOLLO. There are plenty of glib talkers around. Let's try

to make one a mouthpiece for him. Timocles will do the thinking and whisper to him, and he'll put it all in the right words.

MOMUS. Exactly what a beardless juvenile who ought to be back in grade school would say. In a profound philosophic discussion you want to put a mouthpiece alongside Timocles to transmit his ideas to the audience. Damis is to speak his own lines, but Timocles is to use an actor, whisper ideas into his ear, and the actor, who probably won't understand a word of what's said to him, is to make the speeches. If *that* won't hand the crowd a laugh! No, let's think up some other way out. Now you, my admirable Apollo, claim to be a prophet and you've picked up quite a bit of money in that line—even collected some gold ingots once.[29] Why don't you take advantage of this chance to give us an exhibition of your art and predict which of the philosophers will win the debate? You're a prophet; you certainly know how it's going to come out.

APOLLO. Here? How can I? We don't have a tripod or incense or an oracular spring like my Castalia.[30]

MOMUS. See? You're on the spot—and you side-step being put to the test.

ZEUS. Do it anyway, my boy. Don't give this slanderer an excuse to run you down and ridicule your profession. He'll say it's all a matter of tripods, water, and incense and that without them you can't do a thing.

APOLLO. Father, I'd be better off doing something like this my usual way in Delphi or Colophon where I have everything I need. However, even though I don't have a bit of equipment I'll try to predict who'll win. Bear with me, though, all of you, if my verses are a bit rough.

MOMUS. Go ahead, Apollo, but just make it clear or else *we'll* have to have a mouthpiece to interpret. This time it's none of that "boiling lamb and tortoise" business.[31] You know what the discussion's all about.

ZEUS. What are you going to say, my boy? Lord, the pre-
liminaries have me scared already! He's turned white;
he's rolling his eyes; he's tossing his head; he's jumping
around like a madman. The whole thing's weird; it's
frightening; it's like the Mysteries![32]

APOLLO.

> Hear, everyone, a prediction inspired, as the prophet
> Apollo
> Tells of the fate of the battle so bitter 'twixt shrill-
> voiced opponents
> Armed with the might of an army of sentences,
> clauses and phrases.
> Loud is the din—now for this one, now that—of the
> boos and the hisses.
> Many a blow do they strike on the crests of the plow's
> lofty handles.
> But when the cruel-taloned vulture shall carry aloft a
> poor cricket,
> Then will the rain-bearing crows cease for ever and
> ever their cawing,
> Then will the mule win the day, and the ass butt at
> fleet-footed offspring.

ZEUS. What's the big joke, Momus? This is no laughing
matter. Stop that guffawing, damn you, before you
choke.

MOMUS. After hearing an oracle so crystal clear? How can
I?

ZEUS. Then suppose you tell *us* what it means.

MOMUS. Perfectly clear. No Themistocles needed for this
one.[33] The oracle says as plain as day that Apollo here
is a quack, that, so help me Zeus, we're a pack of mules
and asses for believing in him, and that we don't even
have the brains of a cricket.

HERACLES. Father, I may be only a naturalized citizen, but
that's not going to stop me from telling you what I think.
Let's wait until the meeting is called and the debate

begins. Then, if Timocles is winning, we'll let them go
on with this argument about us. But, if it looks as if
it's going the other way, assuming you have no objec-
tions, I'll give the arcade a shake and bring it down on
Damis' head. That way we'll stop the damned scoun-
drel's insults.

ZEUS. So help me Heracles, Heracles, you talk exactly like
some hick from Boeotia. Just to get at one rascal, do
you have to destroy all those people plus the arcade,
Marathon, Miltiades, Cynegirus, and all? If you ruin all
that, how are orators going to orate without their most
important topic?[34] Besides, when you were alive you
might have been able to do something like that, but,
ever since you've been a god, you've come to realize,
I'm sure, that the Fates have exclusive power over such
things and we have none.

HERACLES. You mean that when I killed the Numean lion
or the Hydra I was just acting as agent for the Fates?

ZEUS. Of course.

HERACLES. And if someone insults me today by robbing
my temple or knocking over my statue, I can't squash
the life out of him unless the Fates had so decreed
years before?

ZEUS. You certainly cannot.

HERACLES. Then listen to me, Zeus. I'm going to be frank.
That comic playwright was right about me:

I'm just a hick who calls a spade a spade.[35]

If that's the way things are up here, I'm bidding a long
good-by to all your honors, altar smoke, and gory sacri-
ficial lambs. I'm going to Hades. There I can take my
bow out of its case and at least scare the shades of the
monsters I killed.

ZEUS. Oh, fine. Nothing like your own family for testifying
against you, as they say. Why didn't you pass all this
on to Damis for the debate? You'd have been a great

help. Wait—what's this? Who's that running toward us? It's a bronze. The hair-do is old-fashioned, tooling and design very good. Why, it's your brother, Hermes, the one in charge of public squares who stands by the arcade. See? He's covered with pitch; sculptors are always making copies from him. My boy, why the hasty arrival? Some urgent news from earth to report?

HERMAGORAS.[36] A top priority message, Zeus. Requires maximum attention.

ZEUS. Has there been a second insurrection that we missed hearing about? Speak up!

HERMAGORAS.

> While I was being smeared with pitch just now,
> Applied by bronzesmiths to my chest and back
> To form a silly breastplate round my body,
> One molded and hung with imitative skill
> To capture every impress of the bronze,
> I saw a crowd come by and with it were
> Two men with pallid cheeks but voices loud,
> Two masters of the verbal punch and jab.
> The one was Damis and——[37]

ZEUS. Enough iambics, Hermagoras, please! I know the men you mean. Just tell me this: has the bout been on for very long?

HERMAGORAS. Not yet. They were still skirmishing, sending out long-range volleys of sneers.

ZEUS. Fellow gods, the only thing left to do is to stoop over and listen in. Hours! Will you please draw the bolt, roll back the clouds, and open the gates of heaven? In the name of Heracles! Look at the crowd that's gathered to hear them! Timocles is nervous and confused; I can't say I like that. That man will ruin everything today. No question about it—he'll be no match for Damis. Well, we'll do all we can for him—we'll pray

> Silently, each to himself, so that Damis will not overhear us.[38]

Timocles

Damis, you crook, on what grounds do you claim
gods don't exist and take no thought for mankind?

Damis

Not so quick. First you tell me what the reason-
ing was that convinced you gods do exist?

Timocles

Oh no. Damn you, you answer my question first.

Damis

Oh no. You answer mine.

zeus. This is where our man has the edge. He hands out
insults like a virtuoso. Good work, Timocles! Keep call-
ing him names. That's your forte. Try anything else and
he'll stop your mouth so tight you'll talk less than a fish.

Timocles

So help me Athena, I will *not* answer first.

Damis

All right, then, ask your question. That oath gave
you the first round. But skip the name-calling, if
you don't mind.

Timocles

Agreed. So, damn you, you think the gods ex-
ercise no control over the future?

Damis

None whatsoever.

Timocles

Then, according to you, there's no control at all
over anything that happens?

Damis

That's right.

Timocles

And there's no god taking care of and arranging
everything?

Damis

No.

Timocles

And everything is carried along at random just
by blind chance?

Damis

Yes.

Timocles

Men! Are you going to listen to this and do noth-
ing? Stone the sinner!

Damis

Why this inflaming the public against me,
Timocles? Who are you to carry on like this for
the gods when they don't choose to do so for them-
selves? They've yet to do anything terrible to me
and they've been hearing me talk for years—assum-
ing, of course, that they can hear.

Timocles

They can hear, all right, and they'll go after you
when the time comes.

Damis

How can they have time for me? You've told
me yourself how many jobs they have, how they
have to run the universe with its infinite mass of
things. That's why they haven't gotten around yet
to paying you back for all the times you perjured
yourself in their name and all the times—no, I won't
let myself stoop to name-calling and break our
agreement. Yet I don't know of a better way they
could show their forethought for mankind than by
visiting a horrible death on a horrible sinner like
you. Obviously they must be away on vacation,
across the ocean, maybe, with the blameless Ethi-
opians.[39] They're in the habit of turning up there all
the time for a meal, occasionally without even wait-
ing for an invitation.

Timocles

How do you expect me to reply to such bare-
faced insolence?

[38–39

Damis

By giving me the answer I've been waiting to
hear from you all along: what brought you to be-
lieve in divine providence?

Timocles

First and foremost, the ordered arrangement of
everything that happens. The sun forever travels in
the same orbit. So does the moon. The seasons
come and go in turn; plants grow; living beings are
born and are so ingeniously devised that they grow
up, think, move, walk, build houses, make shoes,
and all the rest. Don't you think that all this is the
work of divine providence?

Damis

That's exactly what has to be proved, Timocles.
You're begging the question: you haven't yet
proved it's divine providence that accomplishes all
this. I don't deny that things happen in the way
you describe. But we need not automatically con-
clude that the cause is some divine prearrange-
ment. It's perfectly possible that things which to-
day have a similar and regular pattern of behavior
were originally totally different. Things have a nat-
ural necessity, and you're calling this an "ordered
arrangement." Obviously you're going to be angry
with everyone who won't go along with you in
enumerating the manifestations of nature, applaud-
ing them, and considering them a demonstration of
how divine providence orders all. So, as the comic
playwright once said,

That answer's not too good; let's have another.

Timocles

I feel I don't need any further proofs beyond
what I've given. No matter, here's one—answer this
question: do you think Homer is our finest poet?

Damis

He certainly is.

Timocles

Well, I was convinced by the way he demon-
strated divine providence.

Damis

My dear Timocles, everybody will agree that
Homer is a fine poet, but not that he—or any other
poet—is a reliable authority for the sort of thing
we're discussing. As I see it, poets are not con-
cerned with truth but with entertaining an audi-
ence. That's why they charm our ears with meter,
make their points through mythical allegories—in
a word, use any and every device to enhance the
pleasure they give. As a matter of fact, Timocles,
I'd very much like to hear just which parts of
Homer convinced you. The one that tells about
the conspiracy against Zeus? How his daughter,
brother, and wife plotted to tie him up and if
Thetis hadn't felt sorry for him and called in Briar-
eus, they'd have grabbed His Majesty and clapped
him in irons? He didn't forget he owed Thetis
thanks for all this, so he sent Agamemnon a mis-
leading dream to deceive him and cause the
slaughter of hundreds of Greeks. You realize, of
course, that he couldn't simply have wiped Aga-
memnon out by tossing a thunderbolt at him; then
everybody would have known what a double-
dealer a god could be. But I know the part that
must have drawn you irresistibly to your faith—
where Diomed wounds Aphrodite and then, with
Athena cheering him on, wounds Ares himself;
pretty soon the rest of the gods have jumped in
and are squaring off—with no distinction between
the sexes: Athena wins over Ares (I presume he
was in a weakened condition from what Diomed
had done to him earlier), and

Stout Eriounian Hermes engages in combat
with Leto.

Or maybe you were convinced by the part about
Artemis? Where that congenital faultfinder got
angry because Oeneus hadn't invited her to a
party and let loose on his land an enormous boar
so powerful no one could overcome it? Tell me, was
it with stories like these that Homer won you
over?[40]

ZEUS. Oh dear! What a shout of applause the crowd just
gave Damis! Our man is shaking with fright; it looks as
if he's at the end of his rope. You can see he's ready to
throw in the sponge; he's looking around for some place
he can slip through and make his getaway.

Timocles

Then I take it you don't think Euripides has
anything worth while to tell us either, when he
puts the gods themselves on the stage and has
them rescue our famous heroes and punish villains
and sinners like yourself?

Damis

Ah, my most noble philosopher, if it was our
writers of tragedy who convinced you with such
stuff, there are only two possible conclusions: either
you must hold that the gods temporarily took the
form of Polus, Aristodemus, and Satyrus[41] or,
what's worse, that they took the form of the masks
with gods' faces, the buskins, trailing robes, cloaks,
long sleeves, belly pads, body pads, and all the
other paraphernalia used to give the proper atmos-
phere to a tragedy. This is ridiculous. As a matter
of fact, when Euripides isn't constrained by the
requirements of his plot and can be himself and
express his own ideas, listen to the frank way he
speaks:

Do you see the air on high, the measureless air,
That holds the earth within its supple arms?
Think this your god, think this your mighty
  Zeus.[42]

or

Zeus—whoever Zeus may be. For him
I only know through other people's words.
and so on.

Timocles

Then the men and nations that believe in gods
and worship them are all mistaken, eh?

Damis

Thank you, Timocles, for reminding me of na-
tional beliefs. They're the best way of demonstrat-
ing how vague the whole subject of religion is. The
confusion is tremendous; each nation has its own
belief. In Scythia they worship a scimitar; in
Thrace Zamolxis, a runaway slave who escaped
there from Samos; in Phrygia Men; in Ethiopia
the day; in Cyllene Phales; in Assyria a dove; in
Persia fire; in Egypt water. The Egyptians, more-
over, though they all worship water, have local
deities, too: in Memphis a bull, in Pelusium an
onion, in some places an ibis or a crocodile, in
others a dog-faced man or a cat or an ape. Even
the villages have their own variations: one will wor-
ship the right shoulder while its neighbor across
the way will worship the left; others worship half
a skull or a clay cup or bowl. Just too silly, isn't
it, Timocles, my friend?

MOMUS. Fellow gods, didn't I tell you all this would come
out and receive a careful going over?

ZEUS. You did, Momus, and your criticism was perfectly
just. And if we ever get out of the danger that's facing
us, I'll personally take steps to remedy the situation.

Timocles

But, you enemy of heaven, what about the

[43–44

oracles and predictions of the future? If this isn't
the work of the gods and their divine forethought,
whose is it?

Damis

My dear Timocles, you keep quiet about oracles
or else I'll ask you which in particular you want
cited. The one Apollo gave to Croesus?[43] The one
that cut two ways, that was as two-faced as those
double Herms that are exactly alike whichever side
you look at? How about it? Which kingdom was
Croesus going to destroy when he crossed the
Halys, his own or Cyrus'? Poor Lydian, he paid
plenty of money for that ambidextrous verse!

MOMUS. Fellow gods, this man is bringing up all the things
I was most afraid of. Where's that good-looking lyre
player of ours now? Apollo, go down there and defend
yourself against these charges.

ZEUS. Momus! This is no time for criticism. Stop turning
the knife in the wound.

Timocles

Watch your step, Damis, you sinner. With that
sort of talk you're just about overturning the very
seats of the gods and their altars.

Damis

I'm not after all altars, Timocles. When they're
full of aromatic incense, what harm do they do?
But the altars of Artemis among the Taurians,[44]
the ones that used to offer the virgin lady those
disgusting feasts she enjoyed so much—I'd like to
see them overturned from top to bottom!

ZEUS. Where did this incubus come from, anyway? There's
no stopping him! There isn't a god that this man spares!
He's as free with his tongue as a soapbox orator; he

Seizes on each one in turn, on the guiltless as well
as the guilty.[45]

MOMUS. You'll find precious few who are guiltless in *our* ranks. And the man might go ahead and even take on a certain very important person.

Timocles

Damis, you god-fighter, don't you ever hear Zeus thunder?

Damis

Of course I hear thunder, Timocles. But whether it's Zeus who's doing the thundering, you'd know better than I since I presume you came here from somewhere near heaven. Of course, people who come here from Crete tell a different story. They say you're shown a tomb and a tombstone there, proving Zeus died ages ago and can't do any more thundering.[46]

MOMUS. I knew all along the man was going to bring that up. What's the matter, Zeus? You've gone pale; your teeth are chattering. You've got to buck up. Contempt is the only thing for pygmies of his ilk.

ZEUS. Momus! What are you saying? Contempt? Look at all those people listening to him! Don't you realize he's already convinced them, that he's leading them by the ears? That Damis!

MOMUS. But after all, Zeus, whenever you want you can let down a golden cord and

Pull them all up from the bowels of the earth and the depths of the ocean.[47]

Timocles

Tell me, damn you, have you ever taken a sea voyage?

Damis

Often.

Timocles

And when you did, as you were carried along by the action of the oars or by a wind which struck

the canvas and filled the sails, wasn't there one
man in charge who piloted the vessel and brought
it safely to port?

Damis

Of course.

Timocles

So, although a vessel can't sail without a cap-
tain, you think this whole universe goes its course
without somebody in command at the helm.

ZEUS. Bravo, Timocles. A good analogy, that.

Damis

But, my super-reverend Timocles, you should
have noticed that the captain of a vessel always
has in mind what is best for him to do and always
has his preparations made, and orders for the crew
ready, well in advance. What's more, his ship car-
ries neither extras nor non-essentials but only what's
needed for use during the voyage. But *your* cap-
tain, the one you want to put in command of this
vast ship, doesn't arrange one detail sensibly or
properly, and neither does his crew. As likely as
not he'll order the forestay made fast to the stern
and both sheets to the prow, have an anchor of
gold and a figurehead of lead, and have the hull
decorated below the waterline but left bare above.
As for the crew, you'll see a lazy good-for-nothing
who knows nothing about his duties and is scared
of them serving as first or second mate, while a
thoroughly trained seaman who's an expert swim-
mer and a skilled hand at going aloft will be the
only one to be assigned to pumping the bilge. The
same is true even of the passengers. You'll see some
jailbird, surrounded by flunkies, seat himself along-
side the captain on the quarter-deck and some
adulterer or parricide or temple robber take over,
amid much bowing and scraping, the best accom-
modations on board. But all the nice people are

crammed into a corner of the hold and trampled
on by their out-and-out inferiors. Suppose Socrates,
Aristides, and Phocion[48] were aboard a ship.
They'd be fed short rations and assigned some bare
planks alongside the bilge where they couldn't even
stretch their legs out. But what a voyage Callias or
Midias or Sardanapalus[49] would have! They'd be
wallowing in luxury, looking down their noses at
everyone below them.

That's the way things are on your ship, my foun-
tainhead of wisdom. Hence the thousands of ship-
wrecks. If there were a captain in charge who kept
his eye on things and arranged every detail, he'd
have first found out who was good and who was
worthless among his passengers and he'd have then
assigned the berths according to merit, giving the
better men the better ones by his side on deck and
putting the worse in the hold, and he'd have picked
his messmates and advisors from the better men.
He'd have done the same with the crew: the eager,
hard-working sailor would be put in charge for-
ward or amidships or given some post of command,
while the lazy good-for-nothing would get half a
dozen strokes of the cat on his back daily. So, my
dear Timocles, your analogy of the ship is in dan-
ger of capsizing because its captain happens to be
no good.

MOMUS. This is making the tide run very strongly for
Damis. A favorable wind's carrying him to victory.

ZEUS. Neatly put, Momus. Timocles can't come up with
an effective idea. All we get from him is bilge—hack-
neyed, banal arguments, one after the other, all of them
a cinch to capsize.

Timocles

Well, if my ship analogy didn't convince you,
then listen to this. Now I'm throwing over the

sheet anchor, as the saying goes. You won't cut this away, no matter what you try.

ZEUS. What in the world is he going to say?

Timocles

See whether this syllogism isn't valid and whether there's any way you can capsize it. If there are altars, then there must be gods. But there *are* altars. Ergo, there must be gods. What do you say to *that?*

Damis

I'll tell you—but first I have to stop laughing.

Timocles

It looks as if you never will. Come on, what strikes you so funny about what I said?

Damis

Simply that you don't realize you've tied that anchor of yours to a thread—your sheet anchor at that. You hitch the existence of altars to the existence of gods and are convinced you've made yourself a safe mooring. Well, since you admit you have nothing more sheet-anchorish than this, we can leave now.

Timocles

Leave? Then you admit you lose.

Damis

Oh yes. Because you took refuge from me at the altars, just the way people do when they feel others pressing them hard. I swear by the god of sheet anchors that I'm ready to sign a truce on those altars of yours to bring an end to this argument.

Timocles

Crook! Swine! Good-for-nothing! Scum! Make fun of me, will you? You think we don't know who your father was? Or that your mother was a whore, that you strangled your brother, that you're a seducer, a corrupter of young men, a lecher, a moral

blot? Don't run away—first I want to give you a
thrashing. Damn you, I'll carve you to pieces with
this broken pot!

ZEUS. There goes Damis on the double, laughing his head
off, with Timocles on his heels, cursing because he can't
stand the way Damis makes fun of him. It looks as if
he's going to bash him on the head with that broken
pot. Fellow gods, what do we do next?

HERMES. I think the comic playwright put it very well
when he said:

You feel no hurt—if you pretend there's none.[50]

What's so terrible if a handful of men go off convinced
by all this? There are lots more who know otherwise—
the Greek *hoi polloi* and all the barbarians.

ZEUS. Still, Hermes, there's a lot to that remark Darius
made about Zopyrus; I'd rather have one Damis on my
side than own ten thousand Babylons.[51]

NOTES

[1] Three of these verses are lines, or adaptations of lines, from
Homer (*Iliad* 8.31, 1.363, 3.35); the rest are Lucian's, done in
Homer's style.

[2] A parody of the opening lines of Euripides' *Orestes*.

[3] A line (538) from Euripides' *Madness of Heracles*.

[4] For Prometheus' services to mankind, see p. 125.

[5] See p. 102, n. 3.

[6] See p. 135, n. 6.

[7] A parody of a line (117) from Euripides' *Phoenician
Maidens*.

[8] Celebrated actors of tragedy who lived in the fourth cen-
tury B.C.

[9] The prophecies at Apollo's oracle in Delphi were delivered
in verse. For their ambiguity see n. 19.

[10] Bendis was the Thracian goddess of the moon, Anubis an
Egyptian god with a human body and jackal's head, Attis a

demigod worshiped in Asia Minor, Mithras the Persian sun-god, and Men a deity of the Phrygians in Asia Minor.

[11] A mountain near Athens that yielded a very fine grade of marble widely used by Greek sculptors.

[12] It was a common practice for sculptors to add small items in gold to a marble statue, e.g., a gold crown and gold lyre pegs to a marble of Apollo. Such things were apparently tempting targets for thieves.

[13] Part of a threat Zeus once made at a meeting to cow the other gods (*Iliad* 8.23–26).

[14] *Iliad* 8.5.

[15] The celebrated Philippics and Olynthiacs delivered by Demosthenes to rouse Athens against Philip of Macedon, father of Alexander the Great.

[16] A parody of some of the opening sentences of Demosthenes' first Olynthiac.

[16a] Lucian has picked an apt name: it means "god-mindful."

[17] The colonnade along the west side of the public square at Athens. It was decorated with wall paintings, including one of Athens' glorious victory over the Persians at the Battle of Marathon. Two of the figures portrayed were Miltiades, the commander-in-chief, and Aeschylus' brother Cynegirus, who had distinguished himself in the action.

[18] Menelaus' taunt to the rest of the Greeks (*Iliad* 7.99) when none came forward to take up Hector's challenge to single combat.

[19] This is the astute reply Apollo's oracle at Delphi gave to Croesus (see also p. 237, n. 15) when, confronted with the possibility of war against Cyrus of Persia, he sought its advice (the prophecy is given in full in Herodotus 1.53). Croesus crossed the Halys and, defeated by Cyrus, destroyed his own kingdom.

[20] Part of the famous "wooden wall" oracle given to the Athenians during the period of their wars with Persia (quoted in Herodotus 7.141). The gifted Themistocles not only interpreted the oracle for them but led them to victory at the decisive Battle of Salamis.

[21] Heracles and Dionysus were sons of Zeus, and Asclepius (the long-bearded god of medicine) a son of Apollo, by mortal mothers. For Ganymede, see p. 103–7.

[22] Theseus was a great, semi-mythical king of Athens. The cleaning up of the coast road between Troezon and Athens was his first great exploit and one of his most celebrated.

[23] King of Tiryns. It was he who assigned Heracles the famous Twelve Labors when the hero, to expiate a crime, was made his servant for a while.

[24] Metrodorus (330–277 B.C.) was Epicurus' pupil and friend.

[25] See the First Olynthiac, 16.

[26] Pheidias' colossal statue of Zeus was at Olympia. There was a famous shrine of Poseidon at Geraestus.

[27] Cronus was Zeus's predecessor, see p. 97.

[28] Mt. Helicon was supposed to be the favorite haunt of the Muses, the nine goddesses of the arts and sciences.

[29] See p. 225.

[30] The sacred spring at Delphi.

[31] When Croesus wanted to test Apollo's oracular powers, he sent messengers to Delphi and asked that they be told what he was doing on a given day. The answer "boiling lamb and tortoise" turned out to be right (see Herodotus 1.47–48).

[32] The Mysteries, centered in the city of Eleusis, about fourteen miles west of Athens, was a religion involving elaborate initiation and secret rites which the members were sworn not to reveal.

[33] See n. 20.

[34] See n. 17.

[35] From some lost play. Heracles portrayed as a drunk and boob was a standard figure on the Greek comic stage.

[36] A pun. The statue was of Hermes of the Agora, and Hermagoras is a common Greek name.

[37] A parody of a messenger's speech in Euripides' *Orestes* (866 ff.; see, in particular, 866, 871, 880).

[38] A parody of *Iliad* 7.195.

[39] The allusion is to *Iliad* 1.423–24.

[40] The illustrations are all drawn from the *Iliad*: 1.396 ff. (the plot), 2.5 ff. (Agamemnon's dream), 5.334 ff. and 855 ff. (the wounds), 20.54 ff. (dueling of the gods), 21.403 ff. (Athena's victory), 9.533 (Artemis). The line quoted is *Iliad* 20.72.

[41] See n. 8.

[42] This and the following are from lost plays.

[43] See n. 19.

[44] The Taurians in Scythia practiced human sacrifice.

[45] *Iliad* 15.137.

[46] There was a legend propagated by the Cretans that Zeus had died and was buried on their island.

[47] *Iliad* 8.24.

[48] Aristides (fifth century B.C.) and Phocion (fourth century B.C.) were noted for their honesty and virtue.

[49] Callias (fifth century B.C.) and Midias (fourth century B.C.) were Athenian millionaires. For Sardanapalus, see p. 210, n. 5.

50 From a lost play of Menander.

51 Zopyrus had made a tremendous sacrifice in order to gain Babylon for the Persian king Darius; see Herodotus 3.153 ff., especially 160.

PLUTO'S WORLD

A Voyage to the Underworld

Dialogues of the Dead

PLUTO'S WORLD

Homer and other early Greek poets gave to Greek literature the mythological conception of the underworld. Lucian, by treating its fanciful elements with a straight-faced literalness, made it the vehicle of what are probably his most famous dialogues.

As the poets described it, the underworld was a vast area of gloomy land and waters (the Lake of Acheron; the hateful Styx; Pyriphlegethon, the river of fire; Lethe, the river of forgetfulness) beneath the earth. Here Pluto and his queen, Persephone, ruled over the hordes of the insubstantial shades of the dead.

Hermes, Zeus's busy factotum, had among his many other jobs that of conducting the shades of the newly deceased down to their future eternal abode. He brought them through the gate past the monstrous triple-headed watchdog, Cerberus, to the shores of the Styx. Here they boarded a ferry under the command of Charon to cross to the underworld proper. The service was not free: the fare was one obol (a bronze coin generally translated "penny" but in purchasing power worth a good deal more), and proper burial theoretically included the placing of this coin on a corpse's tongue. Once across, the shades stood trial before a board of three judges, Aeacus, Minos, and Rhadamanthus, to receive sentence, to be told under what circumstances they were to spend the rest of eternity.

In Lucian's underworld there are a good many departures, since he took whatever liberties suited him. Aeacus, for example, in mythology one of the board of judges, he made gatekeeper and auditor of the ferry receipts. The three Fates—Lachesis, who assigned each mortal's lot, her sister Clotho, who spun the life thread, and her sister Atropos, who snipped it—he occasionally transferred from heaven to the underworld and assigned a number of new duties.

The hero of the underworld dialogues is often a member of the school of philosophers known as the Cynics, a group which, founded about the beginning of the fourth century B.C., was enjoying a widespread revival in Lucian's day. The Cynics professed belief in a plain life and a noble mind. The first they satisfied by dressing in rags, living off scraps, and limiting their possessions to the old coat, sack, and staff which were the standard accoutrements of their order; the second they satisfied by going about aggressively mocking the conventions and mundane ideals men lived by and preaching a harsh righteousness and austerity. Since they made a point of disregarding personal appearance, they were singularly unappetizing to look at, and this may be responsible for their name (kynikos in Greek means "doglike"). The sect was founded by Antisthenes, but the best-known member is probably Diogenes (ca. 400–ca. 325 B.C.), noted for his peculiar choice of abode (a tub) and his cavalier treatment of Alexander the Great (when favored by a visit, he ordered the conqueror of the world out of the way of his sunlight). The Menippus who appears so frequently in the dialogues was another famous Cynic who lived in the first century B.C. He was a prolific writer and his works (now lost) included satires that very likely served Lucian as a model.

The other figures in the dialogues are a mélange, some historical, some mythological, some purely fictitious. For the last Lucian generally selects Greek names that are peculiarly apt: the dictator who received so harsh a sentence he names Megapenthes, "great woe"; the military figure who is stripped of his medals, Strato, "soldier"; the statesman who is stripped of his pomp, Crato, "power."

A VOYAGE TO THE UNDERWORLD
[1–2]

Charon, Clotho, Hermes, and Shades

CHARON. Well, Clotho, I've had the skiff shipshape and
ready for the crossing for hours. The bilge has been
pumped, mast stepped, sail bent to the yard, oars
strapped to the pins—as far as my part's concerned,
there's nothing to stop us from raising anchor and shov-
ing off. It's Hermes who's holding things up; he should
have been here hours ago. Look at that ferry—not a pas-
senger aboard yet, and we could have made three trips
today by now! Here it is almost evening, and there isn't
one obol in the till. And Pluto's going to think I'm lying
down on the job, I know he will, even though it's all
someone else's fault. That fine shade leader of ours must
have joined the others in a glass of Lethe up there and
forgotten all about coming down here. He's probably
wrestling with the youngsters,[1] or plunking away on his
lyre, or giving a speech to show off the brand of non-
sense *he* can spout. Why, the gentleman may even have
taken time off for a little burglary—after all, that's one
of his talents too. He certainly takes liberties with us
even though he's supposed to be on duty down here for
half his time.

CLOTHO. Don't take on so, Charon. For all you know he
may have run into something to keep him busy. Zeus
may have needed to use him a little longer on celestial
matters. He's his boss, too, you know.

CHARON. But, Clotho, we share him fifty-fifty. Zeus should
boss him only when he's supposed to, no more; after
all, *we* never keep him overtime when he's scheduled
to go back. But I know what's behind it all: down here
all we have are flowers for mourning and funeral cakes

and wine, and besides, it's dark and misty and gloomy; up in heaven everything's bright, there's plenty of ambrosia and all the nectar you can drink. If you ask me, he enjoys staying overtime up there. When he leaves us, he flies off as if he was breaking out of jail; when it's time to come back, he takes his time and walks down at a snail's pace.

CLOTHO. You can stop your fussing, Charon. See? Here he comes now. And he's bringing plenty of shades. As a matter of fact, he's driving them with his staff in a pack, like a herd of goats. But what's going on there? I see one shade all tied up and another laughing. And there's one carrying a sack and holding a staff who's keeping a sharp eye on the others and hurrying them along. And look at Hermes! He's dripping with sweat, his feet are all dusty, and he can't catch his breath—at least it looks like that from the way he's puffing. Hermes! What's the trouble? What were you running for? You look all upset.

HERMES. It's this blasted shade that's the trouble, Clotho. He ran away and I've been chasing him. I almost became a deserter from the crew today.

CLOTHO. Who is he? What did he run away for?

HERMES. There's no secret about that: he wanted to go on living. He's some king or dictator. At least I gather so from the way he's been shrieking and wailing about being deprived of all his good fortune.

CLOTHO. So the poor fool thought he could go on living when the thread of life I spun for him was all used up? Tried to run away, did he?

HERMES. Tried? Why, if this very fine fellow with the staff hadn't helped me catch him and tie him up, he'd have gotten away from me. From the moment Atropos handed him over to me, all during the march, he kept resisting and hanging back; he'd dig both feet in the ground, and it was no easy job to get him moving. And every now and then he'd beg and plead, promising me all sorts of things if I'd only let him go for just a little while. Since I knew he was asking for the impossible, naturally I didn't do it. Well, when we came to the entrance and, as we always do, I was counting off the shades for Aeacus and he was checking them against the manifest your sister had sent him, somehow or other this damned rascal managed to make off. So the count showed I was one shade short. Aeacus raises his eyebrows and says, "Hermes, those schoolboy stunts of yours in heaven aren't enough for you, eh? You have to use your thieving tricks on everybody. Our shade records are absolutely accurate; it's impossible to get away with a thing. See here, according to the manifest you're supposed to have one thousand and four shades. You're one short—unless you want to claim that Atropos juggled the figures on you." I was terribly embarrassed by what he said. Then I suddenly remember what happened on the way, look around, and don't see that troublemaker anywhere. I knew right then and there that he had made off, so I lit out at top speed along the road that led to the light. This very nice fellow here took it on himself to follow me; we ran as if we were in a fifty-yard dash, and we caught the runaway just before the exit at Taenarum.[2] He had managed to get that far.

CLOTHO. See, Charon? And we were blaming Hermes for neglecting his duty!

CHARON. Well, what are we waiting for? Haven't we wasted enough time already?

CLOTHO. Right! Let's get them on board. The usual procedure: I'll take the ledger, sit by the gangplank, and ask each one as they embark their name, address, and manner of death. Then you take over and stow them on board. All right, Hermes, carry the infants aboard first; they're not going to have very much to tell me.

HERMES. Here you are, ferryman. Three hundred in all, including those who were exposed.[3]

CHARON. Quite a haul. Pretty tender grapes, this consignment of shades.

HERMES. Clotho, do you want the unlamented next?

CLOTHO. The unlamented? Oh, you mean the aged. Yes. After all, why should I bother asking questions about a lot of ancient history? Everybody over sixty, on board! What's the matter? They're so old they're deaf and don't hear me. You'll probably have to carry them aboard too.

HERMES. Here you are. Three hundred and ninety-eight, all soft and juicy and picked at a ripe old age.

CHARON. No, sir, they're a bunch of dried-up raisins.

CLOTHO. Let's have the wounded next, Hermes. You people there, tell me how you died. No, wait; I'll check you against the entries in the ledger. Yesterday eighty-four were supposed to die in battle in Mysia, including Gobares, the son of Oxyartes.

HERMES. All present.

CLOTHO. Seven suicides over unhappy love affairs, including the philosopher Theagenes, suicide because of that courtesan from Megara.

HERMES. There they are, right near you.

CLOTHO. Where are the men who killed each other over succession to the throne?

HERMES. Standing alongside you.

CLOTHO. And the one who was murdered by his wife and her lover?

HERMES. There he is, next to you.

CLOTHO. Legal cases next—I mean criminals tortured to death or impaled. And, Hermes, where are the sixteen killed by pirates?

HERMES. Don't you see them? The wounded there, standing by you. Do you want their wives at the same time?

CLOTHO. Yes. And all who died at sea, too; same kind of death, after all. And I'll take the victims of fever, including Agathocles, their doctor. But where's the philosopher Cyniscus? He was supposed to die from eating a meal he stole from an altar, plus some eggs he took from a sacrifice, plus a raw squid on top of everything else.[4]

CYNISCUS. My dear Clotho, I've been standing alongside you all this time. What harm did I ever do you that you had to leave me up there so long? You practically spun out your whole spindle for me! Time and again I tried to cut short my thread of life and come here, but for some reason there was no way to break it.

CLOTHO. I left you there to watch over and cure human frailty. Get aboard, and good luck to you.

CYNISCUS. No—not until you put this fellow we tied up on board first. I'm afraid he may get around you with his begging.

CLOTHO. Who is he, anyway?

HERMES. Megapenthes, son of Lacydes, dictator.

CLOTHO. Get aboard.

MEGAPENTHES. Oh no! Please, my dear lady Clotho, let me go back for a little while. Then I'll come of my own accord; you won't have to call me.

CLOTHO. What are you so interested in going back for?

MEGAPENTHES. Just let me finish building my palace. It was only half done when I left.

CLOTHO. Stop driveling and get aboard.

MEGAPENTHES. My lady, I'm asking for only a little time. Let me have just one more day to give my wife instructions about my money. I have an enormous treasure buried up there.

CLOTHO. You can't possibly. The matter's been decided once and for all.

MEGAPENTHES. You mean all that money's going to be wasted?

CLOTHO. It won't be wasted. Don't worry your head about that. Your cousin Megacles is taking it over.

MEGAPENTHES. This is criminal! My enemy, the one I was too good-natured to kill off?

CLOTHO. That's the one. He's going to outlive you by better than forty years. He's taking over your concubines, your wardrobe, and every cent you had.

MEGAPENTHES. Clotho, you can't take what's mine and give it to my worst enemies. That's an illegal act!

CLOTHO. What's yours, my soul of honor? Wasn't it all Cydimachus'? Didn't you take it from him when you murdered him and slaughtered his children while he was still alive to see it?

MEGAPENTHES. But it's all mine now.

CLOTHO. Well, your period of ownership has run out.

MEGAPENTHES. Clotho, listen to me. I'd like to have a word with you in private. Would you people please step aside for a moment? Clotho, if you let me escape, I promise I'll pay you a million dollars in gold this very day.

CLOTHO. So you still have money and gold on the brain, do you? You fool!

MEGAPENTHES. If you want, I'll throw in the two bowls I took when I murdered Cleocritus. Each of them weighs tons. Fourteen-carat gold!

CLOTHO. You people will have to drag him on board; it doesn't look to me as if he'll go by himself.

MEGAPENTHES. I want you all to know that my new wall and shipyards aren't finished yet. And I could have completed the job if I had just five more days of life.

CLOTHO. Stop worrying. Someone else will finish your wall.

MEGAPENTHES. Wait—here's a request that's perfectly reasonable.

CLOTHO. What is it?

MEGAPENTHES. Let me live just long enough to conquer

Persia, make Lydia pay me tribute, and build me a huge tomb with an inscription telling all the great military achievements of my career.

CLOTHO. Look here, now you're not asking for just one day —you want a stay of about twenty years!

MEGAPENTHES. I'm ready to furnish hostages to guarantee I'll come back right away. If you want, I'll even give you as my substitute that young fellow I'm madly in love with.

CLOTHO. You slimy turncoat! Time and again you prayed that you would die before he did.

MEGAPENTHES. That was some time ago. Now I know better.

CLOTHO. It won't be long before he joins you. The new ruler is going to murder him.

MEGAPENTHES. My lady Clotho, please don't refuse me *this* favor.

CLOTHO. What is it?

MEGAPENTHES. I want to know how things are going to turn out, now that I'm gone.

CLOTHO. I'll tell you—because it's going to make you miserable to hear it. Your slave Midas will marry your widow; he's been having an affair with her all along.

MEGAPENTHES. Damn him! I only set him free because she talked me into it.

CLOTHO. Your daughter will be enrolled as one of the new ruler's concubines. The pictures and statues the state set up in your honor so long ago will be knocked down; passers-by will get a good laugh from them.

MEGAPENTHES. Clotho, aren't any of my friends going to resent these acts?

CLOTHO. Who was ever a friend of yours? Why should anyone have been your friend? Don't you realize that all those people who groveled before you and lauded

everything you said or did to the skies only did so be-
cause they were afraid or because they hoped to gain
by it? They were opportunists, friends of your power,
not you.

MEGAPENTHES. I tell you they used to toast me at banquets
at the top of their lungs and pray for my happiness.
Every one of them was ready to die in my place if he
could. Why, they used to swear by me!

CLOTHO. Of course. And then, yesterday, you had dinner
at the house of one of them and died. It was the last
drink served you that sent you down here.

MEGAPENTHES. You know, I thought it tasted bitter. What
did he do it for?

CLOTHO. Enough questions out of you. Time to get aboard.

MEGAPENTHES. Clotho, there's one thing that sticks in my
craw. It's the real reason I want so much to get back
to the upper world even for only a little while.

CLOTHO. What is it? It sounds terribly important.

MEGAPENTHES. It's that servant of mine, Cario. As soon as
he heard I had died, toward evening he came into the
room where I was laid out—he had stopped working;
they all had; no one was even standing guard over me—
bringing that concubine of mine, Glycerium, with him;
I think those two had been having an affair all along.
He shut the door and then, just as if nobody else was
in the room, proceeded to make love to her. When he
had enough of this, he turns to me, says, "Curse you,
you runt, for having beaten me so many times when I
hadn't done a thing wrong," and starts tearing my hair
and punching my face. Finally he hawks up a mouthful,
spits it out on me, says, "I only hope you go where
the damned are kept," and goes off. I was burning with
anger, but there wasn't a thing I could do; I was already
stiff and cold. And that damned chit of a girl—when
she heard the sound of some people coming, she smeared
spit on her eyes to look as if she'd been crying over me

and left the room blubbering and calling my name. If I could only get my hands——

CLOTHO. Stop the threats and get aboard. It's time for you to go to the judgment-seat.

MEGAPENTHES. And who presumes to think he can pass sentence on a dictator?

CLOTHO. On a dictator, nobody; on a shade, Rhadamanthus. You'll find out very soon that he's strictly impartial: he hands out just the sentence each man deserves. Now don't waste any more of my time!

MEGAPENTHES. My lady, you can make me an ordinary citizen—a poor man—even a slave—instead of the king I once was. Just let me live again!

CLOTHO. Where's that fellow with the staff? Hermes, will the two of you grab his feet and haul him? He won't go aboard by himself.

HERMES. Come on, you runaway! Here he is, ferryman. And listen, watch out that——

CHARON. Don't worry. I'll lash him to the mast.

MEGAPENTHES. The mast? I'm supposed to have the best accommodations aboard!

CLOTHO. Why?

MEGAPENTHES. Because, by god, I was a dictator with a bodyguard of ten thousand.

CYNISCUS. How can you be so dumb? You got just what you deserved when that slave pulled your hair out. Dictator, eh? You'll find it a sour role to play when I give you a taste of this staff.

MEGAPENTHES. How dare a Cynic raise his stick against me! Didn't I almost string you up once before for being too free and easy with your strong remarks and criticism?

CYNISCUS. And now it's your turn to be strung up—on the mast.

MICYLLUS. Clotho, don't you people care anything about me? Must I go on board last just because I'm a poor man?

CLOTHO. Who are you?

MICYLLUS. Micyllus, shoemaker.

CLOTHO. You mean you mind waiting? Didn't you hear all the dictator promised he'd give me if I agreed to let him go for just a little while? I'm amazed you're not just as happy at the delay.

MICYLLUS. Listen to me, Lady Clotho. The gift of the Cyclops[5]—I mean that special privilege he gave Noman of being eaten last—doesn't bring any cheer to my soul. First, last—what's the difference? The teeth are always there waiting for you. What's more, people in my situation aren't like the rich. As a matter of fact, we're poles apart, as the saying goes. All his life that dictator was someone people consider a happy man—a person feared and respected who, on dying, left behind piles of gold and silver, clothes, horses, banquets, beautiful women, handsome young boys. Naturally he got angry and carried on when he was pulled away from all this. Somehow or other such things are like glue—the soul sticks to them; it's been attached to them so long it doesn't like to give them up so easily. Or rather, such things are like some unbreakable bond these people happen to be shackled with. When they're finally hauled off by sheer force, they wail and plead; they're brave enough where other things are concerned but, on the road down to the underworld, they turn out to be cowards. They keep twisting around; they want to look back at the world of light, even when it's far away, like a pining lover. That poor fool there is a perfect example: he broke and ran during the march and kept pleading with you after he arrived. I, on the other hand, left no stake behind in life, no farm, no house, no money, no possessions, no reputation, no statues. So I was all ready for the trip;

all Atropos had to do was give me a nod and I threw down my knife and leather with a smile—I was mending a shoe at the time—, jumped up, and followed her without taking time to put on my shoes or wash the blacking off my hands. Followed? I was in the lead and never once took my eyes off the road ahead, since nothing I had left behind made me turn or called after me. And, so help me, I can see already that things down here will suit me fine. This classless society of yours, where no one's any better than his neighbors, seems ideal, at least to me. I gather there are no bill collectors or tax collectors here and, best of all, no freezing in winter, or getting sick, or being beaten up by your betters. Everybody's at peace, and the whole situation is just the reverse of up above: here we poor people laugh, and it's the rich who whine about their troubles.

CLOTHO. Yes, Micyllus, I noticed some time back you were laughing. What was it in particular you were laughing at?

MICYLLUS. My dear goddess, I'll be glad to tell you. Up above I lived next door to a dictator, and I got a good look at everything that happened in his house. When I used to see the lovely purple robes, the crowd of attendants, the gold, the crusted goblets, the couches with silver legs, I considered the man divinely happy; he seemed like a god to me. And the smell of what was cooked for his dinner used to drive me to distraction! He'd hold himself erect, proud of his blessings, and stride along majestically with his head in the air, inspiring awe in everyone he met—it all made him a superman in my eyes, someone thrice blessed, nothing short of an Adonis a foot and a half taller than the rest of mankind. But, when he died and had to take off his trappings, not only did he look ridiculous to me, but I had to laugh even more at how ridiculous I was. Imagine —I had stood in awe of that trash and had jumped to the conclusion that he was divinely happy on the basis of the smell from his kitchen and the color of his robes! My dictator neighbor wasn't the only one. I also got a laugh from Gnipho, the moneylender. He's wailing because only now does he realize he never enjoyed his money; before he could taste it he was dead and his property fell in the lap of that spendthrift, Rhodochares —as next of kin he had first legal claim to the estate. I couldn't stop laughing, particularly when I remembered how pale and wizened and worried-looking Gnipho always was. And he wasn't rich; only his fingers were, the ones he used for counting his thousands and millions —he had scraped it together bit by bit, and Rhodochares, the lucky dog, is soon going to fling it around. But why don't we get going? We can finish laughing during the crossing while we listen to the two of them whimper.

CLOTHO. Get aboard, and then the ferryman can raise anchor.

CHARON. Hey, you, where are you going? The skiff's already full. Wait where you are till tomorrow; we'll take you across first thing in the morning.

MICYLLUS. Charon, you can't leave behind a shade already a day old; that's breaking the law. I'll bring you up before Rhadamanthus on charges of violating the constitution. Damn my luck! They're sailing off. I'm going to be the only one left behind here. If that's the case, why don't I swim after them? I'm not afraid of getting tired and drowning—I'm already dead. Besides, I don't have the obol for the ferry fare.

CLOTHO. What is this? Micyllus, stay where you are! You're not allowed to cross that way!

MICYLLUS. I'm not, eh? I'll probably get to the dock before all of you.

CLOTHO. No, no! Let's put on some speed and catch him. Hermes! Lend a hand pulling him aboard.

CHARON. Now that we've got him, where will he sit? You can see for yourself we're full up.

HERMES. How about putting him on the dictator's shoulders?

CLOTHO. Charon, Hermes has got a good idea there.

CHARON. All right. Climb up, you, and plant yourself on that blasted sinner's neck. Well, let's hope we have a good crossing.

CYNISCUS. Charon, I think I'd better tell you the truth here and now. I'm not going to have the obol for your fare when we land. All I have is this sack you see here and this staff. But I'm ready to bail or take a turn at an oar, if you want. You won't have any complaints to make if you just give me a "sturdy, well-balanced blade."[6]

CHARON. All right then, row. That'll cover your fare.

CYNISCUS. Should I chant the time for the stroke too?

CHARON. Sure, if you know any coxswain's calls.

CYNISCUS. Plenty of them. But listen to all this wailing! I can't compete with it; it'll mess up the whole chant.

SHADES. My property! My fields! The lovely house I had to leave behind! The thousands that heir of mine will throw away! My poor babies! Who'll pick the grapes I planted last year?

HERMES. No wails out of you, Micyllus? No one's allowed to make this crossing without tears, you know.

MICYLLUS. Don't bother about me. I'm enjoying the trip. I've got nothing to wail about.

HERMES. Let's have a groan out of you even if it's just a little one. It's traditional.

MICYLLUS. All right, Hermes, if you think I should. My leather! The old shoes I left behind! The worn-out sandals! Poor me, no longer will I go from dawn to dusk with no food in my belly, or walk around in midwinter barefoot and half naked, with my teeth chattering from the cold! Who'll inherit my knife and awl?

HERMES. That's enough. We're almost there now.

CHARON. Fares, please, before we do anything else. Micyllus, I'll take your fare now; I've collected from all the others. Come on, pay your obol.

MICYLLUS. Charon, looking for an obol from Micyllus the shoemaker? Either you're joking or you're building castles in the air, as the saying goes. I haven't the slightest idea whether an obol's round or square.

CHARON. We had a nice trip today and a profitable one. All ashore! I'm going back for the horses, cows, dogs, and the rest of the animals. It's their turn to cross now.

CLOTHO. Hermes, will you take over and lead the shades ashore? I'm sailing back to the other side to bring over two Chinese, Indopatres and Heramithras; they killed each other in an argument over boundary lines.

HERMES. All right, all of you, let's go. Everybody form a line and follow me.

MICYLLUS. My god, how dark it is! What good do Megillus'[7] good looks do him now? How could anyone tell down here whether Simmiche is better looking than Phryne?[8] Everything's identical, the same color. Being beautiful or more beautiful—such things don't exist here. This rag of a coat that I always used to think looked so awful is as good as a king's robes now. They're both invisible, swallowed up in the same darkness. Cyniscus, where are you, anyway?

CYNISCUS. Right here, Micyllus. Hear me? What do you say we walk together?

MICYLLUS. Good idea. Give me your hand. Cyniscus, I'm sure you've been initiated into the Eleusinian Mysteries.[9] Tell me, what's your impression? Is it like this?

CYNISCUS. You've got a point. At any rate, there's a torchbearer. See? Here she comes—and that look on her face would scare anybody. You think she's one of the Furies?[10]

MICYLLUS. She certainly looks like it.

HERMES. Here you are, Tisiphone—one thousand and four shades.

TISIPHONE. It's about time. Rhadamanthus here has been waiting for you for hours.

RHADAMANTHUS. Have them step up, Tisiphone. And you, Hermes, take over as court clerk and call out their names.

CYNISCUS. Rhadamanthus, I beg you, in your father's name,[11] take me for examination first.

RHADAMANTHUS. Why?

CYNISCUS. I'm terribly anxious to submit charges against a dictator for the misdeeds I happen to know he committed during his lifetime. But I wouldn't make a creditable witness if I didn't first present to the court my own character and the kind of life I've led.

RHADAMANTHUS. Who are you?

CYNISCUS. Cyniscus, your honor, student of philosophy.

RHADAMANTHUS. Step up, then, and face judgment first. Hermes, call for his accusers.

HERMES. Whoever has any charges to make against Cyniscus here, kindly take the stand.

CYNISCUS. No one's moving.

RHADAMANTHUS. But that isn't all, Cyniscus. You've also got to strip. I have to examine you for brands.

CYNISCUS. Brands? On me? How is that possible?

RHADAMANTHUS. Every misdeed any of you commits during his lifetime produces an invisible brand on the soul.

CYNISCUS. Here I am, completely naked. Look me over for these brands of yours.

RHADAMANTHUS. This fellow's absolutely clean except for three or four brands right here, very faint and hard to make out. Wait—what's this? Traces and other signs of a good many places where you had marks which were somehow erased or rather actually cut out. How did this happen, Cyniscus? How did you manage to get a clean skin again?

CYNISCUS. I'll tell you how. A long time ago, because I didn't know better, I lived a bad life and for that reason earned a good many brands. But, as soon as I took up philosophy, with this excellent and most effective medicine I washed my soul clean of all those blemishes.

RHADAMANTHUS. You're to go to the Isles of the Blest to live with the noblest shades. Wait around, however, until you've stated your charges against that dictator you mentioned. Hermes, call the next one.

MICYLLUS. Rhadamanthus, my case is minor; it'll require only a short examination. And I've been naked for some time, so go right ahead, look me over.

RHADAMANTHUS. Who are you, anyway?

MICYLLUS. Micyllus, shoemaker.

RHADAMANTHUS. Very nice, Micyllus. Absolutely clean, no marks at all. You go with Cyniscus here. Hermes, call the dictator now.

HERMES. Megapenthes, son of Lacydes, step forward. Turning away, are you? To go where? Come up here! Yes, it's you I'm calling, the dictator. Tisiphone, take him by the neck and hustle him up here.

RHADAMANTHUS. Cyniscus, now you can state your charges and substantiate them. Here's your man.

CYNISCUS. As a matter of fact, there's no need of my speaking at all since you'll recognize the kind he is immediately from his brands. However, I'll strip the man bare for you myself and make his case clearer with a word or two. I can skip, I think, all that this blackguard did before he entered public life. He made himself dictator by getting together with the most lawless elements, mobilizing a personal bodyguard, and launching an insurrection against the government. Once he was dictator, he killed over ten thousand people without trial, by confiscating their estates arrived at the very pinnacle of wealth, ran the gamut of licentiousness, and practiced every possible form of cruelty and criminal behavior on the miserable populace—ruining young girls, perverting young men, acting toward his subjects exactly like some drunken madman. And his arrogance, delusions of grandeur, and insolence toward everyone he came across deserve a punishment greater than any you can set; looking at him was a surer way to bring tears than looking straight into the eye of the sun. What's more, his ingenuity in thinking up crueler and crueler tortures is beyond description. He didn't even keep his hands off those nearest and dearest to him. All this is not mere unfounded slander—just call to the stand the people he murdered; you'll find out quickly enough how true it is. Or, rather, just take a look: here they come without being called; they're hemming him in on all sides. Rhadamanthus, all these you see here this cursed sinner put to death: some through plots because he had designs on their good-looking wives; some because they resented having their young sons carried off for perversion; some because they had wealth; some because, as decent and thoughtful men, they were opposed to everything he did.

RHADAMANTHUS. What have you got to say to this, you scum?

MEGAPENTHES. Yes, I committed the murders he says I did. But all the rest—adultery, perverting young men, ruining young women—is a lie. Cyniscus made it up to get at me.

CYNISCUS. Very well, I'll produce witnesses to prove these charges, too, Rhadamanthus.

RHADAMANTHUS. Who are these witnesses?

CYNISCUS. Hermes, call his lamp and bed to the stand.

When they get here, they can testify to the acts they were a party to.

HERMES. Will Megapenthes' lamp and bed take the stand. Good, they've answered the summons.

RHADAMANTHUS. Will you please tell the court whatever you know about Megapenthes here. Bed, you speak first.

BED. All Cyniscus' accusations are true. But, your honor, the acts he committed on top of me were such that I'm ashamed to speak further.

RHADAMANTHUS. Can't bring yourself to mention them, eh? That's the clearest possible testimony you could give. Lamp, you may testify now.

LAMP. I didn't see what went on during the day since I wasn't present. But what he did at night, the way he carried on—well, I hesitate to talk about it. I'll say this much: I saw a great deal that was unspeakable, that went beyond all known criminal behavior. Why, time and again, because I wanted to go out, I deliberately refused to drink up the lamp oil. But he made me a witness to all his doings and befouled my light in every possible way.

RHADAMANTHUS. Enough testimony. All right, you, take off that purple robe and let me inspect your brands. Good god! The man's covered with them. Why, he's one mass of scar tissue from his brands! How should we punish him? Throw him into the River of Fire? Hand him over to Cerberus?

CYNISCUS. Oh no! If you don't mind, I'd like to suggest a new form that just fits his crimes.

RHADAMANTHUS. Speak up. I'd be very grateful to you for it.

CYNISCUS. As I understand it, it's the custom for all the dead to drink the water of Lethe.

RHADAMANTHUS. Of course.

CYNISCUS. Then let him be the only one not to.

29]

RHADAMANTHUS. Why?

CYNISCUS. It will be a terrible sentence for him—never to forget who he once was and the power he used to have in the world above; always to remember the luxury he once had.

RHADAMANTHUS. An excellent idea. So ordered: he is to be placed in chains alongside Tantalus[12] and is to remember all he enjoyed in life.

NOTES

[1] For Hermes' duties, see p. 97.

[2] Cape Matapan today, the southernmost tip of Greece. One of the entrances to the underworld was located here.

[3] "Exposing," i.e., abandoning, unwanted infants was still practiced in Lucian's day.

[4] Diogenes was said to have died from eating a raw squid.

[5] When Odysseus and his men were in the cave of the Cyclops, Polyphemus, his host, promised him the privilege of being eaten last; Odysseus had introduced himself under the deceptive alias "Noman" (*Odyssey* 9.369).

[6] The phrase has a Homeric ring.

[7] Noted for his good looks.

[8] Famous courtesans. Phryne lived toward the end of the fourth century B.C.

[9] See p. 169, n. 32. The ceremony was held in the dark of night in a great hall. One of the principals, next in importance to the presiding priest, was the Torchbearer.

[10] The Furies—Alecto, Magaera, and Tisiphone—were the dread goddesses of revenge.

[11] Rhadamanthus was one of Zeus's illegitimate sons.

[12] See p. 237, n. 21.

1

Diogenes and Pollux[1]

DIOGENES. Pollux, I want you to do something for me. I think it's your turn to return to life tomorrow. Well, as soon as you get back to earth, if you happen to see Menippus the Cynic anywhere—you should find him either in Corinth at the Craneum Park or in Athens at the Lyceum, making fun of the philosophers arguing there—, give him this message. Tell him that Diogenes says, "Menippus, if you've had enough of poking fun at things up there, come on down here; there's much more to laugh at. After all, your funmaking now has a bit of uncertainty about it. There's always the question: 'Who really knows what happens after death?' But here you can laugh your head off without any worries, just the way I'm doing now. Especially when you see how the millionaires and the pashas and the dictators have been cut down to size and look just like everybody else —you can only tell them apart by their whimpering and the way they're so spineless and miserable at the memory of all they left behind." Give him that message. Oh, and tell him when he leaves to fill his sack with beans or whatever he can steal from an altar or a sacrifice.

POLLUX. I'll give him the message, Diogenes. But you'd better tell me what he looks like.

DIOGENES. Old, bald, wears a coat so full of holes it lets in every breath of wind and is a crazy quilt of patches, always laughing, and generally to be found making fun of those quack philosophers.

POLLUX. Easy enough to find him from that description.

DIOGENES. How about delivering a message from me to those philosophers?

POLLUX. Say on. No trouble at all.

DIOGENES. Just this: tell them to cut out the nonsense—cut out arguing about the universe and making horns grow on each other and conjuring up crocodiles;[2] stop training the mind to ask such useless questions.

POLLUX. But if I say anything derogatory about those great brains of theirs, they'll call me ignorant and uneducated.

DIOGENES. You tell them I said they could go to the devil.

POLLUX. I'll take your message to the philosophers, Diogenes.

DIOGENES. And here's a message from me to the millionaires, Pollux my friend. Tell them this: "You fools! What are you saving your money for? Why are you wearing yourselves out calculating the interest due you and piling up thousands upon thousands when it won't be long before you've got to come here without a cent more than your ferry fare?"

POLLUX. I'll deliver that message too. I'll tell them.

DIOGENES. Here's a word for the dandies and the athletes. Tell it to that Megillus from Corinth and Damoxenus the wrestler. Say that we down here no longer have such things as blond hair, blue eyes, dark eyes, rosy cheeks, strong muscles, or broad shoulders. Down here everything is reduced to a mote of dust, skulls bare of any beauty.

POLLUX. No trouble at all to pass that on to the dandies and the athletes.

DIOGENES. And, my Spartan friend, here's a message for the poor. There are plenty of them, and they resent the way things are and are sorry about their lot in life. Tell them no more crying and whimpering. Explain that we have a classless society; they'll see that the ones who were millionaires up there are no better off down here than they. And, if you don't mind, tell those Spartans of yours a thing or two for me about the way they've been letting themselves go.

POLLUX. Now don't say anything about the Spartans, Diogenes, because I just won't stand for it. I'll deliver your messages to all the others.

DIOGENES. Let the Spartans go, if that's the way you feel about it. But you report what I said to all those I mentioned.

NOTES

1 See p. 102, n. 2.

2 Lucian felt that philosophy in his day had degenerated to mere verbal quibbling, one symptom of which was the fondness its practitioners had of stumping each other with logical posers such as the riddle of the horns (Anything you haven't lost you still have, right? Have you lost your horns? No? Then you have horns) or of the crocodile (see p. 326).

4

Hermes and Charon

HERMES. Ferryman, how about figuring up right now how much you owe me so we don't have any arguments about it in the future?

CHARON. Let's do that, Hermes. Always better to get things settled. Leaves that much less to worry about.

HERMES. Ten dollars for an anchor delivered as per your order.

CHARON. That sounds like a lot of money.

HERMES. So help me Hades, I paid ten dollars for it. And sixty-five cents for an oar strap.

CHARON. All right, put down ten dollars and sixty-five cents.

HERMES. And a sail needle; I laid out a dollar sixty-five for it.

CHARON. Add that.

HERMES. And wax to calk the seams on the skiff, and nails, and the light line you used to make a brace from—four dollars in all.

CHARON. You got a good buy on those items.

HERMES. That's the story—unless we left something out that should be included. Well, when are you going to pay me back?

CHARON. Hermes, right now it's impossible. If only a plague or a war would send them down in droves, I could juggle the figures for the fare receipts and be able to pick up a little something for myself.

HERMES. What am I supposed to do? Sit around praying for bad times so I can get my money back?

CHARON. There's no other way, Hermes. You can see for yourself I have very few passengers these days. The peace,[1] you know.

HERMES. Well, it's better this way even if it means I have to give you an extension on your loan. Charon, you remember how they looked when they came down here back in the good old days? Real men, every one, and most of them wounded and covered with blood. They're nothing like that nowadays—sallow and spineless, all of them, and they die because their wives or children poisoned them or because they got ulcers or gout from overeating. So far as I can see, it's plotting for each other's money that sends the majority of them down here.

CHARON. That's because money's what they're all mad about.

HERMES. And that's why I don't think I'm doing anything wrong in dunning you for what you owe me.

NOTES

[1] The period in which Lucian lived, characterized by Gibbon as the "golden age," was probably the most peaceful in the history of the Western world.

10

Charon, Hermes, and Shades

CHARON. Your attention, please, while I explain the situation. You can see for yourself the skiff is small. Besides, it's got some dry rot, takes in quite a bit of water, and, if there's too much weight on one side, over it goes. Now there's a big crowd of you people here and each one is loaded down with baggage. If you get on board with it all, I'm afraid you'll be sorry later—especially the ones who don't know how to swim.

HERMES. What should we do to have a safe crossing?

CHARON. I'll tell you. You've got to leave everything behind on shore and get aboard naked. Even that way the ferry'll barely hold you all. Hermes, watch out that from now on you don't take anyone who hasn't stripped bare and thrown away his baggage in accordance with my orders. Stand by the gangplank, look them over, and make sure they're naked when you let them on board.

HERMES. Good idea. Let's do that. You there, the first one in line—who are you?

MENIPPUS. The name's Menippus. See, Hermes? Here goes my sack and staff into the drink. Good thing I didn't bring that old coat of mine[1] with me.

HERMES. Good work, Menippus. On board with you and take the special chair next to the helmsman, the raised one; you can keep an eye on everybody from there. Now who's this beauty?

CHARMOLEOS. Charmoleos from Megara, the boy the men were all in love with. I charged ten thousand dollars a kiss.

HERMES. All right, off with it all: the beauty, the lips— kisses and all—the long hair, the rosy cheeks, every bit of skin. That's the way—now you're stripped for action. Get aboard. Well, who's this impressive fellow with the purple robe and the crown? What's your name?

LAMPICHUS. Lampichus, Dictator of Gela.

HERMES. Well, Lampichus, what are you doing here with all this stuff?

LAMPICHUS. What am I doing—? Hermes, is a man who's a dictator to come here naked?

HERMES. A dictator, no, but a shade, yes. So take those things off, please.

LAMPICHUS. See? There goes all my wealth.

HERMES. Take off the delusions and the arrogance, too, Lampichus. If they go in the boat with you, they'll overload it.

LAMPICHUS. At least let me keep my robe and crown.

HERMES. No, get rid of them too.

LAMPICHUS. All right. What more do you want? See? I've gotten rid of everything.

HERMES. How about your brutality, stupidity, insolence, and bad temper? Get rid of those too.

LAMPICHUS. Look, I'm absolutely bare.

HERMES. Then get aboard. You, there, the heavy-set fellow with all that weight, what's your name?

DAMASIAS. Damasias. I'm an athlete.

HERMES. Yes, I recognize you now. I've seen you lots of times in the wrestling ring.[2]

DAMASIAS. So you have, Hermes. Well, I'm naked,[3] so let me aboard.

HERMES. My dear fellow, naked with all that flesh on you? Take it off, please. Otherwise, if you put just one foot in the boat, you'll sink it. And throw away those trophies and victory speeches.

DAMASIAS. Look, now I'm really naked; I weigh no more than any other shade.

HERMES. Weight zero. That's better; get aboard. You there, Crato! Drop that money and that effeteness and luxury. Take off that fancy winding sheet. Get rid of your ancestors' manly deeds, your genealogy, fame, key to the city, plaques, and statues. And don't start telling me how big a tomb they built for you. Memories like that are heavy.

CRATO. Off they go, much as I hate the idea. What else can I do?

HERMES. Hey, what's this? What are you doing here in full armor? And what are you carrying that monument for?

STRATO. Because I won a great victory. I was a war hero and my state honored me.

HERMES. Leave that monument on earth. In Hades there's always peace; we don't use weapons.

Now here's an important fellow, to judge from that getup and swagger. Who is he? The one buried in thought there, with the supercilious look and the long beard?

MENIPPUS. It's a philosopher—I mean a quack full of tricks. Make him strip too. You'll find a lot to give you a laugh hidden under that cloak.

HERMES. Off with your clothes first and all the rest later. My god! What a load of quackery, ignorance, argumentativeness, conceit, useless questions, thorny words, sophistic ideas! Plus plenty of useless effort, quite a bit of nonsense, humbug, and hairsplitting. What do you know about that! He's got money, too, and easy living, shame-lessness, bad temper, sloth, and effeteness! You can hide them all you want, I can still see them. And get rid of the falsehood and the delusions and this thinking you're better than everyone else. Even a battleship wouldn't hold you if you got on board with all that!

PHILOSOPHER. Well, here it all goes, if those are your orders.

MENIPPUS. Hermes, make him take off that beard. Look how long and shaggy it is. There's at least six pounds of hair there.

HERMES. Good idea. All right, take that off too.

PHILOSOPHER. Who'll cut it?

HERMES. Menippus here. He can take the ship's hatchet and use the gangplank for a cutting board.

MENIPPUS. No, Hermes. Give me a saw. We'll have lots more fun that way.

HERMES. The hatchet will do. Well done! Now you look more like a man and less like a goat.

MENIPPUS. How about my snipping a little off the eye-brows?

HERMES. Absolutely. He's grown them higher than his fore-head. Trying to make himself look important, I guess. What's this? Crying, you scum? Afraid of death? Oh, get aboard!

MENIPPUS. He's still hiding the heaviest thing of all under his arm.

HERMES. What's that?

MENIPPUS. Flattery, Hermes, something he's found very useful all his life.

PHILOSOPHER. Menippus, how about your getting rid of that independence, frank speaking, cheery resignation, high-mindedness, and mockery? You're the only one of us who's enjoying himself.

HERMES. No, you don't, Menippus; you keep them. They're

light, easy to carry, and they'll be useful during the voyage.

You there—the public speaker—get rid of that long-windedness, those balanced and contrasting phrases, sonorous sentences, barbarisms, and the rest of that mass of verbiage.

PUBLIC SPEAKER. See? It's all gone.

HERMES. Good. Ready? Cast off the mooring lines! Secure the gangplank! Heave up the anchor! Mainsail haul! Ferryman, mind your helm! Let's hope we have a good crossing. You fools! What are you whimpering for? Especially you, my new-shorn philosopher.

PHILOSOPHER. You see, Hermes, I always thought the soul was immortal.

MENIPPUS. He's lying. I think there are other things troubling him.

HERMES. What sort?

MENIPPUS. Not being able to go to banquets any more, or to sneak out at night, hiding his head under his cloak, to make the rounds of the brothels, or to spend all day robbing schoolboys by charging them to listen to that wisdom of his. All this is what's troubling him.

PHILOSOPHER. And you, Menippus? You don't mind being dead?

MENIPPUS. I? The man who rushed into death without receiving a summons?[4] By the way, Hermes, don't you hear a noise? As if people on earth were shouting?

HERMES. Yes, and it doesn't all come from one place. In Gela the men have all gathered in the town hall and are laughing and joking because of Lampichus' death; the women have gotten hold of his wife, and the children are raining stones on his poor little tots—even they're getting their share. In Sicyon they're applauding the eulogy that Diophantus, the public speaker, is going through for Crato here. Well, what do you know! There's Damasias' mother leading the women in a dirge for her son; she's brokenhearted. But for you, Menippus, there isn't a tear being shed. Your body's lying there undisturbed—the only one.

MENIPPUS. Oh no. In a little while, when the dogs and crows congregate to bury me, you'll hear heartbreaking howls and a beating of wings.

HERMES. Menippus, you're a brave man. All right, everybody, the trip's over. Next stop the judgment seat; just follow that straight road there. The ferryman and I are going back for another load.

MENIPPUS. Bon voyage, Hermes! Let's go, everybody. What are you all waiting for? We've got to face judgment, and they say the sentences are stiff—wheels, stones, vultures.[5] Everybody's life will be revealed in detail.

NOTES

[1] For the Cynic's traditional clothes and equipment, see p. 174.
[2] Hermes was patron god of gymnasiums.
[3] Greek athletes worked out in the nude.
[4] Menippus was said to have committed suicide.
[5] Three punishments famous in Greek mythology. Sisyphus was condemned to push uphill a stone that everlastingly slipped down just before the top; for the other two, see pp. 107 and 125.

22

Charon, Menippus, Hermes

CHARON. Damn you, pay me my fare!

MENIPPUS. Holler away, Charon, if you get any pleasure out of it.

CHARON. You heard me. I ferried you across. So pay up.

MENIPPUS. How are you going to get it from me? I don't have it.

CHARON. You mean there's someone without money enough for the fare?

MENIPPUS. I don't know about anyone else, but *I* don't have it.

CHARON. Pay or, so help me Hades, I'll throttle that damned neck of yours!

MENIPPUS. And I'll crack your skull with this stick.

CHARON. You pay or you'll find you took this ride for nothing.

MENIPPUS. Let Hermes pay for me. He let me go on board.

HERMES. Me pay for you shades? Oh, fine!

CHARON. You're not going to get away with this.

MENIPPUS. If that's the way you feel, you can just tie that ferry up and settle down right here. If I don't have it, how are you going to get it?

CHARON. You didn't know you were supposed to bring it?

MENIPPUS. Oh, I knew, all right. It's just that I didn't have it. What did you want me to do? Not die because of this?

CHARON. So you're to be the only one to brag you got ferried across for nothing, eh?

MENIPPUS. Not for nothing, my friend. I bailed and I took a turn at the oars. And I didn't cry—the only one of your passengers you can say that for.

CHARON. That has nothing to do with me. You're supposed to pay the fare. Any other arrangement is strictly forbidden.

MENIPPUS. All right, then, take me back. Resurrect me.

CHARON. Very funny. And get a beating from Aeacus for my trouble?

MENIPPUS. Then stop fussing.

CHARON. Show me what you've got in your sack.

MENIPPUS. Beans and some food I stole from an altar. Want a bite?

CHARON. Hermes, where did you get this Cynic? He kept chattering away during the whole trip, poking fun and jeering at all the passengers. While everyone was whimpering he was singing.

HERMES. Charon, don't you know who this fellow you've ferried across is? Completely independent, doesn't give two cents for anybody. He's Menippus.

CHARON. Well, if I ever lay hands on you——

MENIPPUS. *If,* my friend. But you're not going to get a second chance.

18

Menippus and Hermes

MENIPPUS. Hermes, where are all the handsome men and beautiful women? Show me the sights; I've just arrived.

HERMES. I'm busy now, Menippus. Just look over there, on the right. You'll find Hyacinth, Narcissus, Nireus, Achilles, Tyro, Helen, Leda—in short, all the great beauties of long ago.[1]

MENIPPUS. All I can see are bones and skulls without any flesh on them. Most of them look alike.

HERMES. Well, these bones that you seem to look down your nose at are what all the poets have been raving about.

MENIPPUS. Show me Helen's head anyway. I could hardly pick it out by myself.

HERMES. This one is Helen.

MENIPPUS. Well! Is this what launched a thousand ships

from every part of Greece and was responsible for slaughtering so many Greeks and Trojans and destroying so many cities?

HERMES. Ah, Menippus, you never saw her in the flesh. Even you would have admitted that there was no blame in

> Suffering year after year for the sake of a woman like Helen.[2]

If you look at flowers that are dry and faded, obviously they're ugly. But when they're in bloom and have their natural color they're as beautiful as can be.

MENIPPUS. That's what amazes me, Hermes. Didn't the Greeks realize they were going through all those hardships for the sake of something so short-lived, so quick to fade?

HERMES. Menippus, I don't have the time to go into any philosophical discussions with you. Pick a spot, any one you want, and lie down and settle yourself. I'm going after the rest of the shades.

NOTES

[1] Mythological characters noted for their good looks. Hyacinth was a young boy handsome enough to interest Apollo; Narcissus was the youth who ended up falling in love with his own image; Nireus was the best-looking of the Greeks at Troy, and Achilles was a close second; Tyro's looks involved her in an affair with Poseidon and Leda's in one with Zeus.

[2] *Iliad* 3.157.

20

Menippus, Aeacus, and Shades

MENIPPUS. Aeacus, how about showing me around all the sights in Hades?

AEACUS. All? A big order, Menippus. But here are the most important. You know that the dog there is Cerberus; Charon you've met since he gave you your ferry ride; and you saw Styx and Pyriphlegethon when you entered, right?

MENIPPUS. Yes, I know all those. And I know you're the gatekeeper, and I've seen King Pluto and the Furies.[1] Show me the men of olden times, especially the celebrities.

AEACUS. This is Agamemnon, and this Achilles, and this one near them Idomeneus. And here's Odysseus and Ajax and Diomed and the rest of the Greek heroes.[2]

MENIPPUS. Well, what do you know! Homer, the chief characters of your poems have been tossed on the ground, forgotten and ugly, dust signifying nothing, "feeble heads"[3] for real. Aeacus, who's this?

AEACUS. Cyrus.[4] And here's Croesus,[5] and beyond him Sardanapalus, and Midas beyond the two of them. And there's Xerxes.[6]

MENIPPUS. So, you scum, you're the one who made Greece shudder by bridging the Dardanelles and setting your sights on sailing through mountains! And just see what Croesus looks like! And Sardanapalus! Aeacus, may I give him a kick on the ear?

AEACUS. I should say not. His skull's so delicate you'll smash it to pieces.

MENIPPUS. Then I'll spit on it. That half-woman!

AEACUS. Would you like me to show you the wise men?

MENIPPUS. Absolutely.

AEACUS. First of all, this one here is Pythagoras.[7]

MENIPPUS. Hello, Euphorbus. Or Apollo, or whatever name you want.

PYTHAGORAS. Hello, Menippus.

MENIPPUS. No golden thigh any longer?

PYTHAGORAS. No. How about my taking a look in that sack of yours for something to eat?

MENIPPUS. Nothing here for you to eat, old boy—only beans.

PYTHAGORAS. Hand them over. A man changes his ideas when he becomes a shade. I've learned that down here beans have nothing to do with your parents' heads.

AEACUS. Here's Solon, Execestides' son, and that there is Thales, and alongside them is Pittacus and the others. All seven,[8] as you can see.

MENIPPUS. They're the only ones of all the shades who are resigned and bright and cheery. But who's that full of ashes like a loaf fresh from the coals? The one covered with blisters?

AEACUS. Empedocles.[9] He came here from Etna, half roasted.

MENIPPUS. Tell me, my bronze-slippered friend, what did you throw yourself into the crater for?

EMPEDOCLES. A fit of manic depression,[10] Menippus.

MENIPPUS. The devil it was! It was conceit and delusion and a large dose of stupidity. These are what burned you to a crisp, slippers and all—and serve you right. And that smart trick of yours didn't help one bit: people found out you had died. But, Aeacus, where's Socrates?[11]

AEACUS. Talking a lot of nonsense with Nestor and Palamedes.[12]

MENIPPUS. I'd like to see him, anyway, if he's somewhere around.

AEACUS. You see that bald fellow?

MENIPPUS. They're all bald. That's a distinction that applies to every one of them.

AEACUS. I mean the pug-nosed one.

MENIPPUS. Same thing all over again. They're all pug-nosed.

SOCRATES. Looking for me, Menippus?

MENIPPUS. Just the man I want.

SOCRATES. How are things in Athens?

MENIPPUS. A lot of your youngsters call themselves philosophers and, if it's just the getup and walk you consider, they're top-notch.

SOCRATES. I've seen a good number of them.

MENIPPUS. Then you've seen, I think, what Aristippus[13] and Plato[14] himself looked like when they came here—one smelling of perfume and the other an expert in fawning on Sicilian dictators.

SOCRATES. What do people think of me?

MENIPPUS. So far as reputation is concerned, Socrates, you're a lucky man. Everybody thinks you were a wonder, that you knew everything, even though—let's face it, it's the truth—you knew nothing.

SOCRATES. I told them that myself, but they thought it was this business of my Socratic irony.

MENIPPUS. Who are your neighbors there?

SOCRATES. Charmides, Phaedrus, and Alcibiades.[15]

MENIPPUS. Nice work, Socrates! Even here you're up to your old tricks—not passing up the good-looking boys.

SOCRATES. What nicer way to spend time is there? Would you care to lie down with us?

MENIPPUS. Oh no. You see, I'm off to settle down alongside Croesus and Sardanapalus. I think I'll get a lot of laughs listening to them whimper.

AEACUS. And I'm off now too. Don't want any shades giving me the slip and escaping. I'll show you the rest of the sights some other time.

MENIPPUS. Run along, Aeacus. I've seen enough.

NOTES

¹ The terrible goddesses of vengeance.

² Characters from the *Iliad*, the most important commanders on the Greek side in the Trojan War. Agamemnon was commander-in-chief. Idomeneus, Ajax, and Diomed were leaders, respectively, of the contingents from Crete, Salamis, and Argos.

³ Homer several times uses the expression "the feeble heads of shades" (*Odyssey* 10.521, 536; 11.29, 49).

⁴ Cyrus the Great (d. 529 B.C.) was founder of the Persian Empire.

⁵ Croesus, Sardanapalus, and Midas are the examples par excellence of wealth and its power. The first was the fabulously rich king of Lydia (d. 546 B.C.), the second Assyria's last king whose effeteness and luxurious style of living became legendary, and the third the mythical king of Phrygia whose touch could turn to gold.

⁶ The Persian ruler, noted for his arrogance, who, in 480 B.C., launched the Second Persian War against Greece. To transport his enormous army there quickly and efficiently he built a pontoon bridge across the Dardanelles and cut a canal through a mountainous peninsula in north Greece.

⁷ Pythagoras (580–510 B.C.) was one of Greece's earliest and greatest philosophers. He believed in the transmigration of souls and claimed that, in one of his earlier incarnations, he had participated in the Trojan War as Euphorbus, one of Troy's generals. He instituted a brotherhood which had strict rules of behavior and diet, among them a prohibition against eating beans; rumor had it he felt that eating them was tantamount to eating his parents' heads. After he died, legends giving him supernatural qualities were rife, including one to the effect that he had appeared at the Olympic Games with a golden thigh.

⁸ The "seven sages," honored by the Greeks as their wisest men, were Solon, Thales, Pittacus, Bias, Chilo, Cleobulus, and Periander. They lived during the seventh and sixth centuries B.C.

9 Empedocles (ca. 493–ca. 433 B.C.) was another of Greece's great early philosophers. Lucian's remarks refer to the legend that surrounded his death. Empedocles, it was said, wanted to disappear and not be seen to die, in order to convince people he was a god. So he arranged a very special suicide: he put on slippers of bronze that would enable him to walk on hot surfaces, made his way to the edge of Etna's fiery crater, and threw himself in; the volcano, however, belched up one slipper and thereby gave his secret away.

10 Lucian's word is *melancholia*, not the modern "melancholy" with its romantic connotation, but the black depression that, e.g., Burton treats so vividly in his *Anatomy of Melancholy.*

11 Socrates (469–399 B.C.), the key speaker in many of Plato's dialogues, was particularly ugly, with a bald head and turned-up nose. He did not teach for pay but simply held forth in the market place surrounded by devoted disciples. His favorite technique was to interrogate a person on a moral problem, pretending at the same time that he himself knew very little about it—the famous "Socratic irony." He claimed to have one advantage over other men: that, although he and they were equally ignorant, they thought they knew something while he knew he didn't. In 399 B.C. he was brought up on charges of impiety and corrupting the young and was condemned to death.

12 Socrates had argued that death was something to look forward to since it offered the opportunity to meet the great men of old. Nestor and Palamedes are characters from the *Iliad,* Nestor the aged wise counselor of the Greek army and Palamedes one of its generals who, like Socrates, had been tried and condemned on highly debatable grounds.

13 A disciple of Socrates and founder of a school that made pleasure the highest end in life.

14 Plato (428–347 B.C.), Socrates' most famous pupil, made three visits to the court of Dionysius I and II, dictators of Syracuse.

15 Three of Socrates' pupils who were young and particularly good-looking.

2

Croesus, Pluto, Menippus

CROESUS. Pluto, we're not going to put up with this Cynic, Menippus, as a neighbor. So either you move him away or we're shifting our quarters somewhere else.

PLUTO. He's your fellow corpse. What's he done that's so terrible?

CROESUS. We keep remembering what we left behind, Midas here his gold and Sardanapalus his life of luxury and I my treasure, and we moan and groan. Whenever we do, he laughs at us and sneers and calls us slaves and scum. And sometimes he interrupts our moaning with his songs. Frankly he's a blamed nuisance.

PLUTO. Menippus, what about this?

MENIPPUS. Pluto, it's true. I hate them. They're spineless good-for-nothings. The foul lives they lived weren't enough for them; even when they're dead they still remember and cling to what they had on earth. That's why I enjoy needling them.

PLUTO. But you shouldn't. They left a good deal behind. That's why they take it so to heart.

MENIPPUS. Pluto! Are you getting soft in the head too? Agreeing with these whiners?

PLUTO. Oh no. But I wouldn't like you people to get into any fights.

MENIPPUS. Listen, you scum of Lydia, Phrygia, and Assyria, respectively, I want you to get something straight. I'm not going to stop. Wherever you go, I'll follow and make you miserable. I'll drown you out with my songs and poke fun at you.

CROESUS. This is criminal!

MENIPPUS. It is not. But what you people used to do on earth *was*. Making people grovel before you, lording it over free men, never giving the slightest thought to death! Well, you can start whimpering because you've lost it all.

CROESUS. Oh god, all my possessions!

MIDAS. And my gold!

SARDANAPALUS. And my life of luxury!

MENIPPUS. Fine, fine; keep it up. While you whimper I'll sing a song I made up out of the words "Know Thyself."[1] This whining of yours will make just the right accompaniment for it.

NOTES

[1] A maxim that carried such weight with the Greeks they had it inscribed in gold letters in the temple of Apollo at Delphi.

MAN'S WORLD

MEN

Charon

Timon

Alexander the Quack Prophet

MAIDS

Dialogues of the Courtesans

PHILOSOPHERS

Philosophies for Sale

The Fisherman

The Death of Peregrinus

CHARON

Hermes and Charon

Charon meets Hermes in the street of some city, pre-
sumably Athens. It is a day during the middle of the sixth
century B.C.—*not any particular day of a particular year*
since Lucian, to suit his convenience, has conflated events
that took place at widely separated times during the
century.

HERMES. Charon, what are you laughing at? And what's
the reason for leaving the ferry and coming up to our
bailiwick? You're not one for poking your nose into the
goings on up here.

CHARON. Hermes, I wanted to see what life was like—what
men do with themselves during it, and what they give
up that makes them wail so when they come down to
us below. Not one of them, you know, ever makes the
crossing without tears. So, just like that young fellow
from Thrace,[1] I got permission from Pluto for a day's
leave, and I deserted the ship and came up to the sun-
light. It was a lucky break that I ran into you, the man
who knows all about this place. Of course you're going
to take me around and show me everything—give me a
real guided tour.

HERMES. I don't have the time, ferryman. You see, I'm off
on an errand for the commander-in-chief up above, some
business about men. He's got a mean temper, and I'm
afraid if I'm not prompt he'll hand me over to the gloom
—assign me to full-time duty with you people.[2] He
might even do to me what he did to Hephaestus[3] the
other day—grab me by the foot and heave me over "the

threshold of heaven"; then there'd be two of us to give the gods a laugh by limping as we wait on table.

CHARON. You mean you'll stand by and watch me blunder around this place? You, my friend, my shipmate—the man I lead shades with? My dear Hermes, there's a thing or two you ought to keep in mind. Did I ever order you to bail? Did I ever make you take a turn at the oars? You've got all that muscle and yet you either flake out on the deck and snore away or, if you can find some talkative shade, spend the whole trip gabbing, while an old man like me handles the oars all by myself. Please, Hermes, in the name of your father, be a good fellow and don't leave me stranded. Give me a tour of all the things in life so I can at least *see* something before I go back. If you go off and leave me, I'll be just like the blind. You know how they slip and stumble in the dark; well, that's just the way I am, blinking and dazzled by the light. Hermes, please do me this favor. I'll never forget it.

HERMES. I'm liable to get a beating for doing this. I've a good idea right now of the pay I'll receive for your guided tour—and it includes the knuckles of a certain fist. No matter, I'll help you out. I've got to: what else can a person do when it's a friend who's putting on the pressure? But to take a careful look at every single thing is out of the question, Charon. We'd spend years at it. And, if that happened, Zeus would be forced to post notices for my arrest the way they do for runaway slaves, you'd be kept from carrying on your death duties, and, with no deliveries of shades from you over a long period of time, Pluto's affairs would be hard hit. What's more, Aeacus, who handles the receipts, would get good and angry over not taking in a single obol. No, getting you a look at the high spots of what's going on, that's what we've got to work on right now.

CHARON. Hermes, you figure out what's best. I'm a stranger; I don't know a thing about what goes on up here.

HERMES. I'll tell you what we need, Charon: some point high enough to give you an over-all view. Now, if you could only get up to heaven, we'd have no problem; you could look down from there and get a panorama of the world. But, since anyone who associates with shades every day isn't allowed to set foot in Zeus's palace, let's start looking around for some tall mountain.

CHARON. You know what I'm always telling all of you when we're under way. Whenever there's a squall, and the wind shifts and takes the mainsail aback, and the waves run high, all of you, since you don't understand such things, start ordering me to shorten sail or slack the sheet a bit or run before the wind, and I have to tell you to keep quiet, that I know better. The same system applies here: you do whatever you think is right because you're skipper now. And I'll do what passengers are supposed to—stand by in silence, ready to obey your orders to the letter.

HERMES. True enough. All right, I'll see to what has to be done and find us a lookout point that'll serve the purpose. Let's see, will the Caucasus do? Or is Parnassus higher? Or is Olympus over there higher than both of them? By the way, looking at Olympus just gave me an idea that isn't at all bad. But you'll have to pitch in and help.

CHARON. Just give the orders. I'll help all I can.

HERMES. According to Homer,[4] the sons of Aloeus—there were just two of them, like us—when they were still young children, wanted to tear Ossa from its foundations, put it on Olympus, and put Pelion on top of the two; they figured all this would make a scaffold high enough to get them up to heaven. Now both these youngsters were punished because they were wild and up to no good. But what we have in mind has nothing to do with harming the gods. So why don't we do some building too? Roll mountains on top of one another so that we can get up higher and have a better view?

CHARON. You think just the two of us could lift and stack either Pelion or Ossa?

HERMES. Why not? Or maybe you think two gods don't measure up to that pair of babies?

CHARON. Oh no! It's just that the job seems to me to involve an incredible amount of work.

HERMES. Naturally—because you're like the man in the street, Charon; there isn't even a trace of the poet about you. Now our noble Homer has made a "gateway to heaven" for us with just two verses—that's how easily he stacks mountains. I'm amazed that you consider these things so extraordinary. Certainly you know about Atlas[5] —he's only one man and yet he holds up heaven with all of us on it. And you've probably heard how my brother Heracles once took over for that very Atlas and gave him a bit of rest from drudgery by shouldering the load himself.

CHARON. I've heard those stories. But whether they're true or not—you and your poets would know about that.

HERMES. They're absolutely true, Charon. Why would wise and intelligent men tell lies? So let's pry up Ossa first, just the way the poem and our poet-architect tells us, and then

> pile upon Ossa
> Well-wooded Pelion.

See how easily just a bit of poetry did the trick? Now I'll climb up and take a look to see if this is enough; maybe we'll have to do some more building. Oh lord! We're still down in the foothills of heaven. I can barely make out Ionia and Lydia to the east, no further than Italy and Sicily to the west, only as far as the Danube to the north, and Crete very dimly to the south. Ferryman, it looks as if we'll have to add Oeta[6] and then Parnassus on top of them all.

CHARON. Let's do that. But watch out that we don't keep adding to this scaffold beyond the safety point and make it too rickety. If that happens, we'll discover how bad Homer's method of construction can be—we'll come crashing down, scaffold and all, and bash our heads in.

HERMES. Don't worry. It'll be perfectly safe. Shove Oeta over here. Now let's roll up Parnassus. That's it. I'm going up for another look. Fine! I see everything. You can come up now.

CHARON. Give me a hand, Hermes. This is some contraption you want me to climb up!

HERMES. You wanted to see everything, you know. Going in for vistas and keeping out of danger don't mix. Here, hold on to my hand and be careful not to step where it's slippery. Good! See? You made it. Parnassus has two peaks, so let's each take one and sit down. Now turn in a complete circle and take a good look at everything.

CHARON. I see a lot of land surrounded by some sort of huge lake,[7] mountains, rivers that are bigger than Cocytus or Pyriphlegethon, people—but they're very tiny —and things that must be their dens.

HERMES. Dens you call them? Those are cities!

CHARON. Hermes, do you realize we haven't gained a thing? All this shoving around of Parnassus with its springs, of Oeta, and of the other mountains was a sheer waste.

HERMES. Why?

CHARON. I can't see a thing clearly from up here. I didn't want to see just cities and mountains the way you do on maps. I wanted to see the people themselves and what they're doing and to hear what they're saying, just as I was doing when you first ran into me and saw me laughing and asked what I was laughing at. I had just heard something that amused me no end.

HERMES. What was that?

CHARON. This man, as I gathered, had been invited to dinner tomorrow by one of his friends. "Of course I'll come," he was saying, and as he stood there talking, a roof tile fell down—someone must have knocked it loose —and killed him. I burst out laughing at the thought that he wouldn't keep his promise. Well, I think I'll work my way down right now to where I can see and hear better.

HERMES. Hold it. Dr. Hermes can take care of that too. I'll give you the eyes of an eagle in a second by just going to Homer and getting a magic charm for this as well. Now the minute I'm finished reciting, remember—no more blinking; you'll have perfect vision.

CHARON. Start reciting.

HERMES.

> Now I have lifted the mist which has covered your eyes till this moment.
> Now can you clearly distinguish the two—who is god, and who mortal.[8]

How about it? Can you see now?

CHARON. Marvelously! Lynceus[9] was blind compared with me. Now the next step is for you to turn teacher as well and answer my questions. How about my phrasing them *à la* Homer just to show you I'm not exactly an ignoramus when it comes to his poems?

HERMES. You? All your life a sailor, always pulling an oar? How were you able to learn any Homer?

CHARON. See here, that's an insult to my profession. It so happens when I ferried his shade across I heard him recite a lot of his poetry and I still remember some of it—in spite of having had a pretty bad storm during the crossing. You see, he began to recite some poem that wasn't exactly encouraging for people on the water— about how Poseidon gathered the clouds, churned up the waters by using his trident like a ladle, raised the winds, and lots more of that sort of thing.[10] Well, all this poetry started to rile up the sea, clouds came up, and a storm hit us that almost capsized the boat. At which point he got seasick and threw up most of his poetry—Scylla, Charybdis, the Cyclops, and so on. It was no hard job for me to save at least a few things out of all he was sending over the rail. Now then, tell me:

> Who is that man there? The one that's so thickset,
>   so mighty and valiant,
> Towering head and broad shoulders o'er all who are
>   standing about him?[11]

HERMES. Milon,[12] the athlete from the city of Croton. The Greeks are applauding him because he's picked up a bull and is carrying it through the middle of the stadium.

CHARON. Just think how much more they ought applaud *me!* Pretty soon I'm going to take Milon himself and stow him aboard the skiff. He'll come down to us after wrestling with that invincible opponent, Death, who'll pin him to the mat without his even realizing how he was knocked off his feet. And he'll treat us to some wailing, no question about it, when he remembers all his medals and this applause. Now he's all puffed up because everybody's amazed at the way he carried that bull. Well, what are we to think? Doesn't he expect to die some day?

HERMES. When he's at his height? How could he give any thought to death?

CHARON. Let him be. Pretty soon he'll hand us a big laugh when he gets on board the skiff and isn't able to lift a gnat, to say nothing of a bull. Now tell me this:

> Who is that other? The one so majestic and proud?[13]

He's no Greek, at least to judge from his clothes.

HERMES. That's Cyrus,[14] Cambyses' son. All that the Medes used to hold he's turned into Persian territory. Just recently he conquered Assyria and brought Babylon under his control, and now it looks as if he plans a march against Lydia to depose Croesus and become ruler of the world.

CHARON. Croesus? Where is he?

HERMES. Look over there. See that big city, the one with a triple wall? That's Sardis, and you can see Croesus there, stretched out on a golden couch, talking with Solon of Athens.[15] How about listening in to what they're saying?

CHARON. Certainly.

Croesus

Well, my friend from Athens, you've seen my money, treasure, gold ingots, and the rest of my wealth. Tell me, who, in your opinion, is the happiest man in the world?

CHARON. I wonder what Solon will answer?

HERMES. Don't worry. Nothing to be ashamed of.

Solon

Croesus, very few people are happy. In my acquaintance I think the happiest were Cleobis and Biton, sons of the priestess at Argos.

CHARON. He must mean the two who died together, just the other day, right after they had harnessed themselves to their wagon and pulled their mother all the way to the temple.

Croesus

All right, we'll call those two the happiest. Who's next, would you say?

Solon

Tellus of Athens. He lived a good life and died for his country.

Croesus

Damn you, what about me? Don't you think I'm happy?

Solon

I have no way of knowing, Croesus, until you reach the end of your life. You see, death is a sure test in a matter like this, death and whether or not you lived happily right up to the last moment.

CHARON. Good work, Solon! You haven't forgotten us. What's more, you agree there can't be a final decision in a matter like this until a person's alongside my ferry. Hermes, look at those men Croesus is sending out. Who are they? What's that they're carrying on their shoulders?

HERMES. Ingots of gold Croesus is donating to Apollo in return for an oracle—one that's going to destroy him before very long. You have no idea how crazy that man is about oracles.

CHARON. You mean that's gold? The shiny, gleaming stuff there, sickish yellow with a touch of red in it? You see, this is the first time I've laid eyes on it—although I'm always hearing about it.

HERMES. That, friend Charon, is it. Famous in song and story, the seed of so much discord.

CHARON. But I don't see what good it is—unless, maybe, to break the back of whoever carries it.

HERMES. You mean you have no idea of all that's gone on because of it—the wars, plots, freebooting, perjury, murdering, imprisonment, exploring, commerce, enslavement?

CHARON. All because of that? Why, it's not much different from copper. I know what copper is all right because, as you know, I collect an obol from every one of my passengers.

HERMES. That's right. But there's plenty of copper so it's not very much in demand. Gold, however, is scarce; the miners have to go deep down to get it. Except for that it's just like lead and the other metals; it comes from the earth.

CHARON. In effect you're saying that men are fantastically stupid. Yearning so passionately to own something so sickish yellow and heavy!

HERMES. Yes, but Solon over there doesn't seem to be so passionate about it. See? He's laughing at Croesus and the way the fellow brags. I think he's going to ask him something. Let's listen in.[16]

Solon

Tell me, Croesus, do you think Apollo needs those ingots?

Croesus

God, yes! After all, he doesn't have another donation in Delphi like this one.

Solon

So you imagine you're going to make the god supremely happy by letting him own gold ingots along with everything else he has?

Croesus

Of course. Why not?

Solon

Then, according to you, heaven must be pretty hard up. Whenever the gods want gold they have to send to Lydia for it.

Croesus

After all, where else is there as much gold as we have?

Solon

Yes, but tell me this: is iron found in Lydia?

Croesus

Not very much.

Solon

Then you people lack the superior metal.

Croesus

Iron superior to gold? How is that possible?

Solon

You'll find out—if you can answer my questions without losing your temper.

Croesus

Go ahead. Ask them.

Solon

Who are superior, rescuers or the people they rescue?

Croesus

Rescuers, obviously.

Solon

Now then, if Cyrus does as the rumors say and attacks Lydia, will you issue golden swords to your army? In that event, won't you have to use iron?

Croesus

Yes, of course.

Solon

And, if you don't have it available, off goes your gold to be locked up in Persia.

Croesus

Man dear! Don't say things like that!

Solon

God forbid that it turn out that way. But clearly you admit that iron is superior to gold.

Croesus

Then do you want me to send the god iron ingots and take back the gold?

Solon

He won't have any use for the iron either. However, if you do send copper or gold, you'll be making a donation to certain others—you'll be setting up a windfall for the Phocians or Boeotians or the Delphians themselves or for some despot or thief.[17] But the god's not going to care the slightest for this goldwork of yours.

Croesus

You're always attacking me for being rich. You're jealous.

HERMES. That Lydian there can't stand frank speaking and being told the truth. To him it's an unheard-of situation:

a poor man refuses to kowtow and says openly whatever comes into his head. Well, he'll remember this conversation before very long, when Cyrus captures him and makes him mount the funeral pyre. The other day I heard Clotho read off what she had spun for everybody, and there was a note to the effect that Croesus would be captured by Cyrus and that Cyrus himself would be killed by that southern Russian girl over there. See her? The wild barbarian riding on that white horse?

CHARON. You can't miss her.

HERMES. That's Tomyris. That girl's going to cut off Cyrus' head and stuff it into a sack filled with blood. You can see Cyrus' son there, too, a young fellow. There, that's Cambyses.[18] He'll inherit the throne from his father, meet disaster after disaster in Lybia and Ethiopia, finally go mad, kill Egypt's sacred bull, and die.

CHARON. It's so ridiculously funny! Yet, at this very moment, who'd dare look them in the face? Such an air of contempt they have for everyone else! What's more, who could believe that, in a little while, that one there will be a prisoner and this one over here will leave his head in a sack of blood? But who's *that* fellow, Hermes? See? He's wearing a crown, has a purple cloak that fastens on the shoulder, and his cook has just sliced open a fish and is handing him a ring

> There on an isle in the sea. And he proudly asserts he's some chieftain.[19]

HERMES. Parody, eh? And pretty good at that, Charon. You're looking at Polycrates, the ruler of Samos.[20] He thinks he's a completely happy man. Yet his servant Maeandrius, the one standing right alongside, is going to betray him to the Persian vicar, Oroetes, and the poor devil will have a stake thrust through his heart; the bottom will drop out of his happiness in a matter of seconds. I got this from Clotho too.

CHARON. Clotho, you're wonderful! I love you! Burn them, girl, chop their heads off, drive stakes through their hearts until they get it through their heads they're mortals. In the meantime let them raise themselves to the heights; the higher they go, the harder they'll fall. What a laugh I'll get when I spot them aboard the skiff, stark naked, without any purple robe or crown or golden couch.

HERMES. Well, that's what's in store for those people. Now, Charon, can you see the masses? Men sailing, fighting, arguing cases, farming, moneylending, begging?

CHARON. I can see that their way of life is tremendously varied and their world full of confusion. Why, their cities are like beehives—everyone in them has a sting which he uses on his neighbor, while a certain few, like wasps, attack and rob the weaker. But what's that swarm of things they don't notice flitting about them?

HERMES. Hopes, fears, pleasures, acts of ignorance and greed and anger, hatreds, and so on. Ignorance, as a matter of fact, mingles with them down on earth—actually lives side by side with them—as do some of the others, hatred, anger, jealousy, stupidity, helplessness, greed. But fear and hope stay overhead: in that way fear can swoop down and strike them dumb and sometimes even make them cringe in terror, while hope can hover about them and, just when they're convinced they can get their hands on it, fly off and leave them with their mouths agape—the same thing you see the water doing to Tantalus.[21] Now, if you look hard, you can make out the Fates[22] on high twirling for each and every one of them a spindle to which he's attached by a fine thread. See the threads coming down from the spindles to each man? Sort of like cobwebs?

CHARON. Yes, I can see a very fine thread coming down to each. But in most cases the threads are entangled, one with a second, the second with a third, and so on.

HERMES. Naturally, ferryman. You see, it's fated that that second man be killed by the first and the first by the third; that this man here inherit from that one whose thread is shorter and then leave it all to that third one there. It's for reasons like these that the threads are entangled. Notice that everybody hangs by just a hair. Now this fellow here has been drawn up high in the air; pretty soon, when the thread can't support his weight any longer and snaps, he'll come down with a bang. On the other hand, that one there is raised so little above the earth that, if he falls, he'll settle down so quietly even his neighbors will hardly hear it.

CHARON. This is terribly funny, Hermes.

HERMES. You couldn't possibly describe how funny it all is and do it justice. Especially the way they work so hard and earnestly and then, right in the middle of their hopes, off they go in the clutches of our good friend Death. You can see for yourself how well supplied he is with messengers and agents—chills, fever, consumption, pneumonia, swords, bandits, hemlock,[23] juries, despots. Yet people will never give them a thought so long as things are going well. Of course, when things go bad, it's nothing but "Oh, my god!" and "Lord, oh lord!" If they'd only keep in mind right from the very beginning that they're mortal, that after spending this short span of time in life they must leave it, like waking from a dream, and abandon whatever they had on earth, they'd live wiser lives and be less upset about dying. But they look forward to enjoying what they have forever, and so, when one of Death's agents comes calling to clap them in the irons of fever or consumption and lead them away, they get angry at being hauled off because they never expected to be torn from the world. See that man there rushing to finish a new house and hurrying the workmen along? What would he do if he knew what was in store for him? Although the house will get done, as soon

as the last roof tile goes into place, before the poor devil
has a chance even to hold a housewarming, off he's go-
ing to go, leaving it for his heir to enjoy. See that one
there who's so happy that his wife has just given him a
son? He's naming the boy after the grandfather and he's
called in his friends for a celebration. Do you think he'd
be so happy at having a child if he knew it was going
to die at the age of seven? The trouble is, he has eyes
only for someone like that proud father over there whose
son is an athlete with a victory in the Olympics to his
credit; he doesn't notice that his own neighbor is hold-
ing a funeral for *his* son; he has no conception of how
slender a thread that poor boy's life hung on. Look at all
those people arguing about property lines. Look at those
busily grubbing money—the messengers and agents I
told you about will call for them before they have a
chance to enjoy any of it.

CHARON. I see all this, and the thing I can't fathom is what
it is they find so pleasurable in life, what it is they get
so angry about losing. Take their kings who, after all, are
supposed to be the most fortunate among them. Aside
from the fact that, as you mention,[24] there's nothing cer-
tain or stable about their position, you find there's more
bitter than sweet in their lives—suspicions, disorders, con-
spiracies, tempers, enemies, flatterers; these are always
with them. To say nothing of sorrow and disease and
misfortune, which obviously know no class distinctions.
Now, if *their* lives are so bad, you can imagine how
things must be for ordinary people. Let me tell you,
Hermes, what men and their lives make me think of.
You've seen, haven't you, the bubbles that rise where a
spring of water splashes down? The ones that gather to-
gether to form foam? Well, some of them are tiny and
burst and disappear almost immediately. But some last
longer and, when others mass with them, get blown up
to a considerable size—but then these, too, burst apart
all at once, as they inevitably must. Human life is just

the same. All men are inflated with the breath of life, some more, some less. In some this inflation lasts for a little while—it has a short life; in others it comes to an end almost the same moment it came into being. But for everyone the bubble of life must burst.

HERMES. Charon, your simile's as good as Homer's. He compared the race of men to leaves.[25]

CHARON. Yet this makes no difference to them. See how they're carrying on, the way they're fighting to outdo each other in power or honor or possessions, all of which, except for a single obol, they have to leave behind when they come down to us below. Hermes, we're up high right now. How about my shouting at the top of my voice to warn them against going on with these senseless efforts of theirs? To remind them always to keep the image of death before their eyes? I'll say, "Why all this desperate activity, you fools? Stop wearing yourselves out! You're not going to live forever. None of the things that are so terribly important here are eternal, and you can't take any of them with you when you die—you've got to go off stark naked; your house and land and money must change masters continually, falling into one set of hands after another." If I shouted this and a few more things like it from some place they could hear me, don't you think it would help them a great deal in their lives? Make them much wiser?

HERMES. My dear Charon, you have no idea what ignorance and deceit have done to them! Together they've stuffed men's ears with as much wax as Odysseus used on his crew when he was afraid of the Sirens;[26] you couldn't get through with a brace and bit. So, even if you burst your lungs shouting, how could they possibly hear you? On earth ignorance produces the same effect that Lethe does down where you are. Yet there is a handful who have kept their ears free of the wax, who respect the truth, who take a critical look at what goes on and recognize it for what it's worth.

CHARON. Then let's shout to them at least.

HERMES. To tell them what they already know? A waste of time. See how they draw away from the mob and make fun of what it's doing? How they're utterly disgusted by it all? They certainly look as if they're planning to run away from life and come down to us. Why not? Here they're hated for the way they show up people's ignorance.

CHARON. Bravo! You're real heroes! But, Hermes, there's so few of them!

HERMES. They're enough, even so. Well, let's go down now.

CHARON. Hermes, there was one more thing I wanted to see, and if you point it out you'll have given me a perfect guided tour—those storage places where they bury the dead.

HERMES. Ah, you mean the things they call "graves," "tombs," "sepulchers," and the like. Look just outside the cities.[27] See those mounds and stone slabs and pyramids? All those are receptacles for the dead, deposit boxes for corpses.

CHARON. Why are those people laying flowers on the tombs and putting perfume on them? And some are building fires in front of the graves and digging trenches. Why, they're burning all that fine food and pouring wine and mead into the trenches! At least it looks that way.

HERMES. Ferryman, I haven't the slightest idea what good all this does the dead. But men are firmly convinced the shades fly up from below, drink up the mead from the trenches, and eat as best they can by flitting around the aroma from the fire.

CHARON. Shades able to eat and drink? With *their* dried-up skulls? Sorry—I must sound silly telling this to you, the man who escorts shades every day of the year. You certainly know whether they can fly up again once they're in the underworld. What a ridiculous life you'd lead— to say nothing of the work involved—if your job included not only leading them all down but bringing them back to give them a drink. You ignorant fools! Don't you know how great a gulf separates the world of the dead from the living? Don't you know what our world below is like? That there

> Both are just dead men, the king with a tomb and the unburied pauper;
> Irus the begger is equal in honor to great Agamemnon;
> Lowly Thersites takes rank with the son of the lovely-haired Thetis;
> All are alike once they're dead, merely ghosts and the feeblest of shadows,
> Bones bare of flesh, lying whitened and sere in the asphodel meadows.[28]

HERMES. My god, Charon, you certainly bailed up a lot of Homer! Since you've reminded me, I'd like to point out Achilles' tomb.[29] See it there on the shore? The town is Sigeum in the district around Troy. And just across the water Ajax is buried in Rhoeteum.

CHARON. Not very impressive, those tombs. Now show me the famous cities we hear of down below, Sardanapalus' Nineveh, Babylon, Mycenae, Cleonae, and Troy itself. Why, I remember ferrying across so many from Troy I didn't get a chance to haul out the skiff for a cleaning for ten whole years.

HERMES. Nineveh's[30] completely gone now; there isn't a trace of it left, and you can't even tell where it once was. Babylon's[31] that city with the fine towers, the one with the great wall; pretty soon you'll have to search to find it, too, just like Nineveh. I'm ashamed to show you Mycenae[32] and Cleonae and particularly Troy. When you get back below you'll be ready to choke

Homer for the way he exaggerated in his poems, I know
it. Yet once upon a time they were thriving cities. Now
they're dead. You see, ferryman, cities die as well as
men. Strangest of all, even rivers die. You can't even see
the bed of the Inachus[33] in Argos today.

CHARON. Homer! You ought to be ashamed of yourself!
All those glowing adjectives: "sacred," "wide-streeted"
Troy; "strong-built" Cleonae! By the way, Hermes, who
are those people fighting over there? They're slaughter-
ing each other! Why?

HERMES. You're looking at the armies of Argos and
Sparta.[34] And that man half dead there, who's inscrib-
ing a victory monument with his own blood, is Othry-
ades, the Spartan general.

CHARON. But what are they fighting about?

HERMES. The plain where the battle's going on.

CHARON. What stupidity! Don't they realize that, even if
every one of them got possession of the whole of the
Peloponnese, all he'd get from Aeacus is a spot barely
a foot square? And this plain of theirs will be tilled by
one generation after another, and many's the time the
plows will turn up that victory stone.

HERMES. Yes, that's what will happen. Well, let's go down
now and move these mountains back into place. Then
I'll be off on my errand and you to your ferry. I'll be
along in a little while with a delivery of shades.

CHARON. Hermes, you've done very well by me. I'm going
to put up one of those honorary monuments for you. I
learned something from this trip, thanks to you. The
way these poor mortals carry on with their kings and
gold ingots and funerals and fights! But never a word
about Charon!

NOTES

[1] Protesilaus, the first Greek killed at Troy, as a result of his loving wife's prayers was given the privilege of visiting her for three hours.

[2] For Hermes' various assignments, see p. 97.

[3] A reference to *Iliad* 1.590–91, where Homer tells how Zeus, in a fit of anger, took Hephaestus by the foot and hurled him from "the threshold of heaven," crippling him. The sight of the poor fellow limping as he served the wine tickled the gods' sense of humor (*Iliad* 1.597–600).

[4] *Odyssey* 11.305–20 (the quotations "gateway to heaven" and "pile . . . Pelion" are from lines 315–16). The two children, Otus and Ephialtes, were admittedly no ordinary youngsters; when they went in for mountain moving at the age of nine, they were already twenty-seven feet tall. The three mountains, Olympus, Ossa, and Pelion, stand more or less in a line, along the northeastern coast of Greece. Olympus is 9550 feet high, Ossa 6490 feet, Pelion 5095 feet.

[5] Atlas was the Titan who stood forever on the western rim of the earth holding up the heavens. The twelfth labor of Heracles (Hermes' brother because they both had the same father, Zeus) was to fetch the golden apples from the garden of the Hesperides in the far west. Since Atlas knew his way around the place, Heracles took over the heavens while the Titan went and plucked them.

[6] Mt. Oeta is in the southernmost part of Thessaly, not far from the famous battlefield of Thermopylae. It is 7080 feet high.

[7] Since the only bodies of water Charon knows are those of the underworld, he compares the ocean to the Lake of Acheron.

[8] The words of Athena to the Greek hero Diomed (*Iliad* 5.127–28).

[9] One of the Argonauts, the stock example in Greek mythology of keen vision.

[10] A paraphrase of *Odyssey* 5.291–92.

[11] A parody of *Iliad* 3.226–27, in which Priam asks Helen about Ajax.

[12] A famous athlete with a long string of Olympic victories to his credit. His exploit with the bull became famous and is described by a number of ancient authors.

[13] The first half of the line is from *Iliad* 3.226; the second half was made up by Lucian.

[14] Cyrus the Great (d. 529 B.C.), founder of the Persian Empire. He was killed while attempting to conquer south Russia.

[15] Croesus (d. 546 B.C.) was the fabulously wealthy king of Lydia in western Asia Minor. He entered into the war with Cyrus confident of victory because of a prophecy he had received from the oracle of Apollo at Delphi. The prophecy turned out to be disastrously ambiguous; Croesus lost, was captured, and made to mount a funeral pyre; it was kindled—but in the nick of time divine intervention put the flames out.

Solon was an honored Athenian statesman and the most celebrated of the seven wise men (cf. p. 210, n. 8). After retiring from public office (594 B.C.) he decided to see the world and, so the story goes, in the course of his travels visited Croesus and held his frank talk with him. The anecdote is given in full by Herodotus (1.30–33), whose account Lucian has condensed and adapted. As Herodotus tells it, Tellus is first and Cleobis and Biton second. The distance the two boys drew the waggon was better than five miles, all uphill.

[16] The conversation that follows is an invention of Lucian's modeled on Plato's Socratic dialogues.

[17] Delphi with its tempting, rich votive offerings was often plundered, particularly by the Phocians and Boeotians who were the nearest neighbors.

[18] Cambyses reduced Egypt, made unsuccessful attempts against Carthage and Ethiopia, in a fit of passion killed Apis, the sacred bull of Memphis, went mad, and accidentally killed himself with his own sword (522 B.C.).

[19] A parody of *Odyssey* 1.50 (where the island referred to is the mythical Ogygia, not Samos) and 1.180 or 5.450.

[20] Polycrates (d. ca. 522 B.C.), ruler of Samos, was famous for his amazing good luck. Even a ring he had deliberately thrown overboard turned up in the belly of a fine fish that a fisherman had brought him as a gift.

[21] Tantalus was punished by being fixed in water up to his chin under a group of fruit-laden trees: when he bent to drink, the water receded; when he reached for the fruit, the wind blew it out of his grasp.

[22] For the Fates, see p. 173.

[23] The poison used at Athens to execute those condemned to death, as, e.g., in the celebrated case of Socrates.

[24] He is referring to Hermes' description of what the future held in store for Croesus, Cyrus, and Cambyses (p. 228).

[25] Homer's famous simile occurs in *Iliad* 6.146–49.

26 The Sirens were creatures whose song was irresistible to passing sailors. Odysseus, forewarned, stuffed his crew's ears with wax and had himself lashed to the mast (*Odyssey* 12.173–79).

27 Burial was not allowed within the walls of ancient cities. The favored places were along the main roads from the point where they left the city gates.

28 A patchwork made of scraps from various Homeric lines (chiefly *Iliad* 9.319–20; *Odyssey* 10.521, 11.539). Irus was the beggar who sponged off the suitors of Penelope at Odysseus' court. Agamemnon was commander-in-chief of the Greek army at Troy. Thersites was a buck private in the Greek army. Thetis' son is Achilles.

29 Sigeum and Rhoeteum were located on the Asian shore at the entrance to the Dardanelles, on either side of the Scamander River. The Greek camp before Troy was presumably in this area.

30 The capital of Assyria which the combined armies of the Medes and Babylonians destroyed in 612 B.C.

31 Babylon was captured by Cyrus in 539 B.C. and swiftly declined in importance from then on.

32 Mycenae and Cleonae in the northeastern part of the Peloponnese, and Troy in northwestern Asia Minor, were great cities in the days Homer wrote about. Thereafter they dwindled to mere villages.

33 Actually the Inachus still flows during the winter when swollen by rain.

34 The dispute was about a small plain on the border between Sparta and Argos. Three hundred men on each side started the battle; it ended with two Argives and Othryades alive. While the two ran off to announce they had won, Othryades built a victory monument of shields and weapons, inscribed it with his own blood, and then killed himself in order not to survive his companions.

*Timon, Zeus, Hermes, Wealth, Poverty,
Gnathonides, Philiades, Demeas, Thrasycles*

*The scene is a remote spot on the border of Attica, the
district about Athens. The time is the second half of the
fifth century* B.C.

TIMON. O Zeus, god of friends, strangers, comrades, the
hearth, lightning, and oaths; gatherer of the clouds,
thunderer—and whatever else the wild-eyed poets call
you (particularly when they're stumped by their meter
—with all your names strung out you're a big help to a
verse that's short; you plug the gaps in the rhythm).
Well, Zeus, where's your crashing lightning and rolling
thunder and blazing, flashing, terrifying thunderbolt
now? It's become painfully clear that this is all non-
sense, just poetic hot air—the only crash and roar is the
sound of the words. That far-famed, far-flying, ever-
ready missile of yours has somehow or other fizzled
out; it's stone cold; it hasn't a spark of wrath left in it
to descend on the heads of wrongdoers. As a matter
of fact, anyone out to try his hand at perjury would get
more of a scare from an old candle stump than the flame
of that all-consuming thunderbolt of yours. You look so
much like a mere person just wagging a torch that sin-
ners aren't the least bit afraid of the fire and smoke;
the worst hurt they think they can get is a messy smudge
of soot. That's why Salmoneus⁻ had the nerve to set
himself up as a rival thunderer—a perfectly logical thing
to do, considering what a cocksure hothead he was and
how slow-burning your anger is. Why shouldn't he
have? You're as fast asleep as if you'd taken a narcotic;

you don't hear the perjurers or notice the wrongdoers; your eyes are bleary and can't focus on what's going on; your ears are as deaf as any dotard's. When you were young and hot-tempered and in the bloom of your anger, you carried on against the wicked and the violent. You never gave them a moment's peace in those days: the thunderbolt was always in action and the aegis[2] in motion; the thunder rolled, and the lightning flashed so thick and fast it seemed to come in volleys. Quakes tossed the earth like a salad, to use the vernacular; snow came down in bucketfuls, and the hailstones were like rocks. The rain pelted fast and furious, each drop a river. Why, back when Deucalion[3] was alive, in the twinkling of an eye such a flood took place that everything was swamped and only one vessel, some sort of ark, barely came through; it grounded on a peak of Parnassus carrying human seed with its spark of life so that greater wickedness could be propagated on earth. Well, you're reaping the reward of your laziness: men don't sacrifice to you any longer or wear garlands in your honor—someone may do it as an afterthought during the Olympic games, but he hardly thinks of it as an obligation; he's just helping to keep an old tradition alive.

Little by little, my King of the Gods, they're making a second Cronus of you and shoving you off your throne. I won't bother mentioning how many times they've robbed your temple by now. But some have even laid hands on your very image at Olympia[4]—and you, Almighty Thunderer, didn't have the energy to unleash the bloodhounds or call out your neighbors so they could help you catch the criminals while still packing up for the getaway. The noble Destroyer of the Giants and Master of the Titans sat still, his fifteen-foot thunderbolt motionless in his hand, while his golden locks were clipped from his head. Well, Your Highness, when are you going to stop being so careless and indifferent to all this? When are you going to punish such wrong-doing? How much fire and flood do you think you'll need to deal with this rampaging human insolence?

Let me stop talking in generalities and bring up my own case. I raised dozens of Athenians to the heights; I found them in poverty and made them rich. I lent a hand to everyone in need. Even more—I actually poured out my money in a flood to help my friends. But now that all this has left me a pauper, they don't know me any longer, they don't look in my direction—the same people who used to bow and scrape before me and hang on my every word. When I meet any of them on the street they go by me the way people go by some old tombstone overturned by time and lying on its back, without bothering to look at the epitaph. When they catch sight of me from far off they turn up another street—they feel it's a bad omen, it'll bring bad luck, to look at the man who, not so long ago, had been their savior and benefactor. Because of all these troubles I've exiled myself in this remote outpost, put on overalls, hired out as a farm hand for a dollar fifty a day, and deliver my philosophical pronouncements to the solitude and my mattock. I feel I've gained this much: I no longer have to lay eyes upon so much undeserved prosperity; of the two evils, that's by far the worse.

But when, O Lord of the World, will you shake off this deep, sound sleep—you've been at it longer than Epimenides[5]—, stoke the fire in the thunderbolt (or re-light it from Etna), get a mighty blaze going, and show the anger that Zeus used to, in his younger days when he was a real man. Or maybe the stories the Cretans tell about you and your grave there are true.[6]

ZEUS. Hermes, who's that shouting? Down there in the foothills of Mt. Hymettus in Attica. That man there in overalls, covered with grime and dirt. He's bent over; I think he's digging. Talkative fellow with plenty of nerve.

Must be a philosopher—otherwise he wouldn't utter such blasphemy about us.

HERMES. Father, don't you recognize Echecratides' son Timon? He's the one who fed us so often with top-grade sacrificial offerings, that *nouveau riche* who served us whole hecatombs and threw such magnificent parties for us on your festival day.

ZEUS. My, oh my, what a change! You mean the wealthy, fine-looking fellow who always had so many friends around? Why is he like this? Poor devil! It looks as if he's a workman, a farm hand. That's a mighty heavy mattock he's swinging!

HERMES. You *could* say it was his goodness and philanthropy and the way he took pity on everyone in need that ruined him. But the truth of the matter is, it was his senselessness, stupidity, and lack of judgment in choosing friends. The man never realized he was indulging a pack of crows and wolves. The poor devil imagined that all those vultures, who were tearing out his liver, were his bosom friends, who enjoyed eating his food because they liked him so much. When they had stripped his bones, gnawed them clean as a whistle, and carefully sucked out all the marrow inside, away they went, leaving him like a withered tree trunk lopped off at the roots. They don't know him any longer; they won't look at him—perish the thought!—and they're certainly not going to play savior or benefactor in their turn. That's why you see him now in overalls, swinging a mattock. He was ashamed to stay in the city, so he hired out as a farm hand. He's going mad brooding over his troubles, over the way people he made rich pass him by with their noses in the air and don't even remember whether or not his name is Timon.

ZEUS. We simply cannot pass over this man or neglect him any longer. Naturally he's angry at his bad luck. Why, we'd be behaving just like those damned parasites of his

if we forgot about a man who's sacrificed so many fat
haunches of beef and goat on our altars. I can actually
still sniff the aroma in my nostrils. You see, I've been
so busy and there's been such a fuss kicked up by
perjurers and ruffians and bandits, and then there's the
scare the temple robbers have been giving me—there
are so many of them and they're so hard to keep track
of, they don't let me close my eyes for a second—that
it's been ages since I last looked in on Attica. Particu-
larly ever since philosophers and their debates became
the rage there. They wrangle with each other and shout
so loud I can't even listen to prayers; I either have to
sit around with my ears plugged up or let them be the
death of me with their endless hollering about "virtue,"
"incorporeal substances," and all that drivel. That's how
I came to neglect this fellow, who's really not a bad
sort. Hermes, go get Wealth and rush right down to
the man. Tell Wealth to bring Treasure along, and tell
them both to stick with Timon and not be in such a
hurry to leave him this time even if, with that big-
heartedness of his, he tries to chase them out of the
house again. As for those scroungers and the ingratitude
they showed him—I'll look into the matter again and
they'll pay for what they did as soon as my thunderbolt
is fixed. I broke the two biggest flashes and ruined their
edge yesterday: Professor Anaxagoras[7] was trying to
convince his students that we gods are just nobodies,
and I threw it too hard at him. I missed—Pericles had
his hand over him—and it bounced off the temple of
Castor and Pollux and started a fire; it almost broke into
bits on the stone. In the meantime it will be punishment
enough for those parasites when they see Timon rolling
in money.

HERMES (*musing as he goes to fetch Wealth*). That's
what it means to have the nerve to shout and make a
nuisance of yourself. Very useful. Not only in court but
at prayers too. See? Because he raised a holler, said

what was on his mind, and got Zeus's attention, overnight Timon will go from rags to riches. If he had stayed bent over his mattock and kept on digging without opening his mouth, he'd still be digging and nobody would be paying him the slightest attention. (*Gets Wealth and brings him before Zeus.*)

WEALTH. Zeus, I won't go to him.

ZEUS. My dear Wealth, why not? It's my orders, you know.

WEALTH. So help me Zeus, that man insulted me. He squandered me. He cut me up into little pieces—me, an old friend of his father's. He practically booted me out of the house; he got rid of me quicker than you'd drop a hot potato. Go back there and be handed over again to a bunch of parasites, bootlickers, and whores? No, Zeus. Send me to people who'll appreciate the gift, people who'll treat me with respect, who value me and are anxious to have me. Let gulls like him stick with Poverty since they prefer her to me. Let the poor devils take the overalls and mattock she'll give them and be content to pocket their dollar and a half a day—since they so cavalierly toss away gifts worth a hundred thousand.

ZEUS. Timon won't behave that way with you any longer. Unless that back of his is impervious to aches, the mattock's been a good schoolmaster and taught him that you're preferable to Poverty. But what's the matter with you, anyway? You sound to me like a born faultfinder. Now you're blaming Timon because he opened the doors wide to let you circulate freely and didn't guard you jealously under lock and key. Up to now you used to get angry at the rich for doing the reverse—you complained they locked you up so tightly with bolts, bars, and seals you couldn't see a ray of light. You were always wailing about it to me, how they were asphyxiating you in pitch-darkness. It made you look pale and worried, your fingers were cramped from counting money, and you were always threatening to run away if you ever got the chance. All in all, you felt it was a downright outrage to live a virgin's existence in a bronze or iron chamber, like Danaë,[8] under the tutelage of those exacting and rascally schoolmasters, Interest and Bookkeeping. You kept telling me that what the rich do makes no sense: they love you madly yet, though they have every right to enjoy you, they never dare to; you're the object of their passion yet, though they have you in their power, they never lay a finger on you. They stay awake guarding you, staring at the seals and bolts without closing their eyes, thinking it enjoyment enough, not that they have the right to enjoy you, but that they have the right to exclude all others from any share, like the dog in the manger who wouldn't eat the hay himself but wouldn't let the hungry horse have any. What's more, you even used to laugh at the way they scrimp and save, at the incredible fact that they're jealous of themselves, at how it never enters their heads that some damned servant or slave driver of a steward is going to sneak in and have himself a gay party, without a thought for his miserable, despised master who's lying awake the livelong night figuring interest by the light of a dim and skimpy lamp with an oil-starved wick. These are the accusations you used to make. Now you're blaming Timon for just the opposite. I don't think that's fair.

WEALTH. If you look into the truth of the matter, I think you'll find I make sense in both cases. On the one hand, Timon's squandering is, to all intents and purposes, thoughtless and not very considerate toward me. On the other hand, those who put me under lock and key and keep me in the dark, watching over me so I put on weight and become fat as a pig, never touching me or bringing me out to the light for fear someone might see me, those I've always considered not only boobs but criminals: although I've done them no harm, they let me rot in all those chains; they don't realize that, before

very long, they'll pass on and leave me to some of the
luckier ones in life.

No, I'm for neither type, neither these nor the ones
who are so careless with me. I'm for the people who
can set a limit in the situation, who neither hold on to
everything nor throw everything away. That's the best
system. In the name of Zeus, Zeus, tell me this. Suppose
a man marries a young, beautiful woman and then
doesn't keep an eye on her or act the least bit jealous.
Day and night he lets her go wherever she wants and
be with whomever she chooses—or, rather, actually
leads her into adultery by throwing the doors open and
inviting everyone in, like a pimp. Would you say that
man loves her? No, you wouldn't, Zeus, and you've had
plenty of experience with love. Now suppose, on the
other hand, a man takes a respectable woman as his
lawfully wedded wife to be the mother of his children
and then, though she's a beautiful girl in the bloom of
youth, he never lays a finger on her or lets another man
see her but locks her up to drag out a virgin's existence,
barren and childless. Let's say he even keeps telling the
world he's in love with her—and he looks it, too, with
his pale face, loss of weight, and sunken eyes. Wouldn't
you say that such a man is mad? He ought to have
children and enjoy matrimony, yet he lets a beautiful,
alluring girl wither away by treating her, her whole life
long, like a Vestal Virgin. Well, it's behavior like this
that makes me angry—at some people because they have
no respect for me and push me around or gorge on me
or pour me out like water, and at others because they
clap me in irons as if I were a runaway slave.

ZEUS. Why be angry? Both types pay you a handsome
penalty: the one, like Tantalus,[9] goes without food or
drink and, drooling at the mouth, just eyes his gold; the
other, like Phineus, has the food snatched right out of
his throat by Harpies. On your way now. You'll find
Timon a much wiser man.

WEALTH. Timon? He'll never stop acting as if he's in a leaky canoe: he'll bail me out as fast as he can, even before I finish running in; he'll try to beat the inflow so I don't flood in and swamp him. If you ask me, it'll be like filling the cask Danaë's daughters used.[10] I'll be pouring in and getting nowhere since the thing won't hold water; what flows in will practically be out before it gets in. The outlet is so much bigger: it's a gaping hole; it's unpluggable.

ZEUS. Well, if he doesn't plug that gaping hole and it stays open once and for all, it won't take you long to spill out, and he'll have no trouble finding his overalls and mattock at the bottom of the cask. But get going now, and make him rich. And, Hermes, remember on your way back to pick up the Cyclops[11] at Etna and bring them here so they can put my thunderbolt on the grindstone and fix it up. I'm going to need it good and sharp.

HERMES. Let's go, Wealth. What's this? Are you limping? My dear fellow, I had no idea you were lame as well as blind.

WEALTH. Not always, Hermes. Only when I get orders from Zeus to go to someone. Then, somehow or other, I'm lame in both legs and walk so slowly I barely make it to my destination. Sometimes the person expecting me waits around till he's old and gray. But when I have to leave someone, then you see me on wings; I'm swifter than a dream. The starting signal sounds—and at that very moment you hear the announcement that I've won the race. I take the whole course in one jump. Sometimes the spectators don't even see me.

HERMES. That isn't true. I can give you lots of examples of people who yesterday didn't have a penny to buy a rope to hang themselves with and suddenly today they're rich, they're millionaires. Before they didn't even have a pack mule, and now they drive a team of thoroughbreds; they go around in silks and satins and their fingers are full of rings. If you ask me, they themselves find it hard to believe that all this wealth isn't a dream.

WEALTH. That's different, Hermes. In those cases I don't travel on my own legs, and the orders come, not from Zeus, but Pluto. He's another one who likes to give away money and make handsome gifts. You can tell it from his name.[12] Whenever I have to move out of one house into another, people wrap me in a will, sign and seal me carefully, pick me up like a bundle, and transfer me. While the corpse lies in some dark corner of the house with an old sheet tossed over its knees and the cats scrapping over it, the people who hope to get their hands on me hang around in the main square with mouth agape, like twittering swallow chicks waiting for their mother to fly home. The seal is removed, the ribbon cut, the will opened, and my new master announced —a relative, or a parasite, or some pervert of a slave boy who, through his abilities in bed, became the master's favorite and who still shaves to keep that boyish look; in return for the various and multitudinous favors which, even after he became too old for that sort of thing, he furnished the master, our hero now reaps a munificent reward. This unknown grabs me, will and all, quickly changes his name from Pyrrhias or Dromo or Tibius to Megacles, Megabyzus, or Protarchus,[13] and off he runs, leaving behind the disappointed hopefuls looking at each other and mourning—this time for real—because such a fine fish, after gulping down so much of their bait,[14] had slipped out of the bottom of the net. Well, my new owner—a thick-skinned vulgarian who still shudders when he hears the clank of chains, pricks up his ears if some passer-by happens to crack a whip, and genuflects before the treadmill as if it were a shrine— once he's landed on me with both feet, becomes insufferable to everyone he meets. Respectable people he insults, and the slaves he once worked with he has whipped just to prove to himself he can do that sort of thing. He ends up either falling into the clutches of some cheap whore, or going in for breeding race horses, or handing himself over to a bunch of bootlickers who swear he's handsomer than Nireus,[15] comes from a better family than Cecrops or Codrus,[16] has more brains than Odysseus, and is richer than a dozen Croesuses rolled into one. Once that happens, in no time at all the poor devil squanders what took years of lying, cheating, and robbery to scrape together.

HERMES. You're right. That's about the size of it. But tell me, when you walk on your own two feet, how does a blind man like you find your way? When Zeus decides certain people should be rich and sends you to them, how do you recognize them?

WEALTH. Do you think I actually track them down? God, no! In that case I never would have passed up Aristides and gone to Hipponicus and Callias[17] and a lot of other Athenians who didn't deserve a cent.

HERMES. Well, when Zeus sends you down, what do you do?

WEALTH. I walk up and down and wander around until I bunk into someone. The first person who happens to meet me takes me away with him—and offers up heartfelt thanks to you, Hermes, for the unexpected windfall.

HERMES. But Zeus is under the impression you follow his decisions and give money to the ones he thinks merit it. You mean to say you're deceiving him?

WEALTH. Of course—and he's getting what he deserves. He knew I was blind and yet he kept sending me to look for something that became extinct ages ago, something so hard to track down, so small and dim that Lynceus[18] himself would have trouble finding it. So, since there's just a handful of good people while the cities are filled with thousands of good-for-nothings, as I stumble around it's much easier for me to run across that breed and land in their clutches.

HERMES. But when you leave them, how is it you can get away so easily if you can't see where you're going?

WEALTH. Somehow, when it comes to making a getaway —but only then—I become quick as a flash and my vision is perfect.

HERMES. Now explain this one last thing to me. You're blind—it's the truth, let's face it—lame in both legs, and you have a bad complexion. Yet how do you have so many lovers? Everyone has eyes only for you; if they win you they think they're in heaven, and if they lose out they can't bear to stay alive. In fact, I know of quite a few who were so desperately in love with you they went off and threw themselves into the "deep bosom of the sea" or off the "sky-towering cliffs"[19] simply because they got the notion you were deliberately snubbing them when actually you had never even seen them. If you have any idea of what you look like, you'll admit, I'm sure, that they're out of their minds to go wild over an inamorata like you.

WEALTH. Are you under the impression they see me as I really am? Lame, blind, and whatever else is wrong with me?

HERMES. They must—unless they're all blind themselves.

WEALTH. My dear fellow, they're not blind. It's simply that Ignorance and Self-Deceit, two factors having the upper hand everywhere these days, dim their sight. What's more, I take steps on my own not to appear so completely ugly: when I meet them I'm dressed in embroideries and wear a lovely mask gilded and studded with jewels. They think they see my real face, fall in love with my beauty, and destroy themselves if they don't win me. Let someone strip me bare and expose me before them, and they'd kick themselves, no question about it, for being blear-eyed enough to fall in love with something so hideous.

HERMES. But, once they get rich, why do they put on a

mask, too, and go on deceiving themselves? Why, if anyone were to try to take it off, they'd sooner lose their heads than that mask! Once they've seen everything underneath, you wouldn't expect them to shut their eyes to the fact that your beauty is just paint and powder.

WEALTH. There are quite a few things helping me out on that score.

HERMES. Such as?

WEALTH. Whenever someone meets me for the first time and throws open the door to receive me, as I enter, in sneak Delusion, Stupidity, Arrogance, Sloth, Insolence, Deceit, and a thousand others of the same ilk. And once all these take possession of his soul, he marvels at things that aren't the least bit marvelous, longs for what he should shrink from, and goggles adoringly at me—me who begat all these ills that have come over him, me the very captain of the whole band. He'll suffer anything sooner than put up with losing me.

HERMES. It's amazing how slippery-smooth you are. You're hard to hold and quick to get away. There's no way to get a good grip on you; somehow you slither through a man's fingers just like an eel or a snake. Poverty, on the other hand, is sticky and clings. She has thousands of hooks all over her body so that the minute people come near they get caught, and it's not easy to break loose. Oh, damn! During all this chatter we forgot something very important.

WEALTH. What?

HERMES. We didn't bring Treasure, and we particularly need him.

WEALTH. Don't worry about that. I always leave him below on earth when I go up to you people. I give him orders to stay inside with the door shut and, unless he hears my voice, not to open to a soul.

HERMES. In that case let's land now on Attica. Hold on to my coat and follow me; we're going to the frontier.

WEALTH. Good idea, this leading me by the hand, Hermes. If you got separated from me, I might wander around and bunk into Hyperbolus or Cleon.[20] But what's that noise? Sounds like iron on rock.

HERMES. That's Timon digging up a little piece of rocky hillside nearby. Damn! There's Poverty with him. And Toil and Strength and Wisdom and Manliness—the whole gang that's under the command of Hunger. Much better than the ones in your band.

WEALTH. Hermes, why don't we get out of here as fast as we can? We're not going to cover ourselves with glory against a man backed up by an army like that.

HERMES. Zeus has other ideas. So let's not be cowards.

POVERTY. My dear Hermes, where are you taking that fellow you're leading by the hand?

HERMES. To Timon here. Zeus's orders.

POVERTY. So now Wealth comes to Timon, eh? After I picked him up suffering from a bad case of soft living, handed him over to Wisdom and Toil, and made him into a fine, worth-while man? Do I seem so contemptible, so easy to wrong, that, after giving him a complete course of training in virtue, I'm to be robbed of the only possession I have? Robbed so that Wealth can get him in his clutches again, turn him over to Insolence and Delusion, and hand him back to me just as he was at first, soft, spineless, stupid, a worn-out rag of a man?

HERMES. That's the way Zeus wants it.

POVERTY. I'm leaving. Toil, Wisdom, and all the rest of you, follow me. Timon here will find out soon enough what his desertion means—that he loses a fine fellow worker and a teacher of the best things in life. So long as he was with me he was sound in body and sane in mind; he lived the way a man should; he looked to no one else for help, and his basic principle—a perfectly valid one—was that extravagance and plenty were not for him.

HERMES. They're leaving. Let's go up to him.

TIMON. Who the hell are you? What do you mean by coming here and disturbing a workingman who has to earn a living? You're damned nuisances, both of you. You'll be sorry you came: in one minute I'll start heaving clods and stones and smash the both of you.

HERMES. No, Timon, please! Put those stones down. We're not men. I'm Hermes, and this fellow here is Wealth. Zeus heard your prayers and sent us. So, no more of this hard work, take your riches, and good luck to you.

TIMON. Gods, are you? Well, even if you are, you're going to be sorry for this. I hate everybody, you hear, gods and men both. I don't know who that blind fellow is, but I've a good mind to bash his head in with this mattock.

WEALTH. Hermes, in the name of Zeus, let's go now or I won't get away from here under my own power. If you ask me, the man's stark raving mad!

HERMES. Mind your manners, Timon, and stop acting like some country bumpkin. Stretch out your hands and take your good luck. Be rich again; be the top man in Athens. Thumb your nose at those ingrates, and keep your fortune to yourself.

TIMON. I want nothing from either of you. Don't annoy me. This mattock is all the wealth I need. Besides, I'm the happiest man in the world so long as no one comes near me.

HERMES. My dear Timon, how inhuman!

This I'm to bring back to Zeus? A rejoinder so brutal and savage?[21]

To be a man-hater is natural after all you've suffered at their hands, but to be a god-hater is certainly not—not after all they've done for you.

TIMON. Many thanks, Hermes, to you and to Zeus for all

you've done for me—but I cannot accept your friend
Wealth here.

HERMES. Why not?

TIMON. Because he's to blame for endless trouble I
went through earlier. He handed me over to parasites,
brought adventurers to my door, stirred up hatred
against me, ruined me with soft living, made people
envy me bitterly—and wound up by suddenly walking
out on me like a traitor and a hypocrite. But this won-
derful woman Poverty put me in condition with the kind
of labor a man should do, spoke to me truthfully and
frankly, and provided me with the necessities of life—
so long as I worked for them; she taught me to scorn
the plethora of luxuries I once had and to depend on
my own self for all I hoped for out of life. She showed
me what my true wealth was—something no sycophant's
flattery or blackmailer's threats or mob's violence or
voter's ballots or dictator's intrigues can ever take away
from me. And so, toughened by my hardships, I now
work this field—and like it. I see nothing of the wicked-
ness of the city, and I get the bread I need, enough to
keep me going, from this mattock. So, Hermes, turn
right around, go back to Zeus, and take Wealth with
you. If I had my way, I'd be satisfied to make everyone
on earth, young and old, howl with pain.

HERMES. My dear man, not that! They're not all suited for
it. Now stop being so cantankerous and acting like a
child and take Wealth here. Gifts from the gods aren't
to be tossed away.

WEALTH. Timon, may I submit the case for my defense to
you? Or can't you bear hearing me talk?

TIMON. Go ahead. But make it short. No long-winded in-
troductions, like those damned public speakers. For
Hermes' sake I'll put up with listening to a few remarks
from you.

WEALTH. Considering all the accusations you've made

against me, I'd be better off being long-winded. No matter. Just consider whether I've really done you wrong as you claim. In the first place, it was I who was responsible for all the very pleasant things that happened to you: honor, public recognition, medals, and everything else that goes with high society; you were famous, a celebrity, a man sought after, and all because of me. In the second place, I'm not to blame for any harm those scroungers did you—in fact, you've wronged *me* by treating me so disrespectfully and putting me at the mercy of a filthy bunch of fawning double-crossers who plotted against me in every conceivable way. And now your last point, your claim that I treacherously deserted. On the contrary, I could bring that charge against you— you did everything you could to drive me away, you tossed me out of the house on my ear. Result: that lady you think so much of, Poverty, has stripped you of your fashionable clothes and wrapped you in these overalls. Hermes here can bear witness how I pleaded with Zeus not to make me go to you, not after the unfriendly way you behaved toward me. (*Timon shrugs helplessly.*)

HERMES. See how he's changed, Wealth? Don't you worry; start living with him. Timon, keep digging just the way you are. Wealth, make Treasure go under the mattock; he'll listen to you if you call him.

TIMON. I suppose I have to obey and be rich again. What can a man do when the gods put pressure on him? Look what you're getting me involved in! Of all the rotten luck! Up to now I was leading the happiest possible existence, and all of a sudden, though I haven't harmed a soul, I'm to get all this gold and have all the worries that go with it.

HERMES. Put up with it, Timon, for my sake, even if it's hard and you can barely stand it, just to make those bootlickers die of envy. Well, I'm off; I'm flying back to heaven via Etna.

WEALTH. I think he's gone; it feels that way from the beating of his wings. You stay here; I'll go and send Treasure to you. Wait—I've got a better idea. Keep digging. Treasure! Gold! I'm calling you! Listen to Timon here and let him catch you. Dig, Timon. Sink that mattock in. Well, I'll be off now.

TIMON. Come on, mattock. Put some muscle into it now for my sake and don't weaken. Invite Treasure out of the depths into the light of day. O god of miracles! O god of hysterics! O Hermes, you god of windfalls! Where did so much gold come from? Is this a dream? I'm only afraid I'll wake up and find it's just a sack of coal—but no, it's genuine, solid, ruddy gold, the loveliest sight the eye can see:

O gold! The fairest gift a man can get![22]

A blaze of light both night and day, like gleaming fire.[23] Come to me, my sweetest beloved. Now I really believe Zeus once turned into a shower of gold—what girl wouldn't open her arms wide to receive such a handsome lover trickling through the roof?[24] Midas, Croesus, treasures of Delphi[25]—you're nothing compared to Timon and his wealth. Even the King of Persia can't match it. Mattock and overalls, my old friends, if you ask me, the best thing would be to dedicate you to Pan here.[26] For myself I think I'll buy up this whole frontier region right away and put up a tower over my treasure just big enough to be my house while I live and my tomb when I die.

Resolved that the law of my land until my demise be as hereinafter set forth:

that Timon is to cut himself off from society, know nobody, and scorn everybody; that friendship, hospitality, comradeship, and the sacred obligations of pity are all a lot of nonsense;

that compassion for those in mourning and assistance

to those in need are felonies as well as breaches of ethics;

that Timon is to live the life of a lone wolf and have one friend—Timon. All other people are enemies and traitors; to address a word to any shall be a crime and, if I even merely happen to see one of them, the whole day is to be officially declared a day of mourning. In a word, I am to consider them exactly as so many stone or bronze statues: I will accept no messages from them; I will make no truce with them; the desert is to be the boundary between us; "clansman," "kinsman," "fellow citizen," and "fatherland" are cold, useless terms, the prized possessions of the ignorant;

that Timon is to look down on everyone else, keep his money for himself, and live a life of luxury by and for himself, free from parasitism and vulgar flattery;

that, as his own neighbor and boundary sharer, living as far from all others as he can, Timon will conduct sacrifices and celebrate religious holidays all by himself.

Be it further resolved that, when the day comes for Timon to die, he will say good-by to himself and put the winding sheet on with his own hands. "Misanthrope" is to be the name that sounds sweetest in his ears, and his characteristic traits are to be grouchiness, roughness, meanness, temper, and unsociability. If I see someone burning to death and he begs me to put out the fire, I am to put it out—with pitch and oil. If a winter torrent sweeps someone off and he stretches out his hands and beseeches me to take hold, I am to push the victim under water head first to prevent his ever coming up again. That's the way to give them what they deserve.

The foregoing was moved by Timon, son of Eche-

cratides, and seconded by the aforesaid Timon. The ayes
have it. So ordered—and may I abide by the provisions
like a man. And yet I'd give a good deal to have people
know I'm a millionaire; they'd be fit to be tied at the
news. Wait—what's this? Lord, how quick! They're pour-
ing in from all sides, out of breath and covered with
dust. Somehow or other they caught the scent of my
money. Now how about climbing this hill so I can drive
them away by laying down a barrage of stones? Or
should I break my own law code just to the extent of
speaking to them once, so I can show my contempt and
make them even madder? That's a better idea, I think.
All right, Timon, stand your ground and receive them.
Let's see, who's coming first? That scrounger Gna-
thonides,[27] the one who told me to go hang myself
when I asked for a loan the other day. And he used to
puke up whole barrels of my wine at my house! I'm
glad he's come—he'll be the first to howl.

GNATHONIDES. Didn't I always say that heaven wouldn't
neglect a good man like Timon? Hail, Timon, the best-
looking, best-tempered, best all-around good fellow
alive.

TIMON. Hail, Gnathonides, the most greedy, most damna-
ble bloodsucker alive.

GNATHONIDES. Always had to have your little joke, didn't
you? Well, where's the party? I've got a new song to
sing for you. One of the latest hits.

TIMON. Song? You'll be singing funeral dirges. And with
real pathos—this mattock will see to it.

GNATHONIDES. What's this? An attack! I'm calling wit-
nesses. . . . Ow! I'll sue you for assault and battery.

TIMON. Stick around a little longer—you'll be able to make
the charge murder.

GNATHONIDES. I should say not! But at least heal my in-
juries, will you? Just sprinkle a little gold on them. That
medicine has a marvelous way of stopping bleeding.

TIMON. Still here, are you?

GNATHONIDES. No, no, I'm on my way. You're going to be sorry you turned into such a brute. You used to be a wonderful fellow.

TIMON. Who's the bald pate coming up? Philiades—the most repulsive bootlicker of all. Once I sang a song and nobody applauded except him; he raved about it and swore my voice was sweeter than an angel's. I paid for this flattery with one whole farm plus sixty thousand dollars to provide a dowry for his daughter. Yet the other day, when I came to him for help and he saw I was sick, the noble soul gave me the back of his hand.

PHILIADES. Disgraceful! So you all recognize Timon now, do you? So Gnathonides is his bosom friend now, is he? The ingrate! He got just what was coming to him. Even though Timon and I are old, old friends—we went to school together and later were neighbors—I'm taking it easy—I don't want to look as if I'm being pushy. Hello, sir! I warn you to watch out for all these damned bootlickers. They're only mealtime friends; the rest of the time they behave like a flock of crows. You can't trust anybody nowadays; men are ungrateful good-for-nothings, every last one of them. Now *I* was about to bring you ten thousand dollars so you'd have a little something to cover pressing expenses. I was on my way and had almost gotten here when I heard the news that you were rich, a millionaire. I came anyway so I could give you my word of caution. But a smart man like you doesn't need any advice from me—you could tell even Nestor[28] what to do in a tight spot.

TIMON. I'll take your advice, Philiades. But come over here; I want to greet you—with this mattock.

PHILIADES. Help! I give the man some good advice—and the ingrate bashes my head in!

TIMON. Look, here comes a third one, Demeas the politician. He's carrying a copy of some resolution and telling everybody he's my cousin. In one day that man paid the government a fine of a hundred and fifty thousand dollars—with my money. He'd been tried and convicted and, since he couldn't pay, was thrown in jail. I took pity on him and bought him his release. Yet the other day, when it was his turn to issue free theater tickets to all the people in my neighborhood and I came up and asked for mine, he claimed he didn't know I was a citizen.

DEMEAS. Hail, Timon, benefactor of our people, guardian of Athens, bulwark of Greece! The House, Senate, and Cabinet are in session and they've been waiting for you for hours. But first listen to the resolution I'm going to present in your honor:

> Whereas Timon, son of Echecratides, is not only a gentleman and scholar but the wisest man in all Greece,
> and whereas he has devoted a lifetime bestowing benefactions on his country,
> and whereas in one day at the Olympic games he took first prize in boxing, wrestling, running, two chariot events——

TIMON. But I've never even seen the Olympics.

DEMEAS. What's the difference? You will sometime. It sounds better when we tack on a lot of things like that.

> and whereas last year he distinguished himself for gallantry in action at Acharnae and cut down two regiments of Spartans——

TIMON. How? I couldn't afford a suit of armor, so I wasn't even in the army.

DEMEAS. You're too modest. We'd be ingrates if we were to forget what you did.

> and whereas he rendered great service on behalf of his country as legislator, administrator, and military commander,

be it therefore resolved by House, Senate, Supreme
Court, counties, and wards, both individually and
collectively, that, in return for such services, there
be set alongside the statue of Athena on the Acrop-
olis a statue of Timon in gold bearing a thunder-
bolt in the right hand and a halo around the head,
and be it further resolved that he receive as award
seven gold crowns of honor and that public an-
nouncement to this effect be made at the customary
time, to wit, prior to the presentation of new plays
at the Festival of Dionysus—and in his honor we're
to shift the date of the festival to today.

Respectfully submitted by Demeas the public speaker,
Timon's next of kin and his pupil as well, inasmuch
as Timon is an expert in public speaking—and
whatever else he cares to take up.

Well, that's my resolution in your behalf. I wanted to
bring my son to see you. I've named him Timon in your
honor.

TIMON. Son? You're not even married as far as I know.

DEMEAS. But, god willing, I'll get married next year, have
a child, and, since it's to be a boy, I hereby name my
prospective son Timon.

TIMON. Listen, you, I'm not so sure you'll be interested in
getting married—not after this lands on you.

DEMEAS. Ow! What's going on here? Trying to be a dicta-
tor, are you? The son of a slave beating up free citizens,
eh? You'll pay for this, and soon. For burning down the
Acropolis too.

TIMON. Damn you, the Acropolis hasn't burned down. So
it's clear—you're blackmailing me.

DEMEAS. Well, then, you got all this money by breaking
into the treasury.

TIMON. No one's broken into the treasury—so you won't get
away with that either.

DEMEAS. Then you'll do it later. But you've already got everything that was inside there.

TIMON. For that you get another wallop.

DEMEAS. Oh, my back!

TIMON. Stop your yelling or you'll get a third one. The man who, unarmed, cut down two regiments of Spartans not able to break the bones of one godforsaken runt? Ridiculous idea! Those Olympic championships in boxing and wrestling wouldn't mean a thing.

Now what's this? Isn't this Thrasycles the philosopher? Exactly who it is. Here he comes with that flowing beard, those eyebrows up in the air, and that pile of hair on his head, swaggering along, wrapped in his thoughts, and glaring like a Titan—the image of Boreas or Triton in one of Zeuxis'[29] paintings. He dresses in perfect taste, wears a plain dark-colored `coat, has a dignified walk, and, from the crack of dawn on, never stops extolling virtue—he's all for the simple life and against anyone who enjoys a bit of pleasure. But, as soon as he's had his bath and sat down to dinner and the waiter's handed him his drink—a double-sized one, the stiffer the better—you'd think he'd had a swig of Lethe's waters. He proceeds to demonstrate exactly the opposite of the morning's sermons. He swoops down on the dishes like a vulture, elbows his tablemate aside, spills gravy all over his beard, bolts his food like a dog, hunches over his plate as if he expected to find there that virtue he talks about, and wipes the bowls clean as a whistle with his finger so he won't lose a drop of sauce. He can get the whole of a cake or roast all to himself and still not be satisfied—the price a person pays for insatiable gluttony. He's a drunk, too, the kind that doesn't stop with singing and dancing but gets wild and calls people names. What's more, even in his cups he babbles on about temperance and good behavior—that's when he does most of his talking on the topic. He'll hold forth when he's already three sheets to the wind and has such trouble getting the words out it's ridiculous. After all this he'll throw up; they'll finally lift him off the floor and cart him away—and he'll make a grab with both hands for the girl playing the flute as he goes. But, drunk or sober, he yields the palm to no one in lying, nerve, or avarice. He's the king of sycophants, the man most ready to perjure himself; deceit walks before him and shamelessness by his side—in a word, the cleverest thing on two legs, not a flaw anywhere, letter-perfect in all sorts of roles. Well, we'll have some howls from this pattern of virtue in a few moments.

Thrasycles, what's the matter? Why so late in coming to see me?

THRASYCLES. I haven't come for the same reasons as this mob here. They're entranced by your money; they've scurried here en masse, hoping for silver and gold and for fancy parties, prepared to put on a full show of flattery before a simple soul like yourself who's so ready to share everything he owns. But you know very well that a crust of bread is a whole dinner for me, that my favorite dish is a bit of thyme or cress or, when I feel like indulging myself, a pinch of salt. And for drink just cold water. This threadbare coat I prefer to any purple robes. In my opinion gold has no more value than the pebbles on a beach. I've come purely for your sake— to keep your wealth from destroying you. It's the world's worst possession, the one people scheme for most; it's been responsible for irremediable harm to thousands, thousands of times. Now, if you'll listen to me, you'll throw it all into the sea—a good man who can discern philosophy's treasures doesn't need it. But, my dear Timon, not where it's deep. Go into the water just up to your hips and toss it a little beyond the line of breakers—with only me watching. If you don't like this way, I have another, even better, way: hurry and bring the money out of your house—all of it; don't keep a penny for yourself—and distribute it among the needy, a few dollars to this one, a few hundred to that, a couple of thousand to a third. If there are any philosophers it's only fair they get a double or triple share. As for me, I ask nothing for myself but just some to hand out to my needy friends. If you'll fill this sack—it holds less than four bushels—that'll be quite enough. Philosophers should live simply and frugally—and give no thought to anything beyond what's in their sack.

TIMON. I fully agree, Thrasycles. But, if you don't mind, before I fill your sack let me fill your head with fists— after I test its capacity with this mattock.

THRASYCLES. What's happened to our laws? Where's our democracy? This is a free country and this damned rascal is beating me up!

TIMON. My dear Thrasycles, why so angry? I didn't cheat you, did I? All right, here's half a bushel more for good measure.

What's going on here? They're coming in droves! There's Blepsias and Laches and Gnipho—an army of potential howlers. Why don't I climb on this rock, give my mattock a rest—it's put in a hard day—lay in a supply of stones, and pelt them at long range?

BLEPSIAS. Timon! Stop! We'll leave!

TIMON. Not before I draw blood you won't!

NOTES

[1] Salmoneus, son of the god of the winds, imitated thunder (he rolled chariots over a bridge of brass) and insisted that men sacrifice to him as to Zeus.

[2] Zeus's shield, the sight of which inspired terror.

[3] The Greek Noah.

[4] Cf. p. 150.

[5] The Greek Rip Van Winkle.

6 See p. 169, n. 46.

7 A celebrated philosopher who argued that not gods but an intelligent force governed the world. He was brought up on charges of impiety and would have been executed had not Pericles, the all-powerful political leader of Athens at the time, intervened in his behalf.

8 See p. 102, n. 3.

9 For Tantalus, see p. 237, n. 21. Phineus killed his own sons. His punishment was to be victimized by the Harpies "snatchers," monstrous winged creatures that snatched his food from him and devoured it.

10 See p. 124, n. 1.

11 The one-eyed giants who, with Hephaestus as foreman, ran the celestial smithy in the fiery crater of Mt. Etna.

12 *Plouton,* the name of the god of the underworld, is very much like the Greek word for wealth (*ploutos*).

13 Pyrrhias, Dromo, and Tibius were common names of slaves and Megacles, Megabyzus, and Protarchus common names in the best aristocratic families.

14 I.e., the presents they had given the deceased in the hope of being remembered in the will.

15 See p. 206, n. 1.

16 Legendary kings of Athens.

17 For Aristides and Callias see p. 169, nn. 48 and 49. Hipponicus was Callias' father.

18 See p. 236, n. 9.

18 See p. 313, n. 9.

19 Allusions to a poem on poverty by the famous sixth-century Greek poet Theognis.

20 Notorious Athenian demagogues.

21 *Iliad* 15.202, Iris' words to the angry Poseidon.

22 A line from a lost play of Euripides.

23 A paraphrase of the beginning of Pindar's first Olympic ode.

24 Danaë; see n. 8 above.

25 See p. 237, n. 17.

26 As a farmer, Timon maintained a rude shrine to Pan, the farmers' god (cf. p. 107, n. 1).

27 The sycophants are given common Greek names which Lucian has carefully chosen for their etymological associations: Gnathonides, "cheeky"; Philiades, "friendly"; Demeas, "public servant"; Thrasycles, "nervy"; Blepsias, "shark"; Laches, "share-seeker"; Gnipho, "skinflint."

28 An aged chieftain in the *Iliad,* the giver of counsel par excellence.

[29] A celebrated painter of the second half of the fifth century B.C. Presumably he had drawn Boreas, god of the north wind, and Triton, a sea deity, as sailing along with long hair streaming in the wind.

ALEXANDER THE QUACK PROPHET

*In Abonoteichus on the south shore of the Black Sea,
an obscure town in a remote corner of the Roman Empire,
a certain Alexander gained a great reputation in Lucian's
day as mouthpiece of a new god of prophecy.*

*Lucian despised all oracles and rarely passed up a
chance for a joke or sneer at their expense (cf. pp. 140,
225, 322). But this was no joking matter. This was no
shrine going back to hoary antiquity and famous in song
and story but one that had been founded in his own life-
time by a man of intelligence and vast ability, one that,
moreover, was doing an active and very profitable busi-
ness. So, when a person high among the Epicureans, who
were implacable enemies of anything that smacked of the
supernatural, asked Lucian to do a brief life of Alexander,
he went at the task with gusto.*

*This memoir reads as if it had burst white-hot from a
pen burning with righteous indignation. As a matter of
fact, it was written at least fifteen years after the events,
described here so vividly they seem to have happened
yesterday, took place. This immediacy is part of Lucian's
artistry, another stroke of the brush on this portrait in tar
that he deliberately set out to make. For Lucian the ra-
tionalist it was enough that Alexander was passing himself
off as a prophet: it gave him carte blanche to go after the
man with no holds barred.*

*You must, therefore, not believe every word you read
here. Alexander very likely was neither a pederast nor an
oversexed ravisher of women; this is the sort of mud an-
cient pamphleteers slung at their pet hates as a matter of
course. He certainly was no Greek Rasputin with a sinister
influence pervading the entire Roman Empire; this is
Lucian the spellbinding rhetorician at work. The dramatic*

*tale of a face-to-face encounter with Alexander, the bitter
vignette of the Epicurean barely saved from stoning, the
exciting story of the attempted murder—this is Lucian the
master of narrative at work; they may or may not be true.*
Alexander the Quack Prophet *is not a documented tract
against superstition; it is a creative work of art.*

*That there was such a person who ran such an oracle
cannot be doubted. We have incontrovertible proof: the
Abonoteichans, proud of the shrine, embellished their
coins with a likeness of Alexander's new god; specimens
can be seen in many a museum today. Lucian says it was
Alexander who got the emperor's permission to mint these,
and he may very well be telling the truth. And he must be
telling the truth when he names a high-ranking Roman
official as one of the fish Alexander caught—and hooked
so securely he was able to marry off his daughter to the
fool.*

*Alexander's customers came from almost all the key
provinces—as Roman administrative districts were called—
of Asia Minor. The ones Lucian names are: Bithynia and
Pontus (where Abonoteichus was located) along the south
shore of the Black Sea; Galatia and Paphlagonia (which,
very near to Abonoteichus, supplied the bulk of the cli-
entele) in the interior behind; Asia (including the region
of Ionia) and Cilicia on the Mediterranean coast to the
west and south.*

You may be under the impression, my dear Celsus, that
you've given me a minor and trivial assignment in asking
me to compose and send you an account of the life,
schemes, brazen effrontery, and hocus-pocus of Alexander,
the quack of Abonoteichus. Actually, if a man were to do a
detailed study, it would be no less a project than compos-
ing a life of Alexander the Great: the one was as great a
villain as the other a hero. However, if you will read with
indulgence and fill in from your own imagination the gaps
in my narrative, I'll take on the job. I'll try to clean up this

Augean stable—if not all of it, at least as much as I can; I'll haul out a few basketfuls of dung, enough to give you an idea of how vast and unspeakable was the total accumulation that three thousand head of cattle had been able to pile up over all those years.[1]

I feel a sense of shame for both our sakes, yours as well as mine. Yours because you're willing to let the memory of a damned scoundrel be committed to writing and so preserved, mine because I'm spending so much time and energy on such a topic, on the acts of a man who ought not be a subject for the educated to read about but an object for the masses to behold being torn to bits by foxes and apes in some vast theater. However, if anyone criticizes me for what I am doing, I have the following to offer as precedent. Arrian, Epictetus' disciple, an outstanding Roman and a man who devoted a lifetime to culture, can come to my defense as well as his own.[2] He did the same thing; he was willing, for example, to draw up a biography of Tilliborus the bandit. I'm doing a memoir of a much more vicious bandit—mine didn't do his plundering in forests and on mountainsides but in cities and, in his marauding, didn't range over merely Mysia and Ida and a few of the more barren areas of Asia Minor but, in a sense, saturated the entire Roman Empire with his brigandage.

First I want to paint for you a word picture of the man, making as exact a likeness as I can, though I'm not much of a literary portraitist. In physical appearance, to give you an idea of that as well, he was tall and had good looks with a genuine godly quality about them. His skin was white, his beard was long but not shaggy, and his flowing locks were partly real and partly a wig he wore, but one so well matched that few people were aware his hair wasn't all his own. His eyes were piercing and had an inspired gleam, his voice very soft, yet at the same time perfectly clear.

That was his outward appearance and, in all of it, there

[4

isn't a single flaw to be found anywhere. But that soul
and mind of his! O Heracles the Protector, O Zeus the
Guardian, O Castor and Pollux the Saviors! Throw a man
in with his worst enemies, and keep him away from some-
one like Alexander! You see, in brains and shrewdness and
keenness there wasn't anybody like him. Energy, grasp,
memory, a natural aptitude for learning—he had more than
his due of each. But he used these endowments for the
worst possible ends. Though he had such a wealth of
noble talents, he lived in a way that outdid all the no-
torious evildoers of history—he was worse than the Cer-
copes, worse than Eurybatus or Phrynondas or Aristode-
mus or Sostratus.[3] Once, in a letter to his son-in-law
Rutilianus, when he was being modest about himself, he
claimed he could be compared with Pythagoras. With all
due respect for Pythagoras, who was a wise man with an
inspired mind, had he been a contemporary of this fellow,
believe me, he would have looked like a child in compari-
son. Now, in the name of all three Graces, don't imagine
for a moment that I say this to insult Pythagoras or be-
cause I'm trying to pair the two men for having achieved
similar ends. If you were to take the vilest actions Pythag-
oras' detractors have attributed to him to ruin his good
name—actions I, for one, don't believe are true, but no
matter—if they were all lumped together, the whole batch
would amount to only a minuscule part of Alexander's in-
genious scheming. All in all, you must conceive of, you
must conjure up in your mind, a soul composed of the
most varied ingredients, one that blended deceit, trickery,
lying, sharp practices, carelessness, nerve, recklessness, and
tirelessness in carrying out plans with trust, reliability, and
the knack of acting a better role, of looking white when
the end in view was black. As a matter of fact, everyone
who met him for the first time left with the impression
that this was the finest and most decent person alive, even
the most simple and naïve. On top of all this, he was a
man whose ideas were on the grand scale: he never paid

attention to anything small but always kept his mind on the big things.

When a young boy Alexander was extremely good-looking—not only could you hear this from people who told his story but you could see for yourself the traces left in the grown man. He made an out-and-out prostitute of himself: he went to bed with whoever wanted him and would pay. Among the many lovers who took him on was some quack, one of those who offer magic, miracle-working incantations, charms to snare a lover, tricks to defeat an enemy, places to dig for buried treasure, and ways to inherit a fortune. This fellow observed that the youngster not only had a natural talent and all the qualifications to be of help in his business but that the boy was as much in love with his dirty tricks as he was with the other's blooming youth. He took the youngster under his wing and used him constantly as servant, attendant, and assistant. He himself had been a government doctor supposedly and, like the wife of Thon of Egypt, knew the

> Brewing of many a potion most healthful and many most harmful.[4]

To all this Alexander became sole heir. His teacher-lover, a native of Tyana, belonged to the circle of Apollonius of Tyana and knew all the ins and outs of the act Apollonius used to put on.[5] You see now the school that produced the subject of this memoir!

Our friend from Tyana died just when Alexander was of an age to grow a beard. He was left penniless, and at the same time the good looks by which he could have made a living lost their bloom. But he no longer had his mind on anything small. Instead he went into partnership with a worse scoundrel than himself, someone from Byzantium who used to cast horoscopes for contestants in the games held on festival days—"Nutsy," I think he was nicknamed. The two of them went around masquerading as magicians, pulling off swindles, and fleecing the "fat-

heads," as the public is called in the magicians' argot.
Among their victims was a wealthy woman named Macetis
who had outlived her attractiveness but still had the urge
to be alluring to men. Once they had discovered her, they
made a very good thing out of it and followed in her
tracks when she left Bithynia to go back to Macedonia.
She came from Pella which long ago, during the days of
the kings of Macedon, was a flourishing spot but today
has the merest handful of miserable inhabitants. Here
their eye was caught by certain enormous snakes which
were perfectly gentle and tame—they were fed by the
women, slept with the children, allowed themselves to be
stepped on, didn't turn fierce when petted, and took milk
from the breast just like any infant. These serpents are ex-
tremely common there, a fact that very likely gave rise, in
bygone days, to the story about Olympias when she be-
came pregnant with Alexander;[6] I imagine that one such
snake had been sleeping with her. The partners bought one
of these creatures, the finest available, for a few pennies,
and, to quote Thucydides, "this was the starting point
of the war."[7]

As you'd expect of a pair of out-and-out rascals who
were ready to stoop to anything and stop at nothing and
who had gotten together for the same ends, it didn't take
them long to figure out that two all-important factors,
hope and fear, tyrannize every man's life and that anyone
able to make use of either for his own good could become
rich overnight. They saw that what both the fearful and
the hopeful needed and wanted the most was knowledge
of the future, that this was the reason Delphi and Delos
and Clarus and Didyma had ages ago become rich and
famous:[8] men, because of the two tyrants I mentioned,
hope and fear, were forever coming to these shrines and
asking to know the future, and, in payment, they sacrificed
whole hecatombs and donated ingots of gold. After turning
this discovery over in their minds and pondering it, the
partners laid plans to set up an oracle, a seat of prophecy.

They hoped, if things went well, to become prosperous and wealthy in short order; what actually occurred far surpassed their initial expectations and was much greater than anything they had ever looked for.

Next they took up two questions: first, where to locate their enterprise, and, second, how to launch and operate it. "Nutsy" voted for Chalcedon[9] as a likely spot since it was a commercial town near to both Thrace and Bithynia and, in addition, wasn't far from Asia and Galatia and all the peoples in the hinterland. Alexander, on the other hand, was in favor of his home town. His point—a perfectly valid one—was that, in its initial stages, they needed "fatheads" and boobs to fall for such an operation as this, and, he claimed, the natives of Paphlagonia who lived beyond Abonoteichus, superstitious and well-heeled—yokels for the most part, were ideal; all a man had to do was come along, at his heels someone tootling a flute or beating a drum or clashing cymbals, and offer to tell fortunes with a sieve,[10] as the saying goes, and the next minute all their jaws would drop and they'd stare at him like a god from heaven.

After a bit of a squabble over this Alexander finally won out. They first went to Chalcedon—in spite of their decision they felt the city could serve a useful purpose. Here, in the sanctuary of Apollo, the oldest in Chalcedon, they planted some bronze tablets with an inscription to the effect that Asclepius and his father Apollo were moving forthwith to Pontus and were going to settle down in Abonoteichus.[11] The opportune unearthing of these tablets spread the news for them the length and breadth of Bithynia and Pontus with no effort on their part. The first place it reached was Abonoteichus, whose townspeople promptly voted to erect a temple and started at once to dig the foundations. At this point "Nutsy" was left behind in Chalcedon, busily turning out ambiguous, equivocal, and enigmatic oracles. Not long after that he died, of snake bite I think.

Alexander went on ahead. By now he had long, flowing locks, wore a white-trimmed purple shirt with a white mantle over it, and carried a scimitar à la Perseus, whom he had added to his genealogy as a maternal ancestor. The Paphlagonians, poor devils, though they knew perfectly well that both his parents were low-class nonentities, willingly believed the oracle that said:

Hail the descendant of Perseus, the dearly beloved of Apollo,

Heir to the great Podalirius' blood—Alexander the godly!

(Podalirius,[12] I take it, was so oversexed and woman-crazy he produced an erection which reached from Tricca to Alexander's mother in Paphlagonia.) By now Alexander had also come up with an oracle according to which the Sibyl purportedly had long ago prophesied that:

Near to Sinope upon the long shore of the Pontus Euxinus,

Born will there be by a Tow'r, in the days of the Romans, a prophet,

One who will show, first, the primary unit, then a decade thrice over,

Followed by five other units, then twenty plus twenty plus twenty;

Numerals four which add up to the name of a man to defend us![13]

So, after a long absence, Alexander descended upon his home town accompanied by all this fanfare. There he made himself a celebrity and leading light by pretending to have fits of madness and even managing to froth at the mouth at times. For him there was nothing to it—he simply masticated soapwort root, the plant dyers use—but to the onlookers this foam was something fearful from heaven. There was also ready for use—it had been made up a while back—a linen mask in the form of a serpent's head with a more or less human face. It was all painted over to look most lifelike; its mouth, rigged with horsehair strings,

opened and closed, and a black forked tongue like a ser-
pent's could be made to stick out, also by means of strings.
The snake from Pella was there, too, being cared for in
his house until the moment when it would be revealed to
the public and assigned a role—or rather the leading role—
in the act.

It was by now time to get under way. The scheme he
worked out was this. One night he stole out to the ex-
cavation that had just been dug for the foundations of
the new temple. There was a puddle of water standing in
it which was either the result of a rainstorm or had seeped
in by itself from somewhere. He had with him a goose
egg that, emptied of its contents, now carried inside a newly
hatched snake. He set it down, buried it deep in the
mud, and took off. At the crack of dawn into the main
square he tore, wearing not a stitch of clothes except a
G string of gold brocade over his genitals (but carrying his
scimitar, of course) and tossing that head of hair around
as wildly as a fanatic collecting money for Cybele.[14] Clam-
bering up on a high altar, he launched into a speech con-
gratulating the city on the visit it was very soon to receive
from the god in person. His audience—practically the whole
town, women, old men, children, and all, had collected
there—was dumfounded; they all fell on their knees and
began to pray. Then he mouthed some gibberish—Hebrew
or Phoenician words perhaps—which left them awe-struck:
they had no idea of what he was saying; all they could
catch were the "Apollos" and "Asclepiuses" he slipped in
everywhere. The next minute he was off like a shot for
the site of the new temple. Coming to the excavation with
its oracular spring already in place, he jumped into the
puddle and, in a loud voice, sang some hymns to Asclepius
and Apollo and called on the god to "Come to the city and
bring it blessings." Then he asked for a sacrificial saucer;
somebody handed him one; he dipped it in and, presto,
in a bowlful of mud and water hauled up his god-bearing
egg, the crack where he had opened it sealed carefully

with white wax and white lead. Picking it up, he an-
nounced that he now held Asclepius in his hands. Every-
body, already overwhelmed by the discovery of the egg a
moment ago, waited, goggle-eyed, for what would happen
next. When he cracked the shell and let the tiny snake fall
into the palm of his hand, and they saw it wriggle and
curl about his fingers, they raised a cry to heaven, wel-
comed the god, congratulated the city, and, to a man, be-
gan praying their hearts out, begging this deity for money,
health, and every other kind of blessing. Our sprinter then
dashed off to his house, taking with him his fledgling
Asclepius, who

> Twice had been born whereas once is the lot of us other
> poor mortals,

and not from a Coronis, not even from a crow, but from a
goose.[15] The mob followed him en masse, everyone in a
frenzy and crazed with expectations.

Alexander kept to his house for a few days and hoped.
He was not disappointed: the word got around, and most
of the population of Paphlagonia promptly came to him
on the run, leaving their hearts and brains behind and look-
ing not like "men who eat of the fruits of the earth"[16] but,
in everything save shape, exactly like a flock of sheep.
When the city was filled to bursting with them, he dressed
himself up like a god, seated himself on a couch in some
small room, and took his Asclepius from Pella to his
bosom. The snake, an enormous and magnificent specimen
as I mentioned, he wound about his throat, except for the
tail which was so long it streamed over his breast and
dragged for part of its length on the ground. The head
alone he hid, keeping it under his arm—all this the crea-
ture put up with—and, in its place, beside his beard he
displayed that linen mask, making it look for all the world
as if it belonged to the body everyone could see.

Now picture in your mind a dim cell with insufficient
light and a motley, excited mob, already overawed on ar-

rival and floating in air with hope. Naturally, when they entered the whole affair seemed like a miracle: the snake, a tiny infant a few days ago, had, in so short a span, grown into this enormous serpent, one that was tame and had the face of a man in the bargain. And the next minute, before they had time to get a good look, they were shoved toward the exit and pushed out by the unbroken stream of spectators entering. You see, he had had an exit cut in the wall opposite the doorway, the way we're told the Macedonians did in Babylon during Alexander the Great's illness, when he was failing and everyone was standing around the palace, anxious for a last look and word. According to reports, the scoundrel put on this act not once but a number of times, particularly when fresh arrivals from the ranks of the wealthy came along.

To tell the truth, my dear Celsus, in all this we can't be too hard on those poor people from Paphlagonia and Pontus for being taken in. They were uneducated "fatheads"; they actually touched the snake—this privilege Alexander extended to whoever wanted it—and in a dim light they saw what was presumably the head with the mouth opening and closing. To see through such a set-up would have taken the brains of a Democritus or of Epicurus himself or of Metrodorus or of anyone else who had a mind that was adamant against this sort of thing, someone who would be instinctively suspicious and either guess at what was involved or, if he couldn't discover the trick, would at least be convinced that it was some magician's stunt he couldn't fathom, that it was all a hoax and simply couldn't be true.[17]

Before long all Bithynia, Galatia, and Thrace poured into the place; I'm sure everybody who brought back the news went on record that he had seen the god born and then had touched it when, a few days later, it had grown into an enormous serpent with a man's face. Next came pictures, models, and statuettes, in silver as well as bronze, and the giving the god a name. He was dubbed Glycon as the result of a command which Heaven delivered in meter. Alexander proclaimed that:

Glycon am I, of Jove's blood once removed, and a light unto mortals.

Now came the big moment, the culmination of all his scheming: to follow the lead of Amphilochus in Cilicia and supply oracles and prophecies for whoever wanted them. Amphilochus, you see, after his father Amphiaraus' death and disappearance in Thebes, had been banished from his home town; he made his way to Cilicia and there came out of it all very nicely by going into oracle making himself and foretelling the future for the Cilicians at a charge of seventy-five cents per prediction.[18] Taking his cue from him, Alexander announced to all visitors that the god was going to prophesy on such and such a day. He instructed them to write down whatever wishes they had or whatever they most wanted to know on a scroll, to tie it up, and to seal it with wax or clay or the like. He would take the scrolls and go into the inner sanctum—by now the temple was up and he had a stage setting at his disposal—listen to what the god had to say, have an announcer and an assistant prophet call in the clients in order, and hand back each scroll with seal absolutely intact and response added below (the god delivered an individual answer to each question). It was a trick which, to someone like yourself or, if it's not presumptuous to say so, someone like myself, was obvious and simple to understand, but to those poor slobs it was a miracle, something beyond belief. You see, since he had figured out all sorts of techniques to open the seals, he simply read each question, appended whatever answer he thought best, then rolled the scroll up again, sealed it, and handed it back, to the vast amazement of the recipient. Time and again you'd hear, "How could he have known what I gave him sealed tight under seals that couldn't be counterfeited unless he really is a god who knows everything?"

"What were those techniques of his?" you may ask. Listen then, so you can be in a position to expose this kind of thing yourself. The first, my dear Celsus, was the one everybody knows. He would remove the seal by cutting through the wax beneath it with a hot needle; then, after he had read the contents, with the same needle he'd warm the wax under the string and on the under side of the seal and, with no trouble at all, stick the two together again. Another way involved what is known as collyrium plaster, a preparation made from south Italian pitch, bitumen, powdered glass, wax, and mastic. After making up the plaster from all these ingredients, he would warm it over a fire, smear the seal with saliva, then apply the compound to the seal and make a mold of it. Since this hardened instantly, he would go right ahead and break the seal, read the contents, then smear on wax and, using his mold just like a seal-stone, make a new impression that looked exactly like the original. Here's still a third method. He would add marble dust to bookbinder's glue, make a paste out of it, apply it when still moist to the seal, and then remove it. This would instantly dry harder than bone or even iron, and he would use it to make a new impression. He had thought up a good many other tricks to handle the problem, but I needn't mention them all—I don't want to seem to be overdoing it, particularly since you've gone into the subject sufficiently and presented far more material than this in that exposé of magicians you wrote, an excellent and most useful work which should pound some sense into whoever opens it.

So Alexander gave out oracles and made prophecies, using a great deal of resourcefulness and combining guesswork with inventiveness. To some questions he delivered enigmatic and ambiguous answers, to others absolutely unintelligible ones; this, he felt, had the proper oracular touch. Some people he encouraged or discouraged, depending on which course he guessed was the best to take; for other people he prescribed therapy or diets since, as I

mentioned at the outset, he knew a good many useful
drugs. His favorites were his "cytmides," a name he coined
for a cure-all he compounded from a base of goat grease.
However, hopes and improved prospects and the inheriting
of fortunes he invariably put off into the future, adding
the statement that "All this will come to pass when I so
wish, and Alexander my prophet pleads and prays in your
behalf." The fee he charged was two dollars and thirty
cents per oracle. Don't imagine for a moment, my dear
friend, that this brought him any small or modest income.
With customers avid enough to put in for ten to fifteen
oracles each, his total annual receipts ran between a hun-
dred and fifteen and a hundred and thirty thousand dol-
lars. What he took in he didn't spend solely on himself or
put away for his own private fortune; by this time he had
a large staff—assistants, servants, investigators, oracle writ-
ers, oracle recorders, secretaries, seal makers, interpreters
—and he gave each whatever share he deserved.

Pretty soon Alexander was even sending agents into
neighboring lands to spread the word about his oracle
among various peoples. These men advertised that he
offered general prophecy, recovery of runaway slaves, de-
tection of thieves and bandits, discovery of buried treasure,
healing of the sick, and, on occasion, raising of the dead.
The result was a stampede from all sides plus sacrifices
and offerings—with double allotments for the prophet and
disciple of the god. You see, among the oracles he issued
was this one:

Honor, I bid you, my servant, the one who gives voice
to my sayings;
Care have I none for possessions, all my care is reserved
for my servant.

By this time a good many men of sense, as if coming
out of a drunken stupor, got together to attack him, par-
ticularly the followers of Epicurus, of whom there were
quite a number. In the cities they gradually unmasked all

his hocus-pocus and the act he was putting on. When this happened, Alexander began a campaign of intimidation against them. He announced that Pontus was full of atheists and Christians who had the effrontery to utter the worst possible slanders about him, and he ordered everyone who wanted to stay in the good graces of his god to stone the offenders. And this is the oracle he issued when someone asked how Epicurus was faring in the underworld:

In filthy slime he sits with leaden shackles on his ankles.

(Do you wonder that that shrine of his was able to reach the heights when you see how intelligent and informed the clientele's questions were?) In a word, it was war to the death against Epicurus. And no wonder—what man had a better right to be the bitter enemy of a quack who loved humbug and loathed truth than Epicurus, the one who delved into the nature of things, the only one who discerned the truth in it all? The Platonists and Stoics and Pythagoreans were Alexander's friends; between them and him a profound peace reigned. But the "unmitigated" Epicurus, as Alexander called him, was his worst enemy and rightly so—Epicurus had laughed at everything the man stood for and treated it as child's play. That's why, of all the towns in Pontus, Alexander hated Amastris the most: he found out that Lepidus and his disciples and sympathizers, a sizable group in all, lived there.[19] He never prophesied for people from Amastris. Once he took a chance and gave out an oracle to the brother of one of its aldermen and he ended up a laughingstock. He couldn't make up the right oracle himself or find anybody able to turn one out on the spur of the moment; he wanted to tell the man, who was complaining of a pain in the stomach, to eat pig's foot cooked with mallow, and it came out:

Mallow of pig in a trough that is holy besprinkle with cummin.

As I mentioned before, he often displayed the snake to people who asked to see it. He didn't expose it all but chiefly the tail and the rest of the body, keeping the head out of sight in his robe. But he wanted to impress his public even more, so he issued a promise that he would have the god deliver prophecies in person without any intermediary. Whereupon, with no trouble at all, he joined together some cranes' windpipes and fitted one end into the artificial head, making it all look very natural; in answer to the questions, a confederate outside bellowed into the tube, and the voice issued from the linen Asclepius. Oracles of this sort he labeled "self-spokens." They were not given out indiscriminately to everyone but were reserved for the notable, the rich, and the openhanded. For example, the one given to Severianus about his march into Armenia was a "self-spoken." The oracle, encouraging him to make the attempt, went:

> After thy spear has laid low both Iran's and Armenia's peoples,
> Home wilt thou go to the city of Rome and the Tiber's bright waters,
> Decked on thy brow with a garland of victory rayed like a sunburst.

That numbskull from Gaul was convinced and launched an attack. When he ended up cut to ribbons, he and his whole army, by Chosroes, Alexander removed the above from the records and inserted this instead:

> March not thy men—for it augurs not well—'gainst Armenia's peoples.
> Lest by a man in the garb of a woman be shot the fell arrow
> Fated to sever thy soul from its life and thine eyes from the daylight.[20]

As a matter of fact, this was a very shrewd idea of his, these ex post facto oracles to help out bad predictions that had missed the mark. Time and again he would prophesy recovery for the sick before their end and then, when they died, have his recantation all ready in a second oracle:

Seeketh no longer for succor against the dread scourge
  of thy sickness—
Now is thy destiny manifest, gone every chance to
  escape it.

He found out that the priests at Clarus, Didyma, and
Mallus enjoyed a great reputation for the same brand of
divination as his. So he made friends with them and sent
them a good many of his clients by giving such responses
as:

Now unto Clarus begone, to give ear to the voice of my
  father,

or

Wendest thy way to the shrine of Didyma and list to its
  prophet,

or

Get thee to Mallus. 'Tis there that Amphilochus tells of
  the future.

Up to now he had stayed within the borders of Ionia,
Cilicia, Paphlagonia, and Galatia. But soon the fame of
his shrine made its way to Italy and descended on Rome.
Every soul there, one on the heels of the other, hurried
either to go out in person or to send an envoy, particularly
the most influential and important personages in the city.
The leader and prime figure in this movement was Ruti-
lianus.[21] Rutilianus, in every other respect a fine and cul-
tured man and a proven public servant in many a Roman
governmental post, was, when it came to religion, a serious
mental case willing to accept on faith the most outlandish
claims. All he had to do was see somewhere a stone
smeared with holy oil or crowned by a wreath, and down
on his knees he would go, making obeisance, and then
stand there for hours, praying to it and beseeching it for
blessings. He heard about the shrine and practically threw
up his current public office to fly off to Abonoteichus; as
next best thing he sent off one envoy after another. The
people he used, ordinary servants who were no trouble at

all to fool, came back with paeans of praise: they reported not only what they had seen but what they thought they had seen or heard—and then increased the dimensions all around for good measure in order to raise themselves in their master's estimation. They had the poor fellow on fire; they whipped him up into a mad frenzy. He then made the rounds of the city's notables, most of whom were in his circle of friends, and told them what he had heard from his envoys plus some trimmings of his own. He filled the city with talk of Alexander and threw it into an uproar. He got the people at the emperor's court so worked up most of them promptly rushed out to hear something about their own futures. Alexander greeted all comers with great cordiality, won them over with lavish hospitality and expensive gifts, and sent them home not only with the answers to their questions but ready to sing the praises of his god and fabricate miracles on behalf of the shrine and himself.

All this led the damned scoundrel to concoct a canny scheme well beyond the capacity of any ordinary swindler. As he opened and read the scrolls sent him, if he came across any in which something indiscreet or risky had been asked, he didn't hand them back—he held on to them. The idea was to throw a scare into the senders, who remembered very well what their questions were, and thereby get them under his thumb and practically make slaves of them; you know yourself the sort of inquiries the rich and powerful are likely to make. Plenty of blackmail came his way from the victims; they knew he had them trapped.

Let me tell you about some of the oracles he gave Rutilianus. Rutilianus had a son by his first marriage who was the right age to start higher education. So he asked the oracle which teacher he should select for the boy's studies. The answer was:

Choose thou Pythagoras. Choose the great poet and teacher of battle.

Then, just a few days later, the boy died. Alexander was stymied and had nothing to say to his critics: his oracle had been refuted right on the heels of its delivery. But Rutilianus, that goodhearted soul, rushed to its defense. He explained that the god had predicted precisely what had come to pass in that he had ordered him to choose for the boy, not any living teacher, but Pythagoras and Homer, who had both been dead for ages and with whom the youngster was probably studying at that very moment down in Hades. How can you blame Alexander for deciding to devote his time to such pathetic creatures as the likes of this? On another occasion Rutilianus asked, "Whose soul have I inherited?" The answer was:

First as Achilles thou entered the world, and thou next wert Menander,
Third came the man thou art now, and in time thou shalt shine in the heavens.
Eighty more years shalt thou live, when thou once hast completed a hundred.

Actually he died of manic depression when he was seventy, without waiting to make good the god's promise. And this oracle was a "self-spoken," no less. Once he asked about marriage; he was told in no uncertain terms:

Marry the daughter that goddess Selene has borne Alexander.

Alexander had long ago given out the story that the mother of the one daughter he had was Selene: she had once seen him when he was asleep and had been overcome with love for him—it's her tradition, after all, to fall in love with sleeping beauties.[22] Rutilianus, that epitome of wisdom, didn't hesitate a minute. He promptly sent for the girl, celebrated the wedding—the groom was now sixty— and lived with her, making up to his mother-in-law Selene with whole hecatombs and regarding himself as officially entered into the ranks of the heavenly host.

Once Alexander had gained a foothold in Italy, his ideas

grew ever bigger and bigger. He sent his oracle agents to all the cities of the Roman Empire with a warning to be on guard against plagues, fires, and earthquakes; he then offered to furnish assistance guaranteed to keep any city safe from such things. One particular oracle—a "self-spoken"—he sent to every area that had been hit by the plague.[23] It was just a single verse:

Long-tressed Apollo it is who protects against plague's blighting shadow.

This line you could see written on doorways everywhere, as a charm against the plague. In most cases things turned out the other way around: through some quirk of fate the households that had put up the inscription were the ones wiped out. Now don't think I'm trying to say they were destroyed on account of the verse. It just worked out that way. Perhaps most of them, overconfident because of their line of poetry, took things easy and were careless and did nothing to help the oracle combat the disease, figuring they had all those metrical feet fighting for them plus long-tressed Apollo keeping the plague off with his magic bow.

In Rome itself Alexander stationed a good number of his accomplices to serve as undercover agents. They sent him reports about the character of all clients and gave him advance notice of what they were going to ask and what they wanted most. Envoys found him all ready with the answers—they had been composed even before the questions arrived.

Also aimed at the Italian trade was the following scheme. He worked up a mystery ceremony of his own, complete with torchbearers and presiding priests. It lasted three whole days in a row. On the first there was, as at Athens, an initial proclamation. Here it took the form: "If any atheist, Christian, or Epicurean has come here to spy, let him be gone. And may the true believers of the god conduct their rites with heaven's blessing." Immediately thereafter the ceremony led off with an expulsion ritual. Alexander opened it with the words, "Christians, begone!" and the crowd responded with one voice, "Epicureans, begone!" Then came the acting out of Leto in labor, of the birth of Apollo, his mating with Coronis, and the birth of Asclepius. On the second day there was the birth and presentation of the god Glycon. On the third day came the marriage of Podalirius and Alexander's mother; this was called Torch Day, so torches were burned. The finale was Alexander's love affair with Selene and the birth of Rutilianus' wife. Alexander alias Endymion was torchbearer and officiating priest. He lay in the center of the scene, ostensibly asleep. Flying down to him from the roof, as if from heaven, came, not Selene, but Rutilia, a beauty married to one of the imperial procurators. She was actually in love with Alexander and he with her, so there, with everybody around, before her poor husband's very eyes, the pair exchanged kisses and embraces. And, if there hadn't been lots of torches burning, Alexander probably would have carried on some under-the-dress lovemaking as well. A little later he reappeared in the officiating priest's regalia and, amid a dead silence, cried in a loud voice, "Hail, Glycon!" Whereupon the garlic-reeking Paphlagonian clodhoppers who were presumably his Eumolpidae and Ceryces responded with, "Hail, Alexander!"[24]

At frequent intervals during the torchlight parades and mystic jigging he made sure his thigh was bared so everyone could see it was golden; apparently he had wrapped around it a piece of gilded leather which glittered in the lamplight. A pair of brainless academes once undertook to do research on whether his golden thigh meant he actually had Pythagoras' soul or one similar to it.[25] They brought the problem to Alexander himself, and Lord Glycon settled all difficulties with an oracle:

Sometimes the soul of Pythagoras waxeth and sometimes it waneth.

Prophets, however, are blessed with a fragment of
    heavenly spirit
Sent by the father of gods as an aid to all god-fearing
    mortals.
Homeward to Zeus doth it hasten when Zeus's swift
    thunderbolt strikes it.

Alexander used to issue warnings to the public to refrain
from pederasty on the grounds that it was a sin. Yet he
himself, noble soul, worked out the following scheme. He
ordered the cities in Paphlagonia and Pontus to send choir-
boys who for a three-year period would be quartered at
his house and sing for the god. They were to be carefully
screened, and only those judged perfect in family qualifica-
tions and age, and unrivaled in looks, were to be sent.
Alexander kept those boys behind closed doors and used
them like so many slaves, sleeping with them and behav-
ing like a drunken degenerate with them. He had made
it a general rule never to greet anyone over eighteen on
the lips or welcome them with a kiss. They got his hand
to kiss; his mouth was reserved for the fresh flowers, to
whom he gave the official title "Receivers of the Kiss." Such
were the pleasures he enjoyed at the expense of the poor
dupes about him; life was a continuous round of ruining
young women and sleeping with young boys. All hus-
bands without exception considered it a most desirable
mark of distinction to have the prophet notice their wives,
and, if he decided they were worth a kiss, the poor devils
were sure their households would be swamped by a wave
of good fortune. Many of the wives boasted of having had
children by him—and their own husbands were willing to
testify they spoke the truth.

I'd like to quote for you a dialogue that took place be-
tween Glycon and a certain Sacerdos from Tium,[26] whose
intellectual capacity you'll gauge from the questions he
asked. The whole thing was inscribed in letters of gold on
a wall of Sacerdos' house in Tium, which is where I read
it:

"Tell me, Lord Glycon, who are you?"

"I am the new Asclepius."

"What do you mean? Different from the former one?"

"You are not allowed to know that."

"How many years will you remain with us and give us your prophecies?"

"One thousand and three."

"Then where will you go?"

"To Bactria and the lands there. For foreigners, too, must reap the benefits of my presence among them."

"Does your forefather Apollo still abide in the other seats of prophecy, at Didyma and Clarus and Delphi, or are the oracles now issued from there all false?"

"Do not seek to know this either. It is forbidden."

"What will I become after this life?"

"A camel, then a horse, and then a wise man and prophet as great as Alexander."

This was the dialogue that took place between Glycon and Sacerdos. The god, knowing Sacerdos was a friend of Lepidus', ended up with an oracle in meter:

Trust not in Lepidus—ill-fated doom is his constant companion.

You see, as I mentioned before, Alexander was terribly afraid of Epicurus as a professional rival and counteracter of all his hocus-pocus. One Epicurean, for example, who had the courage to show him up in front of a large crowd, he placed in a position of mortal danger. The man had gone up to him and said in a loud voice, "Alexander, you talked so-and-so of Paphlagonia into bringing his servants up for the death penalty before the governor of Galatia on the grounds that they had murdered his son in Alexandria where the boy was attending school. But the son is alive, he has returned in the flesh—and you have already had those servants handed over to the wild beasts and destroyed." What had happened was this. The boy sailed to Egypt and pushed on to Suez; here a ship was just leav-

ing for India and he was persuaded to go along. Since he
took a long time getting back, his poor servants, convinced
he had drowned in the Nile or been captured by pirates—
they were rife at the time—went home and reported his
disappearance. Then came the oracle, the trial, and, after
that, the boy's reappearance with the explanation of his
absence. The man spoke his piece. Alexander's reaction
was to fly into a rage at being exposed—the rebuke was
true, and that was what he couldn't take. He shouted to
the audience that, if they didn't stone the fellow, he would
put them under a curse and brand them all Epicureans.
Just as everybody began throwing, a certain Demostratus,
a prominent citizen of Pontus who was in town on a visit,
threw himself in front of the man and barely saved him
from being stoned to death. But he deserved to die! What
right did he have to take advantage of Paphlagonia's im-
becility and be the only person with sense among all
those madmen?

So much for what happened to one Epicurean. For the
others there was this. The clients for oracles used to be
presented one by one the day before the prophesying took
place, and the announcer would ask, "Do you have a
prophecy for this man?" If the answer from within was,
"A curse on him!" then nobody would ever again receive
the rejected applicant under his roof or share fire or water
with him—he was to be hounded from one land to the
next; he was unclean; he was godless; he was—the most
horrible epithet of all—an Epicurean.

As a matter of fact, Alexander did one extremely silly
thing in this connection. He came across a copy of
Epicurus' *Principal Doctrines,* his finest work, as you know,
and the one that embraces the key tenets of his philosophy.
Alexander carried the book into the main square and
burned it on a pyre of fig logs, presumably feeling he was
destroying the author in the fire. The ashes he dumped
into the sea, adding an oracle for good measure:

Hear my command: to the flames with the thoughts of
a visionless dotard.

The damned fool had no conception of the great benefits
that book holds for all who open it, how much peace and
calm and freedom it builds up in the reader by ridding
him of the fear of specters and portents, of vain hopes
and excessive desires, by implanting in him understanding
and a feeling for the truth, by cleansing his mind for real,
not with torches and squills and such nonsense, but with
honest thought and truth and candor.

Of all the acts of colossal nerve the filthy rascal
pulled the greatest was this. Through Rutilianus, who
stood so high there, he had easy entree to the palace and
court. When the war in Germany was in full blaze and
the late Emperor Marcus Aurelius had already come to
grips with the Marcomanni and Quadi,[27] Alexander for-
warded an oracle. It stated that two live lions should be
thrown into the Danube along with a lot of expensive
spices and other sacrificial offerings. But I'd better quote
it verbatim:

Into the churning and eddying stream of the rain-
swollen Danube,
Cast, I do bid you, a pair of the beasts that are
Cybele's servants,
Mountain-bred lions. And cast in the plants and the
sweet-smelling blossoms
Nourished in India's climes. Whereupon there shall
come in an instant
Victory, glory abounding, and with it the peace we so
cherish.

His instructions were carried out. The first result was that
the lions swam for the enemy shore where the barbarians,
taking them for gods or a new kind of wolf, finished them
off with clubs; the second was that there "came in an in-
stant" the greatest loss our forces sustained, the destruction
en masse of close to twenty thousand men. This was fol-

lowed by the campaign around Aquileia in which the town escaped capture by a hair. To explain what happened, Alexander coolly produced for his defense the Delphic oracle and its answer to Croesus: the god had simply prophesied a victory without specifying whether it was to be Rome's or the enemy's.[28]

By now droves of people were pouring in. The city was bursting at the seams with the crowds coming in to consult the oracle, and there wasn't enough food to go round. So Alexander hit upon the idea of "nocturnals," as he called them. Taking the scrolls, he slept on them, so he said, and the answers he gave were ostensibly what he had heard in a dream from the god. They certainly weren't very clear; the majority were enigmatic and confused, particularly when the prophet noticed that a scroll had been sealed with extra care. Alexander, you see, was running no risks: he would write down the first thing that popped into his head, since he considered material of this sort as suitable as any other for oracles. Special interpreters were on hand who collected a nice fee from the recipients of "nocturnals" for solving and elucidating them. This concession they enjoyed cost money: each interpreter paid Alexander ten thousand dollars.

Every now and then, to dumfound the brainless, he would issue a response to someone who hadn't submitted a question either in person or through an envoy and who, as a matter of fact, didn't exist at all. Here is an example:

> Who is it, all unbeknownst to thyself, on the bed in thy chamber
> Layeth fair Calligeneia, thy wife? Dost thou want me to name him?
> Know 'tis Protogenes, know 'tis the slave thou implicitly trusted.
> *Thou* got thy loving from him, wherefore *he* turns for his to thy madame.
> Such is the recompense, paid thee in kind, for the insults he suffered.

Horrible drugs have been brewed by these two in their
   battle against thee,
Potions that close both thine eyesight and mind to the
   things they are doing.
These thou'lt discover against the back wall underneath
   thine own bedstead
Near to the head. And Calypso, thy handmaid, has been
   their accomplice.

Wouldn't even a Democritus have been disturbed at hear-
ing the specific names and places?[29] But then, a minute
later, realizing it was all just a scheme, he'd have been
revolted.

Here's another instance. He issued, in prose, not verse,
the following injunction to return home: "This very day he
who sent you has fallen by the hand of his neighbor
Diocles in league with the bandits Magnes, Celerus, and
Bubalas, who have already been arrested and thrown into
jail." No recipient was around and, in fact, no recipient
existed.

Very often, when people submitted questions in a na-
tive tongue, Syrians or Galatians, for example, Alexander
would prophesy in a foreign language, going to a great
deal of trouble to locate among the visitors in town fellow
nationals of the clients. Because of this there was quite a
lapse between the handing in of such scrolls and the de-
livery of the response, an interval long enough to give him
plenty of time to unseal the questions safely and find peo-
ple able to provide letter-perfect translations. Here is an
oracle, for example, that he gave to some Scyth:

Morphi ebargulis eis skien chnenchikrank leipsei phaos.

Let me tell you about a few of the oracles he gave me.
Once, making it obvious that I had sealed my scroll care-
fully, I asked whether Alexander was bald. I got back a
"nocturnal":

Sabardalachu malach Attis was different.

Another time I submitted two separate scrolls under two different names but with the same question on both: "Where was Homer born?"[30] Taken in by my servant—Alexander asked the boy why his master had sent him and was told, "To find how to treat a pain in the side"—to one of them he gave the answer:

> Rub it, I bid, with a "cytmis" plus foam from the mouth of a race horse.

To the second, since we had let him overhear another piece of information, that the sender wanted to know whether it was better for him to sail to Italy or go on foot, he gave this answer—and it had very little to do with Homer:

> Ships I forbid thee—the way across land with thy feet shalt thou follow.

Yes, I personally played lots of tricks of this kind on him. Here's another example. I submitted a scroll with a single question. On the outside, for the brief customary identification, I wrote "Request for Eight Oracles from So-and-So," adding a false name. I enclosed eighteen dollars plus the change and sent it all off. He took on faith the amount of money I had forwarded and the information on the scroll and, in answer to my single question—it was: "When will Alexander the quack magician be caught?"—sent me eight oracles, every one of which was unintelligent, unintelligible, and totally unconnected with anything under heaven or on earth, as the saying goes.

When he later found out not only about all this but that I had tried to dissuade Rutilianus from his marriage and from leaning on the bright prospects offered by the oracle, naturally he hated me and considered me his worst enemy. Rutilianus once submitted a question about me; the answer was:

> Colloquies whispered at night does he relish, and vicious liaisons.

All in all, I was, as you'd expect, his worst enemy.

When he got word that I was in his city and found out
that I was *the* Lucian—I even had an escort of two soldiers,
a spearman and a pikeman, assigned by the governor of
Cappadocia, who was a friend of mine, to accompany me
as far as the nearest seaport—he promptly sent me a very
cordial and most friendly invitation. On my arrival I found
him with a considerable crowd standing around. By a
stroke of luck I had my soldiers with me. He stretched
out his hand for me to kiss, as he did with his public, but
I, bending over as if to kiss it, gave it one beauty of a
bite that practically crippled it. At that the crowd closed
in to throttle me and beat me up as a sacrilegious dese-
crater; I had raised their hackles even earlier by addressing
him as Alexander instead of "Prophet." He bore up under
it all nobly. He held back the mob, assuring them he
would have no trouble taming me and demonstrating
Glycon's greatness, the god who turns even the bitterest
enemies into friends. Then, sending everybody off to the
side, he argued his case before me. He told me he knew
all about the advice I had given Rutilianus and he asked,
"Why did you do this to me? I could have made you
stand very high with that man." In view of the dangerous
spot I had gotten into, I was glad by that time to accept
this overture. A few minutes later I stepped forth his fast
friend. The ease with which I had been converted seemed
no mean miracle to all beholders.

Then, since I had elected to go by sea—I was alone with
Xenophon at the time; my father and the rest of the family
I had sent ahead to Amastris—Alexander, along with a
load of souvenirs and gifts, sent an unsolicited offer to sup-
ply a boat and rowers to take me home. I took it as a
straightforward, friendly gesture. But when, in the middle
of the crossing, I noticed that the captain, with tears in his
eyes, was arguing with the crew, my hopes for the future
sank: they had received orders from Alexander to heave
me over the rail into the sea. Had it gone off as planned
he'd have had an easy end to his war against me. The

captain's tears, however, convinced the men not to do me any harm or wrong. "I'm sixty years old, as you can see," he told me, "a man with a wife and children. I've always led a clean, decent life and, at this point in it, I wouldn't like to filthy my hands with a murder." And he confessed to me the reason he had taken me aboard and the orders he had gotten from Alexander. He set me ashore at Aegiali, a town even the noble Homer has mentioned, and turned back. There I came on some men from the Bosporus who were sailing along the coast, a delegation from King Eupator en route to Bithynia for the delivery of their annual levy, and I explained to them the danger I was in.[31] Luckily I had fallen in with decent people: I was taken aboard and, after coming so close to death, arrived safely at Amastris.

From that moment on I was up in arms against Alexander, and I moved heaven and earth in my desire to get even with him. Even before this plot of his I had hated the man and looked on him with loathing because of his despicable character. We set out to file charges against him, I and a large group of co-plaintiffs, particularly people from the circle of Timocrates, the philosopher from Heraclea.[32] However, Avitus, the governor of Bithynia and Pontus at the time, put a stop to it by practically getting down on his knees and beseeching me to give it up. He was on good terms with Rutilianus and because of that, he claimed, he wouldn't be able to punish the man even if he caught him red-handed.[33] So my attempt was cut short, and I stopped pounding the table since it served no purpose in front of a judge who felt that way.

Here is an act of brazen nerve that stands out even among all his others: Alexander requested the emperor to change the name of Abonoteichus to Ionopolis and to issue a new coin, one side to be engraved with the likeness of Glycon, the other with himself holding the insignia of his grandfather Asclepius and that famous scimitar of his maternal ancestor Perseus.[34]

Although he once predicted in an oracle about himself that he was destined to live for a hundred and fifty years and then be killed by the thunderbolt's stroke, he came to a miserable end, and before he had reached even seventy. The son of Podalirius died because his leg (*poda-*) was alive with maggots and had rotted through and through right up to the groin. It was then that we found out he was bald: he was in such pain he let the doctors put wet compresses on his head, which they couldn't do without removing his wig.

Such was the finale of Alexander's act, the denouement of his whole drama. Even though it happened totally by chance, you could almost believe it had been somehow pre-arranged that way. And he was to have a funeral contest worthy of his career: a struggle over the oracle arose among the leading lights in that pack of accomplices and fellow quacks he had. They came to Rutilianus for a decision: he was to pick one of them to inherit the shrine and assume the crown of priest and prophet. The group included even Paetus,[35] a doctor by profession and a grayish little man, who never in his life did anything worthy of a doctor or a graybeard. Referee Rutilianus sent them all home uncrowned and preserved the office intact for the soul of the defunct.

The above, my dear Celsus, just a few instances out of many, will serve as samples. I felt it right to put them in writing for two reasons. The first was the wish to give pleasure to a dear friend and comrade, a man whom I have admired above all others for his wisdom, love for the truth, gentleness, decency, serene way of life, and warmth toward those about him. The second, more important reason, one that will appeal to you even more than to me, was to avenge Epicurus, a man who was *genuinely* holy and possessed of a divine nature, who alone perceived the truly beautiful and passed his knowledge on, and who became thereby the emancipator of those who were his disciples. But all who read this account will, I think, find it useful, as much for the encouragement it gives to men of good sense as for the exposures it makes.

NOTES

[1] Cleaning these stables had been one of Heracles' most disagreeable labors.

[2] A well-known Roman historian of the early second century A.D. A number of his writings have been preserved, but this life of Tilliborus failed to survive.

[3] The Cercopes were thieving imps who robbed Heracles in his sleep. Eurybatus and Phrynondas were proverbial evildoers. Aristodemus and Sostratus may possibly be identical with two figures lampooned by Aristophanes for immorality.

[4] *Odyssey* 4.230.

[5] Apollonius, born at Tyana in southeastern Asia Minor around the beginning of the Christian Era, acquired a great reputation for wonder-working and clairvoyance.

[6] Olympias was Alexander the Great's mother. The story had it that Zeus visited her in the form of a serpent and her celebrated son was the product of the union.

[7] Thucydides 2.1.

[8] Sanctuaries of Apollo that were famous seats of prophecy. Delphi was in Greece, Delos on an isle in the Aegean, Clarus and Didyma in Asia Minor.

[9] Chalcedon lay just across the Bosporus from modern Istanbul. The province of Thrace corresponded roughly to what is today Turkey in Europe.

[10] Coscinomancy, a very simple, everyday way of telling fortunes, enjoyed a great vogue in the ancient (and medieval) world.

[11] Apollo was the god of oracles par excellence (cf. p. 152). It was one of Alexander's master strokes to turn the son Asclepius, usually only a god of healing, into a source of prophecy as well.

[12] One of the two doctors attached to the Greek army during the Trojan War (*Iliad* 11.833). He was a son of Asclepius and lived in Tricca in north Greece.

[13] This gibberish all works out to the greater glory of Alexander. "Born by a Tow'r," i.e., a fortified spot, refers to Abonoteichus; the second element in the name, *-teichus,* means

"wall." The four numbers in the second and third lines—1, 30, 5, 60—in Greek, which used letters of the alphabet to represent numerals, would be written A,L,E,X. And "a man" (*andr-*) + "to defend" (*alex-*) = Alexander.

14 The cult of Cybele, the mother-goddess, was one of the most violent in the ancient world. The goddess's cart was drawn by lions, her priests practiced self-castration, and her followers went in for bouts of frenzy.

15 The quotation is a parody of *Odyssey* 12.22. Coronis was Asclepius' mother. There is a pun here: the Greek word for "crow" is *corone.*

16 *Odyssey* 9.191.

17 Three philosophers. For Democritus, see p. 332, n. 8; Epicurus, p. 333, n. 12; Metrodorus, p. 169, n. 24.

18 Amphiaraus had been a seer during his lifetime. After a mysterious death (Zeus clove the ground in front of his chariot and he was swallowed up), he continued prophesying from a famous shrine in central Greece. The son's oracle was located in the town of Mallus.

19 Tiberius Claudius Lepidus was a local notable and apparently a dedicated Epicurean. Amastris was a city on the coast west of Abonoteichus.

20 Marcus Sedatius Severianus, of Gallic extraction, was governor of Cappadocia. In 161 a serious war broke out between Rome and Parthia. Severianus marched into Armenia to meet the enemy, and Chosroes, commanding the Parthians, wiped the expedition out. Chosroes is given the "garb of a woman" because, in Greek and Roman eyes, all oriental costume seemed effeminate.

21 Publius Mummius Sisenna Rutilianus was a well-born, prominent Roman whose long and successful career in the imperial service included the governorship of several provinces.

22 See p. 54, n. 5.

23 From 165 to 168 A.D. a great plague ravaged most of the Roman Empire.

24 Alexander's homemade mystery religion was modeled on the famous Eleusinian Mysteries (cf. p. 169, n. 32) which began with an expulsion ritual to rid the congregation of foreigners, homicides, and the like, and then presented a dramatized version of the life of Demeter and Persephone. The Eumolpidae and Ceryces, ancient and distinguished families, had the hereditary right to supply priests for the cult.

25 Cf. p. 210, n. 7.

26 Tium lay on the southwest shore of the Black Sea, west of Amastris and Abonoteichus.

[27] Between 167 and 169 A.D.

[28] See p. 147.

[29] Democritus (cf. n. 17 above) was the proverbial hard-headed skeptic.

[30] See p. 41.

[31] The little kingdom of the Bosporus (i.e., the Cimmerian Bosporus, the modern Crimea) maintained its independence by paying tribute to the empire, delivering it apparently to the governor of Bithynia. Tiberius Julius Eupator ruled ca. 154–171 A.D. Aegiali lay somewhat west of Amastris.

[32] Timocrates was a distinguished philosopher and teacher. Heraclea was an important city on the southwest shore of the Black Sea.

[33] Lucius Lollianus Avitus, governor of Bithynia in 165 A.D.

[34] A good example of the coin and a bronze statuette of Glycon (cf. p. 277), both from the collection of the Boston Museum of Fine Arts, are pictured in F. Allinson's *Lucian, Satirist and Artist* (Boston, 1926), opposite p. 108. The town's name actually *was* changed; it's called Ionopolis on the coins, and the modern Turkish village on the site is Ineboli.

[35] Paetus is otherwise unknown.

DIALOGUES OF THE COURTESANS
[3.1–2]

From 300 B.C. on, a type of comedy known as Greek New Comedy flourished throughout the Greek-speaking world. It had an almost fixed cast of characters, prominent among whom was the courtesan. Lucian has deliberately given his courtesans the same names as the girls in the plays and has occasionally put them in the same situations. But here the resemblance ends: the courtesans of Greek New Comedy were onstage; in these dialogues we are backstage.

3

Philinna and her Mother

MOTHER. Philinna, did you go mad? What got into you at the party yesterday? This morning, at the crack of dawn, Diphilus came to me, moaning, with a long story of what he had to put up with from you: you got drunk; you jumped up and started to dance in the middle of the room even though he tried to stop you; you kissed his best friend Lamprias and, when that made Diphilus flare up, you left him and walked over and threw your arms around Lamprias. He said he was fit to be tied at what happened. And I got the impression you didn't sleep with him last night. You left him to moan and groan while you went to bed by yourself on the cot alongside, singing to yourself just to give him a bad time.

PHILINNA. He didn't tell you what *he* did, did he? The way he humiliated me? You wouldn't have been so ready to take his side. He forgot all about me and got

very chummy with Thais, Lamprias' girl—this was be-
fore Lamprias got there. And when he saw me getting
mad about what he was doing, and giving him dirty
looks, he took Thais very daintily by the ears, bent her
head back, and kissed her so hard he had trouble prying
himself loose. I began to cry, and he laughed and kept
whispering in her ear, about me, of course. And she
kept staring at me and grinning. By the time they saw
Lamprias coming they had had enough kissing to satisfy
them both. In spite of everything I still went over and
sat down beside him just so he wouldn't have an ex-
cuse for making a fuss later on. Thais was the one who
got up and danced first. And she pulled her dress way
up to show off her legs—as if she's the only girl in the
world with nice ones. When she was done, Lamprias
didn't applaud or say a word, but Diphilus raved about
how graceful she was, what an interesting dance she did,
how well she kept time to the music, her beautiful
ankles, and so on and so forth, as if she was Venus di
Milo instead of Thais. I don't need to tell *you* what
she's like—we've both seen her at the baths. And do you
know the dirty crack she made right to my face? "If
someone wasn't so ashamed of her skinny legs, *she'd*
get up and dance too." I'll admit it, Mother, I got up
and danced. What else was I going to do? Sit there and
make it look as if she was telling the truth? Let that
Thais lord it over the whole party?

MOTHER. You always want to be the best. You shouldn't
have paid any attention to her. But then what happened?

PHILINNA. Everyone applauded except Diphilus. He just
stretched out on his back and looked at the ceiling.
After a while I got tired and stopped.

MOTHER. Did you really kiss Lamprias? And move over
next to him and throw your arms around him? That's
unforgivable. Come on, tell me.

PHILINNA. I wanted to get back at that Diphilus.

MOTHER. And then you didn't sleep with him? You actually sang while he was moaning and groaning? My dear daughter, don't you realize we're paupers? Have you forgotten all we've gotten from him? What a winter we'd have had last year if Lady Venus hadn't sent him along?

PHILINNA. What do you mean? Is that any reason for me to let him insult me?

MOTHER. Get angry with him, yes. But don't insult him back. You don't realize that an insulted lover simply walks out on a girl and blames himself for making the wrong choice. You've always been too hard on that boy. Watch out or, like the proverb, you'll add the straw that'll break the camel's back!

5

Clonarium and Leaena

CLONARIUM. We've been hearing queer things about you, Leaena. They say Philippa, that millionaire lady from Lesbos, feels about you the way a man does and that the two of you have been making love, doing lord knows what to each other. What's this—blushing? Tell me, is it true?

LEAENA. Yes, Clonarium. But I'm so ashamed of myself! It's all so unnatural!

CLONARIUM. In the name of Venus, what's it all about? What's the woman after? What do you two do when you make love to each other, anyway? See? You're not really my friend. You wouldn't have kept a thing like that secret from me.

LEAENA. You *are* my friend; there isn't another girl I like as much. But this woman is so like a man it's frightening.

CLONARIUM. I don't know what you're talking about—un-

[5.2–3]

less you mean she's one of those Lesbians. I hear that the women on that island look just like men and that they never go through the act with men; they make love to other women the way men do.

LEAENA. Something like that.

CLONARIUM. But tell me this: how did she get a chance to sound you out? How did she talk you into it? And what happened after that?

LEAENA. She arranged a little dinner party with Demonassa from Corinth—she's rich, too, and the same type as Philippa. They invited me along to play the lyre for them. When I got done it was very late, past bedtime. Both of them were drunk, and Philippa said, "Leaena, we'd better go to sleep. You can spend the night here; just stretch out between the two of us."

CLONARIUM. And you did? What happened then?

LEAENA. First they kissed me the way men do. Not just pressing lips, but with our mouths open. Then they hugged me and squeezed my breasts. And Demonassa kept kissing me and biting at the same time. I had no idea what in the world was going on. After a while Philippa got a little warm and took off her wig—a very convincing one that sat on her head perfectly naturally —and I could see she was shaved to the skin like the tough types among our athletes. I looked and didn't know what to make of it. And she said, "Have you ever seen a boy this beautiful?" And I said, "I see you, Philippa, not a boy." And she said, "Don't you make a woman out of me! My name's Philip. Years ago I married Demonassa here; she's my wife." That made me laugh, and I said, "You mean you're really a man and you kept it a secret from us, the way they say Achilles did when he dressed in fancy gowns and passed for one of the girls on Scyros? Do you have what men have, and do you go through the act with Demonassa the way men do with women?" "No," she said, "I don't

have what men have. But I don't need it—I have my
own way of making love, and it's lots nicer. You'll see."
"You're not a hermaphrodite," I asked, "half man and
half woman, the way I hear so many people are?" You
see, Clonarium, I still didn't know what this was all
about. "No, I'm not," she said. "I'm all man." Then I
said, "Ismenodora, the girl from Boeotia who plays the
flute, once told me, when she was talking about things
back home, that there had been someone in Thebes
who changed from a woman into a man. Some wonderful
prophet. Teiresias, I think his name was. The same
thing didn't happen to you, did it?" "No," she said,
"but, though I was born a girl like all of you, I have a
man's mind and instincts and everything else." "Ah," I
said, "are instincts enough?" "If you don't believe me,"
she said, "just take me on. You'll quickly find out I'm
as good as any man. Instead of what men have I have
something else. Just take me on. You'll see." Well,
Clonarium, she begged so and gave me such presents—
a beautiful necklace and some very sheer gowns—that I
did. I took her in my arms just as I would a man, and
she kissed me and breathed hard and went through the
act and seemed to enjoy herself no end.

CLONARIUM. Went through *what* act, Leaena? How?
That's what I want you to tell me!

LEAENA. Don't ask questions like that. The whole business
is too shameful. As heaven's my witness, I can't even
talk about it!

6

Crobyle and Corinna

CROBYLE. Well, my daughter, now you know that losing
your virginity and becoming a woman wasn't nearly as
terrible as you thought. And you had yourself a good-

looking boy and earned your first money—a hundred and
fifty dollars! I'll go right out and buy you a necklace
with it.

CORINNA. Oh yes, Mommy! One with shiny red stones like
Philaena's.

CROBYLE. One just like hers. But first I have something
else to talk to you about: what you have to do, and how
you have to behave with men. You see, Corinna, we
have no other way to support ourselves. Have you any
idea how we stayed alive during the two years since
your poor dear father died? When he was living we
had everything we needed. He ran a bronze foundry,
and he had a fine reputation in the city—everybody you
talk to swears there'll never be another smith like Phi-
linus. Well, after he died, at first we lived off three hun-
dred dollars I got by selling his tongs and his anvil and
hammer. Then I barely managed to get us enough to eat
by doing some weaving and spinning. But, my daughter,
I kept you fed, and I waited—and I hoped.

CORINNA. Hoped for this hundred and fifty dollars, you
mean?

CROBYLE. Not quite. My idea was that, once you got this
old, you'd not only support me but you'd find it easy to
live like a lady yourself. You'd be rich and have lovely
gowns and lots of servants.

CORINNA. What do you mean, Mother? How?

CROBYLE. By going out with young men. Going to parties
with them and sleeping with them—for money.

CORINNA. Like Daphnis' daughter Lyra?

CROBYLE. Yes.

CORINNA. But she's a courtesan!

CROBYLE. What's so terrible about that? It means you can
have lots of lovers and be as rich as she. What are you
crying for, Corinna? Don't you realize how many girls
are courtesans? How the men run after them, and how

much money they make? God forgive me for bringing it up, but I know for a fact that that Daphnis dressed in rags until her daughter grew up. Now look at how she's getting on: gold jewelry, embroidered gowns, four servants.

CORINNA. How did Lyra make all that money?

CROBYLE. First of all, she dresses like a lady, smartly and with good taste. Then she's gay with everybody: not that she giggles at the least little thing the way you used to; she has a way of smiling sweetly and enticingly. When men come and visit her or take her out, she knows how to talk to them, and, without throwing herself at them, she gives them what's coming to them. Whenever she's invited to a dinner party as a paid escort, she never gets drunk—that's making a fool of yourself; men can't stand women who do that—and never behaves like a pig and gorges herself. She handles her food with the tips of her fingers, doesn't smack her lips over a mouthful, and doesn't gobble away with both cheeks full. She drinks slowly, never gulping, but just sipping.

CORINNA. Even when she's thirsty?

CROBYLE. Especially when she's thirsty. She never says more than she should, never makes fun of the other guests, and always has eyes only for the man who's paying her. That's why they all think so much of her. When she has to sleep with someone, she's never lewd but never acts as if she doesn't care. The one thing she's always on the watch for is to lead a man on and make him passionate about her. So they all rave about her. Now, if you'd only learn these things, we could be on top of the world too. When you think that, in everything else, you're so superior—no, god forgive me for boasting; you're alive and well, and that's enough.

CORINNA. But, Mother, are all the men who hire girls like Eucritus, the boy I slept with last night?

CROBYLE. Not all. Some, of course, are even nicer. Some
are more masculine. And some aren't good-looking at
all.

CORINNA. Do I have to sleep with those too?

CROBYLE. Certainly. They'll even pay you a better price.
The good-looking ones care about one thing only, their
good looks. And you must always keep your eye on the
better price if you want to hurry the day when people
will point you out and say, "Look, that's Corinna,
Crobyle's daughter. She's so rich! And she's made her
mother so happy!" What do you say? Will you do it?
You will, I know you will, and you'll be the best of all
of them, easily. You'd better run along and take your
bath now if your Eucritus is coming today too. He
promised, you know.

7

Musarium and her Mother

MOTHER. Well! If we find one more lover like that Chaereas
of yours, we're going to have to get on our knees and
thank Lady Venus. Lady Luck, too. We'll be so happy,
so blissful! Look at all we're getting from him! Why,
he hasn't given us a penny, not a stitch of clothing, not
a pair of shoes or drop of perfume. All we get is ex-
cuses and promises, great hopes for the future, a lot of
"If my father would only er-ah, and I get the estate in
my hands, everything's yours." You say he even swore
he'd marry you?

MUSARIUM. He swore it, Mother. Gave me his solemn oath.

MOTHER. And you believe him, of course. So, at yesterday's
dinner, when he couldn't pay his share, you gave him
your ring without telling me anything about it. He sold
it and got drunk on the money. Last time it was those

two long necklaces that that shipowner from Chios, Praxias, had made for you in Ephesus; there was five pounds of gold in each. Of course—Chaereas had borrowed from his classmates and had to pay back. And what about all the shirts and jackets? Oh, he's been a windfall for us, he has, a real treasure-trove.

MUSARIUM. But he's good-looking and doesn't have a beard, and he cries and says he loves me, and Judge Laches is his father, and he does say he's going to marry me, and we can expect great things from him as soon as the old man passes away.

MOTHER. So if you need your shoes repaired and the shoemaker asks for his three dollars we'll tell him, "We don't have any money, but here, have a few of our great expectations." We'll say the same thing to the baker. And when the landlord wants the rent we'll tell him, "Please wait till Judge Laches dies. We'll pay you after the wedding." You're the only courtesan who doesn't have earrings or a necklace or a decent evening gown. Aren't you ashamed?

MUSARIUM. Does that make the other girls any happier or better looking?

MOTHER. No, but they're smarter. They know how to be courtesans. They don't listen to the prattle of youngsters with sworn promises ready on the tip of the tongue. You're too trusting and sentimental, and you won't let anyone come near you except Chaereas. Yesterday that farmer from Acharnia—he didn't have a beard either—came here with three hundred dollars in his hands, all the money he'd gotten for the wine his father sent him to sell, and you turned up your nose at him. *You* had to sleep with Mr. Adonis.

MUSARIUM. What are you saying? That I should have ditched Chaereas and taken on that farm hand? He stank like a goat! Give me an Acharnian pig, as the saying goes; it has no beard either.

MOTHER. All right, he was a hick and he did smell awful. But what about Antiphon. He offered you a hundred and fifty dollars and you turned him down. And he was a good-looking boy and a gentleman and no older than Chaereas.

MUSARIUM. Yes, but Chaereas threatened to cut both our throats if he ever caught me with him.

MOTHER. As if they don't all make threats like that! Is that any reason why you have to be without lovers and live the life of a Vestal Virgin instead of a courtesan? Let's forget about everything else. Today is Harvest Day. What did he give you for the ball?

MUSARIUM. He doesn't have any money, Mommy.

MOTHER. The only boy in the world who's never found a way to get around his father or never used a tricky servant to get money out of him! Who's never gone to his mother and threatened to join the foreign legion if she didn't come across! No, he sits around here to be the ruination of us. Not only does he give us nothing—he doesn't let us get from those who will give! Do you think you're going to stay eighteen all your life? Or that Chaereas is going to feel the same way when he gets to be a rich man and his mother finds some heiress for him to marry? You think he'll still remember the tears and the kisses and the sworn promises then? When he's got his eye on a dowry of, say, fifty thousand dollars?

MUSARIUM. He won't forget. Not he. If you want proof, just look at how he never got married. They put the pressure on him and tried to force him, but he wouldn't.

MOTHER. Let's hope he's not lying. I'll remind you about all this, Musarium, when the time comes.

11

Tryphaena and Charmides

TRYPHAENA. Now why would anyone take a girl out, pay her ten dollars, go to sleep with her—and then roll over to the other side of the bed and cry his eyes out? I suspect you had no fun during the drinking either, and you were the only one who didn't want to eat at dinner. You were weepy all during the meal. I saw it. And now you can't stop blubbering like an infant. What's behind all this, Charmides? Don't hide it from me; let me at least get this much out of staying awake all night with you.

CHARMIDES. Love, Tryphaena. It's terrible; it's destroying me. I can't stand it any longer.

TRYPHAENA. It's not me you're in love with. That's for sure. Otherwise you wouldn't ignore me when I'm here for the taking, shove me away when I want to put my arms around you, and end up by hanging your coat up between us like a wall because you're afraid I'll touch you. Tell me, who is she? I may be able to do something for this grand passion of yours. I know how affairs like this have to be handled.

CHARMIDES. You know her, all right, and very well. She knows you too. She's one of the big names among you girls.

TRYPHAENA. What is her name?

CHARMIDES. Philematium.

TRYPHAENA. Which Philematium? There are two of them. You mean the one from the Peiraeus who lost her virginity just the other day? The one who goes around with Damyllus, the son of the general? Or do you mean the other, the one they call "Mantrap?"

CHARMIDES. That's the one. And I'm the poor devil she caught. She's got me.

TRYPHAENA. You're crying your eyes out over *her?*

CHARMIDES. Of course.

TRYPHAENA. Has this affair been going on very long or is it something recent?

CHARMIDES. Very long. Ever since I first saw her on Dionysus Day almost seven months ago.

TRYPHAENA. Have you gotten a good look at all of her or just her face and whatever other portions of her anatomy a woman of forty-five will put on view?

CHARMIDES. Why, she swore to me she was going to be twenty-two next month!

TRYPHAENA. Which would you rather believe, her word or your eyes? You look at her carefully some day. Take a good look at her temples. That's the only place she has her own hair; all the rest is just a thick wig. But around the temples, when the rinse she uses starts to fade, it's almost all gray. And what about making her strip so you can see her in the nude?

CHARMIDES. But she's never permitted me anything like that!

TRYPHAENA. Naturally. She knows you'd be disgusted at how scabrous she is. She's as spotted as a leopard from her neck to her knees. So you were crying your eyes out because you never slept with someone like that, eh? I suppose she gave you a hard time. Kept looking down her nose at you, didn't she?

CHARMIDES. That's right, Tryphaena, and after all the presents I gave her! And now she's asking for two thousand dollars and I'm having trouble getting it for her because I'm on an allowance and my father's stingy, so she's shut the door on me and taken up with Moschion. That's why I invited you. I wanted to get back at her.

TRYPHAENA. Well! So help me Venus, I'd never have come

here if anyone had told me *that* was the reason you invited me, to get back at someone else, especially that old bag Philematium! I'm leaving. As a matter of fact, the cock has already crowed for the third time.

CHARMIDES. Don't be in such a hurry, Tryphaena. If all the things you say about Philematium are true—I mean that she has splotches and uses a wig and dyes her hair —I couldn't bear to look at her.

TRYPHAENA. Just ask your mother whether she's ever seen her at the baths. And your grandfather can tell you about her age—if he's still alive.

CHARMIDES. Well, since that's what she's like, down comes this wall. Into my arms now, and let's kiss and make love for real. Philematium—good-by!

PHILOSOPHIES FOR SALE
[1–2

Zeus, Hermes, Buyers, Philosophers

The scene is an imaginary slave market in which Zeus, with the aid of his factotum Hermes, puts various philosophers on the block.

ZEUS. Hey, you, set up the benches and get the place ready for the buyers when they come. And you there, line up the items for sale. Pretty them up so they'll look good and attract a big crowd. Hermes, make the announcement—invite the buyers to step this way, please, into the salesroom.

On sale today, a miscellaneous lot of philosophers from a variety of schools. Credit for one year available to those who can't pay cash; security required.

HERMES. There's quite a crowd already. Let's not waste time and hold them up.

ZEUS. Start the sale then.

HERMES. Who'll we put on the block first?

ZEUS. This long-haired fellow from Ionia. He's such an impressive item.

HERMES. Hey, Pythagoras![1] Step down here and let the people look you over.

ZEUS. Make your pitch, Hermes.

HERMES. For sale, one top-grade philosopher, the most impressive you can find. Any takers? Any of you gentlemen want to be more than a man? Want to know the harmony of the universe? Want your soul to transmigrate?

1ST BUYER. He looks pretty good. What's his specialty?

HERMES. Arithmetic, astronomy, magic, geometry, music, and humbug. You also have here the best prophet in the business.

1ST BUYER. May I ask him a few things?

HERMES. By all means.

1ST BUYER. Where are you from?

PYTHAGORAS. Samos.

1ST BUYER. Where did you get your education?

PYTHAGORAS. At the side of the sages of Egypt.

1ST BUYER. Now then, if I buy you, what will you teach me?

PYTHAGORAS. Teach thee? Nought. I'll *remind* thee.

1ST BUYER. Remind me? How?

PYTHAGORAS. First by purifying thy soul and cleansing it of its filth.

1ST BUYER. All right, assume I'm purified. What's your system for "reminding?"

PYTHAGORAS. The first step is a long period of silent contemplation. Not one word to be uttered for five whole years.

1ST BUYER. My dear man, you ought to be teaching Croesus' son.[2] I like to talk; I don't want to be a statue. Well, go on anyway, what comes after the five years of silence?

PYTHAGORAS. Thou must practice music and geometry.

1ST BUYER. Oh, fine! To become a wise man I must first learn to plunk a lyre, eh?

PYTHAGORAS. Next thou wilt learn to count.

1ST BUYER. I already know how to count.

PYTHAGORAS. What is thy way of counting?

1ST BUYER. One, two, three, four . . .

PYTHAGORAS. See? What thou takest to be four is ten. It's the perfect triangle. We swear by it.

1ST BUYER. Well, so help me Holy Four, I've never heard anything more pious and devout in my life.

PYTHAGORAS. Then wilt thou learn of the rotations of the earth, air, water, and fire, and what shape each has and how it is set in motion.

1ST BUYER. Fire, air, and water have shapes?

PYTHAGORAS. Certainly. For, without shape or form, there can be no motion. Next thou wilt learn that god is number, mind, and harmony.

1ST BUYER. Marvelous!

PYTHAGORAS. After all this that I have set forth thou wilt learn that, though thou thinkest thyself one, thou art two—one in appearance and another in reality.

1ST BUYER. What's this? I'm not the same as the person talking to you right this minute?

PYTHAGORAS. At this minute, yes. But before this thou didst appear under another name and in another incarnation. And the time will come when thou wilt transmigrate to still another.

1ST BUYER. Do you mean to say I'll be immortal, changing into one shape after another? Enough about all this. What are your views on diet?

PYTHAGORAS. Nought with the breath of life will I eat, but all else—save beans.

1ST BUYER. Why? Don't you like beans?

PYTHAGORAS. It's not that. It's because they are holy, their nature is a marvel. In the first place, they are pure procreation. Shell a bean when it is still green and thou wilt find it groweth like unto the male genital organs. Cook one and put it out in the light of the moon for a fixed number of nights and thou wilt produce blood. And, most important of all, in Athens government officials are elected by beans.[3]

1ST BUYER. You answered all questions very well, as good as any priest. Now strip; I want to look you over in the nude. Oh, my god! He's got a golden thigh! He's no man; he's a god! I'm buying him, all right. Hermes, what's the price of this one?

HERMES. Fifteen hundred dollars.

1ST BUYER. I'll pay it. Give him to me.

ZEUS. Hermes, get the purchaser's name and address.

HERMES. Seems to be Italian, Zeus, from Croton or Tarentum or one of the Greek towns around there. But it's not one buyer; about three hundred have chipped in.

ZEUS. Let them have him. Put the next one on the block.

HERMES. How about that dirty fellow?[4] The one from the Black Sea?

ZEUS. Fine.

HERMES. Hey, No-Sleeves! You with the sack! Come over here and walk around the room. For sale, one fine, manly, noble specimen, no slave. Any takers?

2ND BUYER. What's that, mister? You're putting someone on the block who's not a slave?

HERMES. I certainly am.

2ND BUYER. You're not afraid he'll have you up for kidnaping? Even hale you before the Supreme Court?

HERMES. Being sold doesn't bother him. He feels he's free no matter what happens.

2ND BUYER. What can you do with anyone so filthy and miserable looking? Make him a ditchdigger or a water carrier, that's about all.

HERMES. No, you can also make him a gatekeeper. You'll find he's more reliable than a watchdog. As a matter of fact, he's even called "dog."

2ND BUYER. Where's he from? What philosophy does he practice?

HERMES. You'll do better to get the answer from him.

2ND BUYER. But his face is so grim and sour. I'm afraid

he'll start barking if I go near him. Damn it all, he might even nip me. See? He's raised his staff and he's glowering; he's got an angry, mean look.

HERMES. Don't be afraid. He's tame.

2ND BUYER. First of all, my good man, where are you from?

DIOGENES. Everywhere.

2ND BUYER. What do you mean?

DIOGENES. That you see in me a citizen of the world.

2ND BUYER. What's your ideal?

DIOGENES. To be like Heracles.

2ND BUYER. You've got the club, all right. But where's the lion's skin?

DIOGENES. See this old coat? That's my lion's skin. Like Heracles I wage war, but against pleasure. And he was a draftee; I'm a volunteer. My goal is to purify life.

2ND BUYER. Excellent goal. Now then, what shall we say is your specialty? What's your profession?

DIOGENES. I'm an emancipator of men, a doctor of their sorrows. In a word, I want to be the exponent of truth and candor.

2ND BUYER. All right, Mr. Exponent, if I buy you, what training will you give me?

DIOGENES. First I'll take you in hand, strip off all the soft living, swathe you in poverty, and throw an old coat around your shoulders. Then I'll put you through hardship and toil: you'll sleep on the ground, drink nothing but water, and fill your belly with whatever you can lay your hands on. In case you have any money, my advice will be to toss it in the sea. You won't give a second thought to marriage, children, fatherland—all this will be just so much nonsense to you. You'll leave your home and family to live in a tomb, an abandoned tower, or a tub. Your sack will be full of beans and of scraps of paper covered with scribbling. And you'll say you're happier in this sort of life than the Pasha of Persia. If someone flogs or tortures you, you won't find it the least bit bothersome.

2ND BUYER. Flogged and not get hurt? What are you talking about? I don't have the back of a turtle or a lobster, you know.

DIOGENES. Follow what Euripides says—with some slight revisions.

2ND BUYER. What does he say?

DIOGENES.

My heart will hurt; my tongue will be unhurt.[5]
The things you must concentrate on are these: always be bold and reckless and jeer indiscriminately at everybody, from kings on down. That way people will look up to you and regard you as a man. Speak in a harsh, rough voice; let yourself sound just like a dog. Wear a scowl and walk with the sort of gait that goes with it. In a word, behave exactly like a wild beast. Forget about shame, propriety, moderation. Wipe the blushes from your face forever. Make for the places where crowds gather but, in their very midst, remember to be solitary and aloof, to stay away from friend and stranger alike; otherwise you'll be undermining our empire. Don't hesitate to do in the sight of all what the ordinary man wouldn't do even in private; pick the more amusing perversions for your sexual pleasures; and, finally, if you care to, kill yourself off by eating a raw octopus or squid.[6] This is my kind of happiness. And I'll guarantee it for you.

2ND BUYER. Get away from me! Everything you've said is nauseating. It's inhuman.

DIOGENES. But, listen. It's so easy. Anyone can do it. No course of study required, no debates, no nonsense; my road is a short cut to fame. You can be just plain John Doe—tanner, fishman, carpenter, money-changer—and there's nothing to stop you from being acclaimed as a wonder—provided you have brass, no sense of shame, and know how to jeer with finesse.

2ND BUYER. Can't use you for anything like that. But in a pinch you might do as a boatman or gardener—if this man here is willing to let you go for fifty cents. That's my top price.

HERMES. He's yours. Glad to get rid of him. He's always making a nuisance of himself with his hollering and his tirades. He insults everyone in creation.

ZEUS. Put the fellow from Cyrene[7] on the block next. The one with the fancy clothes and the garland on his head.

HERMES. Your attention, everybody. Here's an expensive item that costs money: one charming philosopher, blissfully happy. Who's interested in a life of luxury? Any buyers for a grade-A fop?

3RD BUYER. Come over here and tell me what you know. If you're any use to me, I'll buy you.

HERMES. Please, mister, don't annoy him, and don't ask him any questions. He's drunk. See? How can he answer? He can't talk straight!

3RD BUYER. Now who in his right mind would buy such a degenerate and undisciplined slave? Look at him reel! He's tipsy. And he reeks of perfume. Well, Hermes, you'll have to tell me yourself what his accomplishments and aims are.

HERMES. Easy to live with, good company at parties, and a perfect companion for an amorous spendthrift out for a night on the town with a chorus girl. Besides, has a good knowledge of pastry, is an excellent chef—in short, a professor of soft living. Attended school at Athens. Served as slave to various dictators in Sicily and has excellent references from them. Key tenets of his philosophy: scorn everything, exploit everything, beg, borrow, or steal pleasure wherever and whenever you can.

3RD BUYER. Better look for someone else, Hermes, one of the plutocrats in the crowd. I'm in no position to buy such gaiety.

HERMES. Zeus, he's unsalable. It looks as if we're stuck with him.

ZEUS. Take him away and bring on the next. No, make it those two, that laugher from Abdera and that weeper from Ephesus.[8] I want them sold as a pair.

HERMES. Step down here, you two. For sale, two excellent items, the wisest we have to offer.

4TH BUYER. My god! What a contrast! This one won't stop laughing and that one looks as if he's in mourning; he's crying his eyes out. Hey, you, what's the joke?

DEMOCRITUS. The joke? That ye and all that ye do seemeth ridiculous to me.

4TH BUYER. What's that? You're laughing at us all? You consider all our affairs meaningless?

DEMOCRITUS. They *are* meaningless. For there is nothing in them to be taken seriously. The whole world is merely void, infinity, and atoms in motion.

4TH BUYER. Oh no. Your head's the void. An infinity of void. Of all the insults—stop laughing, you! I say, my dear fellow, what are you crying about? I think I'm much better off talking to you than him.

HERACLITUS. As I see it, everything that hath to do with men is full of misery and tears and none of it will endure; it will all pass away. Wherefore I pity men and weep for them. Methinks what they suffer now is not very great, but what will come to pass in time—oh, horrors! I refer to the final conflagration and destruction of the world. And I weep that all things are in flux, that all things are mingled as in a salad, that all things are one and the same—joy and sorrow, knowledge and ignorance, the great and the small—whirling about, up and down, and forever changing, the playthings of eternity.

4TH BUYER. Just what is eternity?

HERACLITUS. A child at play. With checkers. Making combinations. Unmaking combinations.

4TH BUYER. What are men?

HERACLITUS. Mortal gods.

4TH BUYER. What are gods?

HERACLITUS. Immortal men.

4TH BUYER. Hey, are you playing riddles or conundrums with me? None of what you say makes sense—just like Apollo.[9]

HERACLITUS. Who cares? Ye mean nothing to me.

4TH BUYER. If that's the case, nobody in his right mind is going to buy you.

HERACLITUS. Hear ye, young and old, prospective buyers or not, may ye all howl with pain!

4TH BUYER. This fellow's suffering from a near case of manic depression. I'm not buying either one of them.

HERMES. Zeus, they're unsalable; we're stuck with them too.

ZEUS. Put up the next one.

HERMES. How about that Athenian?[10] The one that never shuts up?

ZEUS. Fine.

HERMES. Hey, you! Come here. For sale, one good, intelligent item, 100 per cent devout. Any takers?

5TH BUYER. Tell me, what's your specialty?

SOCRATES. I'm a pederast. Very knowledgeable in matters of sex.

5TH BUYER. Then I can't buy you. I'm after a tutor for my son; he's a handsome young boy.

SOCRATES. I'm the best person in the world to leave with handsome young boys. I don't love their bodies—it's the soul I consider beautiful. They can even be under the same blanket with me, and you won't hear a word of complaint from any one of them.

5TH BUYER. A pederast who meddles with nothing more than their souls? Even when they're under the same blanket and there's nothing to stop him? I can't believe it.

SOCRATES. So help me Dog and Plane Tree, it's the truth!

5TH BUYER. My god! What outlandish divinities!

SOCRATES. What do you mean? You don't think the dog is a god? Don't you realize how important Anubis is in Egypt?[11] And how about the Dog Star in heaven and Cerberus in the underworld?

5TH BUYER. You're right. My mistake. Now, tell me, what sort of life do you lead?

SOCRATES. I live in a state I made up myself. It's an unusual form of republic. I pass my own laws.

5TH BUYER. I'd like to hear one of your statutes.

SOCRATES. Here's the most important, the one about women: no woman is to be the exclusive property of just one man; anyone who wants may share the privileges of marriage.

5TH BUYER. What's that? You've done away with laws against adultery?

SOCRATES. I certainly have. Plus all the hairsplitting that goes on about the subject.

5TH BUYER. What are your views about young boys?

SOCRATES. They're to be awarded as lovers to heroes who have distinguished themselves for gallantry in action.

5TH BUYER. Pretty generous! What are the key tenets of your philosophy?

SOCRATES. My theory of ideas and of the images of reality. I mean this: whatever you see—the earth, the things on the earth, the heavens, the sea—each and every one of these has an invisible form which exists outside the universe.

5TH BUYER. Where do they exist?

SOCRATES. Nowhere. If they existed somewhere, they wouldn't be what they are.

5TH BUYER. I can't see these forms you're talking about.

SOCRATES. Of course you can't. The eye of your soul is blind. Now *I* see the forms of everything, the invisible you, the other me—I see everything double.

5TH BUYER. You've not only got brains but the eye of an eagle! I've got to buy you. Let me see—Hermes, what price will you make me for this fellow?

HERMES. Give me twenty thousand dollars.

5TH BUYER. It's a deal. But I'll have to have credit.

HERMES. What's your name?

5TH BUYER. Dion. From Syracuse.

HERMES. He's yours, and I wish you luck. Epicurus,[12] your turn now. Any buyers for this one? He's a disciple of the laugher and the drunk I had on the block a little while ago, but he outdoes them both in one respect: he's more of an atheist. Besides, he's a nice fellow and likes his food.

6TH BUYER. How much is he?

HERMES. Three hundred dollars.

6TH BUYER. Here you are. Incidentally, I'd better know what he likes to eat.

HERMES. Sweets, honey cakes, and dried figs. They're his favorite.

6TH BUYER. Not bad. I'll buy in fig cakes from Caria for him.

ZEUS. Put up the next one. That fellow with the scowl and the cropped head.[13] The one from the Stoa.

HERMES. Good idea. Looks as if he's the one most of the crowd we have here has been waiting for. For sale, virtue and perfection personified. Who's interested in being the only one to know everything?

7TH BUYER. Why do you say that?

HERMES. Because this fellow here is the only man in the world who's wise, good, just, brave, the only king, orator, millionaire, jurist, or what have you.

7TH BUYER. Then he's the only cook. And, damn it all, the only tanner, carpenter, and so on.

HERMES. Looks that way.

7TH BUYER. Come over here, my friend. Let's assume I've bought you; tell me what you're like. First I want to know this: aren't you unhappy at being a slave? At being up for sale like this?

CHRYSIPPUS. Not at all. Such things are beyond our control. And what's beyond our control is a matter of indifference.

7TH BUYER. How do you mean? I don't understand.

CHRYSIPPUS. What's that? You don't understand that, in matters of this sort, we have to deal with preferitives and rejectives?

7TH BUYER. I still don't understand.

CHRYSIPPUS. Naturally. You're not familiar with our terminology. You don't have the apperceptive image. But any serious student of our system of reasoning not only understands all this but also understands predicates and incidental predicates and the distinction between them.

7TH BUYER. In the name of all that's wise, I hope you won't mind explaining to me what predicates and incidental predicates are. I'm somehow struck by the ring of the words.

CHRYSIPPUS. Don't mind in the least. Assume that a man who has a crippled foot stubs it on a rock and unexpectedly injures himself. We *predicate* his crippled foot, but we *incidentally predicate* its injury. Because it was an incident.

7TH BUYER. What a mind! What else do you specialize in?

CHRYSIPPUS. Word nets. I use them in arguments to trip,
    gag, silence, practically muzzle my opponents. How can
    I do it? By using my far-famed syllogism.

7TH BUYER. Good god, it must be something unbeatably
    powerful.

CHRYSIPPUS. Here's an example. Do you have a child?

7TH BUYER. What if I do?

CHRYSIPPUS. Let's assume he wandered too near the river
    and a crocodile found him and caught him. Let's also
    assume the crocodile promised to release him provided
    you could correctly state in advance what its intentions
    were, whether to release the boy or not. Which would
    you say it had made up its mind to do?

7TH BUYER. That's a hard one to answer. Which shall I
    say to get my boy back? I don't know! In god's name,
    hurry and give the answer yourself! Save my child be-
    fore he gets gulped down!

CHRYSIPPUS. Don't worry. Now I'm going to teach you
    some others even more remarkable.

7TH BUYER. Which?

CHRYSIPPUS. The Reaper, the Owner—even better, the Elec-
    tra, and the Masked Man.

7TH BUYER. What masked man are you talking about?
    Who's Electra?

CHRYSIPPUS. *The* Electra, Agamemnon's daughter.[14] She
    both knew and didn't know the same thing at one and
    the same moment. You see, Orestes incognito was
    standing next to her. She knew Orestes was her brother
    —but she didn't know that the man standing beside her
    was Orestes. Now I'll give you the Masked Man, a really
    remarkable exercise in logic. Tell me, do you know your
    own father?

7TH BUYER. Certainly.

CHRYSIPPUS. Now then, if I put a masked man alongside you and asked you if you knew who it was, what would you say?

7TH BUYER. That I don't know, of course.

CHRYSIPPUS. Ah, but the masked man is your father. So, if you don't know him, obviously you don't know your own father.

7TH BUYER. Not at all. I'd take the mask off and learn the truth of the matter. Never mind. What's the end result of your philosophy? What will you do when you arrive at the pinnacle of virtue?

CHRYSIPPUS. By that time I'll be as nature intended me to be in the most important respects, e.g., health, wealth, and so on. But before that a lot of preliminary spade-work must be done—sharpening the eyes over books in fine script, collecting learned notes, getting stuffed with solecisms and outlandish phrases. Most important of all —you can't become a wise man until you've had three successive doses of hellebore.[15]

7TH BUYER. All this is very noble and terribly manly. But I notice that you go in for shylocking and usury. How do you square this with drinking hellebore and being a paragon of virtue?

CHRYSIPPUS. Easily. No one's better suited for moneylending than the wise man. His forte is the manipulation of syllogisms; moneylending is the manipulation of interest, so the two are very close. The serious scholar is the one man to handle both together. And he'll charge not only simple interest, like all the others, but interest on interest. Perhaps you're not aware that interest produces a second interest upon itself, its offspring, as it were. You see, the syllogism goes this way: if simple interest is charged, compound interest is, too; simple interest *will* be charged; ergo, compound will be too.

7TH BUYER. Then we can say the same for the tuition fees your students pay you for your philosophy. Obviously only a serious scholar can collect tuition for his virtue.

CHRYSIPPUS. You're catching on. But I don't do it for my own benefit, only for the young man who pays me. People, you see, are either spenders or savers; charging tuition provides practice for my pupil in spending and for me in saving.

7TH BUYER. It ought to be just the other way around: you, the world's sole millionaire, should be the spender and the young fellow the saver.

CHRYSIPPUS. Being funny, eh? Watch out—I'll shoot you down with my Indemonstrable Syllogism.

7TH BUYER. Sounds terrible. What happens to the victim?

CHRYSIPPUS. Bafflement, stopped mouth, and severe dislocation of the brain. My best, though, is this: if I want, I can turn you to stone this instant.

7TH BUYER. Stone? How? You don't look to me like Perseus,[16] my friend.

CHRYSIPPUS. This way. Tell me, is a stone a substance?

7TH BUYER. Yes.

CHRYSIPPUS. Something animate is a substance, right?

7TH BUYER. Right.

CHRYSIPPUS. Are you something animate?

7TH BUYER. I should think so.

CHRYSIPPUS. Then you're a substance—which makes you a stone.

7TH BUYER. No, no! For god's sake, reverse the logic and turn me back into a man!

CHRYSIPPUS. Not hard. Ready to be a man again? Is every substance animate?

7TH BUYER. No.

CHRYSIPPUS. Now, then, is a stone animate?

7TH BUYER. No.

CHRYSIPPUS. Are you a substance?

7TH BUYER. Yes.

CHRYSIPPUS. Are you a substance that's animate?

7TH BUYER. Yes.

CHRYSIPPUS. Ergo, since you're animate, you're not a stone.

7TH BUYER. Thank you, thank you! My legs were already getting cold and stiff, just like Niobe's.[17] I'm buying you. Hermes, how much do I have to pay for this fellow?

HERMES. Two thousand dollars.

7TH BUYER. Here you are.

HERMES. Are you buying him all by yourself?

7TH BUYER. Good god, no. All these men you see here are in on the deal.

HERMES. Quite a crowd. And all husky specimens. They'll go well with the Reaper.

ZEUS. You're wasting time. Bring on the next, that Peripatetic.[18]

HERMES. Hey, rich and handsome, it's you I want! Any buyers for the smartest man in the world? The man who knows absolutely everything?

8TH BUYER. What's he like?

HERMES. Even-tempered, restrained, adaptable in his habits. Best of all, he's double.

8TH BUYER. What do you mean?

HERMES. Apparently he's one thing as seen from the outside and another thing inside. So, if you buy him, always remember to specify "inner" or "outer."

8TH BUYER. What's his most important contribution?

HERMES. That there are three forms of the good: in the soul, in the body, in the things about us.

8TH BUYER. He has ideas a man can understand. How much is he?

HERMES. Three thousand dollars.

8TH BUYER. That's high.

HERMES. My dear man, not at all. If you ask me, he comes with money of his own, so don't lose a minute, buy him. Besides, in no time at all he'll teach you how long a gnat lives, how far down sunlight penetrates sea water, and what sort of soul oysters have.

8TH BUYER. My god! What scholarship!

HERMES. Ah, wait till you hear about other things, things that require a much keener eye than these do. Such as conception and birth and the formation of the embryo in the womb, the fact that man is a laugh-emitting animal but donkeys are neither laugh-emitting nor house-building nor ship-using animals.

8TH BUYER. Most impressive and help-producing bits of information. I'll pay the three thousand.

HERMES. Very good.

ZEUS. Who's left?

HERMES. The Skeptic here.[19] Hey, boots, up here! Let's get you sold, and quickly. Everybody's leaving; there's only a handful left for the sale. Well—anybody interested in this one?

9TH BUYER. I am. First tell me what you know.

PYRRHO. Nothing.

9TH BUYER. How can you say that?

PYRRHO. Because, as I see it, absolutely nothing exists.

9TH BUYER. You don't know whether we exist?

PYRRHO. No, I don't.

9TH BUYER. Not even whether you exist?

PYRRHO. I'm even less sure about that.

9TH BUYER. How bewildered can a man get? What are you doing with that set of scales?

PYRRHO. I use it to weigh arguments. I get them to balance and, when I see they're exactly equal, then I'm once and for all sure I don't know which is right.

9TH BUYER. What else are you good at?

PYRRHO. Everything—except chasing runaway slaves.

9TH BUYER. Why can't you do that?

PYRRHO. Because, my friend, I can't grasp *anything*.

9TH BUYER. I'm not surprised. You look pretty slow to me. What do you consider the end result of your philosophy?

PYRRHO. Ignorance, deafness, blindness.

9TH BUYER. You mean the lack of both sight and hearing?

PYRRHO. And of judgment and feeling. In short, being exactly like a worm.

9TH BUYER. For that I must have him. Hermes, what shall we say he's worth?

HERMES. A hundred and fifty dollars.

9TH BUYER. Here you are. All right, you, what do you say? Do I own you or not?

PYRRHO. Who knows?

9TH BUYER. *I* know. I bought you. Paid cash down, too.

PYRRHO. I reserve judgment. I'll look into it.

9TH BUYER. In the meantime, follow me the way a slave of mine should.

PYRRHO. Who knows if you're telling the truth?

9TH BUYER. The salesman, the hundred and fifty dollars, and the other people here.

PYRRHO. You mean there are other people here?

9TH BUYER. Look here, I'll take the weaker side and still prove I'm your master—I'll put you on the treadmill.

PYRRHO. Don't. Reserve judgment on the point.

9TH BUYER. God, no. I've already declared myself on the point.

HERMES. Stop arguing and follow him. He bought you. Gentlemen, please come back tomorrow. We're putting up for sale a selection of plain people, workmen, and shopkeepers.

NOTES

[1] Pythagoreanism was rather a museum piece in Lucian's day. Pythagoras (580–510 B.C.) was born in Samos, traveled in Egypt, and founded at Croton in south Italy a sect that was as much a religious order as a philosophical school. He taught that the basic principle of the universe was number and proportion, and he gave mystic value to certain digits (e.g., 4; its four integers [1+2+3+4] add up to ten, and, if the integers are represented by dots, the result is a perfect,

i.e., equilateral, triangle · · ·). He held that the soul was immortal and transmigrated from body to body, so a man's knowledge was the sum total of his recollections from his soul's previous incarnations. He made his neophytes observe silence for five years. For the legends about him see p. 210, n. 7.

[2] A mute. The story goes that he suddenly cried out in time to save his father from an assassin (Herodotus 1.85).

[3] Government offices were filled by lot. Black and white beans were put in an urn, and those who drew whites won.

[4] Diogenes, born in Sinope on the Black Sea, represents the Cynics. For this school see p. 174.

[5] *Hippolytus* 612 ("My tongue did swear; my heart remained unsworn").

[6] See p. 193, n. 4.

[7] Aristippus, born in Cyrene toward the end of the fifth century B.C., founded the Cyrenaic school which held that pleasure was the greatest good. He spent some time at the court of Dionysius, the famous dictator of Syracuse.

[8] The philosophies of both Democritus of Abdera (460–361 B.C.) and Heraclitus of Ephesus (ca. 500 B.C.) had long been passé by Lucian's time. Democritus propounded the theory that the world was made up of countless atoms in an infinity of void. Heraclitus held that fire is the first principle of the world and that consequently all things are constantly changing. He expressed himself in language often obscure and enigmatic.

[9] See p. 167, n. 9.

[10] Socrates (469–399 B.C.), whom Lucian lumps together with his famous disciple Plato (428–347 B.C.). One of Socrates' idiosyncrasies was to swear queer oaths; "by the dog" was a favorite. See also p. 211, n. 11. It was Plato who developed

the theory of ideas, i.e., of ideal abstract categories distinct from individual discernible objects. Among his most famous works were the *Laws* and the *Republic;* in the latter he advocated a community of women. He taught in a lovely garden, the Academy, in the suburbs of Athens. Dion, a wealthy citizen of Syracuse, was one of his most devoted pupils.

[11] See p. 167, n. 10.

[12] Epicurus (342–270 B.C.) derived from Democritus the theory of the atomic structure of the universe and from Aristippus the view that pleasure was the highest good. He rigidly excluded the gods from any important place in the world order; cf. p. 136.

[13] For Chrysippus and the Stoics, see p. 55, n. 29.

[14] Electra had sent her brother away from home as an infant in order to save his life. He returned as a young man, came before his sister, but did not immediately reveal his identity.

[15] Hellebore was the standard ancient remedy for insanity.

[16] Perseus had possession (for a while) of the head of the Gorgon Medusa which could turn to stone whoever beheld it.

[17] See p. 10, n. 7.

[18] Aristotle (384–322 B.C.) founded the Peripatetic school of philosophy which was located in the Lyceum, a public garden in Athens. For a while he was tutor to Alexander the Great and was presumably well rewarded for his services. He was a man of vast learning whose writings included pioneer works on biology and natural history.

[19] Pyrrho (ca. 300 B.C.) was the founder of Skepticism, which held that knowledge of reality was unattainable and advocated perpetual suspension of judgment. Lucian, punning, calls him "Pyrrhias," a common slave name.

Lucian, Socrates, Empedocles, Plato, Chrysippus, Diogenes, Aristotle, Other Philosophers, Philosophy, Truth, Good Sense, Virtue, Syllogism, Argument, Priestess of Athena, Platonists, Pythagoreans, Stoics, Peripatetics, Epicureans, Academics

This piece is a sequel to "Philosophies for Sale." The scene is first the Potter's Quarter in Athens and then the porch of the Erechtheum, the temple on Athens' Acropolis that Athena, Goddess of the City and Watcher over the City, shared with Erechtheus. For the philosophers involved see the notes to "Philosophies for Sale."

SOCRATES. Stone him! Stone him, damn his hide! Don't spare the rocks! Throw clods! Broken crockery too! Slug the sinner with your sticks! Watch out—don't let him get away! Plato, start throwing! You, too, Chrysippus! You, too, there! Let's all stand shoulder to shoulder together

> Thus making sack protect sack, mighty staff-butt protect mighty staff-butt.[1]

We're all against him; there isn't one of us he hasn't humiliated. Diogenes, use that stick of yours as you never have before! Don't let up. He's to get what's coming to him, the slanderer. What's this? Tired already, Epicurus? And you, too, Aristippus? This is no time for it—

> Show yourselves men, O philosophers! Pour out your anger in torrents![2]

Faster, Aristotle, faster! Good work! We've captured the beast alive. Well, damn you, we've got you. You'll

find out very soon now the caliber of the men you've
been slandering. How can we revenge ourselves on him?
Let's think up some complicated death that'll satisfy all
of us. He deserves to die seven times over for each one
here.

FIRST PHILOSOPHER. I move we nail him to a cross.

SECOND PHILOSOPHER. Right. But first let's flog him.

THIRD PHILOSOPHER. And tear his eyes out before that.

FOURTH PHILOSOPHER. And cut his tongue out even before
that.

SOCRATES. What's your idea, Empedocles?[3]

EMPEDOCLES. Throw him into the volcano. That'll teach
him not to malign his betters.

PLATO. You know what would have been best? We should
have let him, like Pentheus or Orpheus,

Be rent apart and die among the crags.[4]

Then we could have each walked off with a chunk of
him.

LUCIAN. No, no! In the name of Supplication, spare me!

SOCRATES. The matter's been decided. There's no escape.
You know very well what Homer said:

Sworn and strict covenants cannot exist between hu-
mans and lions.[5]

LUCIAN. All right, then, I'll use Homer too. Maybe you'll
have some feeling for his verses, maybe you'll pay me
some attention after I've struck up an epic tune:

Give me my life, for I'm not a bad man, and I'll pay
a rich ransom:
Copper and gold—these are things that a wise man
will certainly cherish.[6]

PLATO. Ah, but we can match that with a Homeric reply.
Listen to this, for example:

Villain, you blabber of gold, but I warn you: all
thought of escaping

Cast from your mind; it will do you no good—you are now in our clutches.[7]

LUCIAN. O woe, woe! Homer, my best hope, is no use to me! I'll have to fly into the arms of Euripides. Maybe he can save me:

The suppliant's slayer sins—so slay me not![8]

PLATO. Is that so? Well, this comes from Euripides too:

It is no wrong to wrong the doers of wrong.[9]

LUCIAN.

And will you slay me now for words alone?

PLATO. God, yes! As a matter of fact, Euripides himself says:

For the tongue with no bridle,
For the head crazed with folly,
The sole end is ill-fortune.[10]

LUCIAN. Well, since you've made up your minds to kill me, and there's no way I can escape, the least you can do is tell me what this is all about. Who are you? What have I done to you that's so terrible you're nursing this bitter grudge against me and hauling me off to execution?

PLATO. Damn you, you want to know the crimes you've committed against us? Look into your own conscience. Or look into those charming dialogues you wrote in which you not only slandered Philosophy herself but humiliated us by hawking us like slaves on the block— philosophers, mind you, and, even more important, free men! It made us so mad we put in a request for a short leave from Hades and came up here to get you. I'm Plato; here's Chrysippus and Epicurus; there's Aristotle; the silent one here is Pythagoras; and here's Diogenes and all the others you tore to bits in your dialogues.

LUCIAN. Hurray, I breathe again! You see, you'll never kill

me, once you know how I really have felt toward you.
So drop those stones—wait, I have a better idea. Keep
them; you can use them against the people who deserve
them.

PLATO. Drivel! Today you die. This very moment

Clothed shall you be in a tunic of stone for the wrongs
you have done us.[11]

LUCIAN. Gentlemen! Understand one thing—if you kill me,
the man who has suffered so much on your behalf, you'll
be killing the one person in the whole world who de-
serves your cheers, your kinsman who thinks and feels
as you do, and—if it's not vulgar to bring it up—the
agent of your best interests. Watch out that you don't
behave like the philosophers of today and treat a bene-
factor with a display of ingratitude, bad temper, and
lack of consideration.

PLATO. Of all the nerve! So, on top of everything, we're
supposed to thank you for your slanders, eh? You really
think you're dealing with slaves, don't you? All the in-
sults and sodden rant in your dialogues you're going to
put under the heading of doing us a service, eh?

LUCIAN. How have I ever insulted you? When? All my
life I've stood in awe of philosophy, sung your praises
to the skies, kept the works you left behind always by
my side. As a matter of fact, where have I gotten the
very words I write if not from you? I draw them the
way a bee does honey and display them to men; they
applaud—but they know where and how I plucked each
flower and whose it was originally. Ostensibly it's me
they envy for the bouquets I've garnered, but actually
it's you and your garden; the blooms you have produced
are of such beautiful and varied tints—if people only
knew how to pluck them and mix and arrange them so
that one wouldn't clash with another! Would a man who
has received so much good from you try to malign his
benefactors? The very ones to whom he owes what

reputation he has? It's out of the question! He'd have
to have the character of a Thamyris or a Eurytus, be
ungrateful enough to take on the Muses, who had given
him the gift of song, in a musical contest, or challenge
Apollo, who had taught him to use the bow, to an
archery match.[12]

PLATO. Spoken, my soul of honor, just like a lawyer. To
wit, it's clean contrary to the facts and just goes to show
that you have even more barefaced nerve than we
thought: to injustice you're adding ingratitude. On your
own say-so you're using *our* arrows to shoot at us and
making your one and only target the maligning of us
all. This is the thanks we get for opening that garden of
ours to you and not stopping you from picking happily
and walking off with both arms full. For this you cer-
tainly deserve to die.

LUCIAN. See? You listen to me in anger; you stop your
ears to the justice of my cause. And yet I would never
have thought anger could reach Plato or Chrysippus or
Aristotle; I considered you to be the only people in the
world above that sort of thing. But, gentlemen, don't kill
me without a trial. First give me a hearing. As a matter
of fact, it was your own idea that governments shouldn't
use force or superior power but should resolve differ-
ences through courts of justice where a party sets forth
its side and lets the opposition do likewise. So pick a
judge and submit your case, either all of you together
or any spokesman you choose, and I'll defend myself
against the charges. If I'm shown to be in the wrong,
and the court so decides, I shall obviously be punished
as I deserve, and you'll steer clear of any violence. But
if, after rendering my accounts, they're found to be
spotless and above reproach, and the court releases me,
then you must shift your anger to the ones who de-
ceived you and inflamed you against me.

PLATO. What? Invite the duck to take to water? Give you

the chance to bamboozle a jury and get off scot-free?
We've heard about your being a trial lawyer and a
damned good man at putting words together. And just
who will you be willing to accept as judge if it's to be
one you can't bribe into giving a crooked verdict the
way your ilk does so often?

LUCIAN. Don't worry about that. I won't ask for any such
shifty, two-faced judge who'll sell me his vote. Look,
I'll even pick Philosophy herself. She can be Madame
Chief Justice and you can be her associates.[13]

PLATO. Who'll do the prosecuting if we're to be judges?

LUCIAN. You can be prosecuting attorneys as well as
judges. It doesn't frighten me one bit. I have so much
justice on my side, I figure I can defend myself and
still have some left over.

PLATO. Well, Pythagoras and Socrates, what should we
do? He claims the right to a trial. It's not an unreasona-
ble demand.

SOCRATES. What else *can* we do? We'll have to go to court,
invite Philosophy there, and hear his defense. This no-
trial business is not for us. It's terribly amateurish. It's
for the kind of people who lose their tempers and leave
justice to their fists. If we stone a man without letting
him defend himself, we'll open ourselves to attack from
everyone who's out to run us down—especially after all
our talk about how we cherish justice. What will we be
able to say about my accusers Anytus and Meletus or
the men who sat on my jury if this fellow here dies
without getting his share of courtroom time?

PLATO. Excellent advice, Socrates. So let's go get Philoso-
phy. She can be judge. Whatever she decides will suit
us fine.

LUCIAN. Very good, Gentlemen of Wisdom. Much better
this way, and much more legal. Hold on to your stones,
though, as I suggested; you'll need them a little later
in the courtroom.

But where do you find Philosophy? I have no idea
where she lives and I've wandered about for years look-
ing for her house so I could stay with her. I'd run into
certain worthies with old coats and long beards who'd
tell me they had come from the lady in question and,
figuring they could give me the answer, I'd ask them
for directions. But they knew far less than I, so they'd
either give no answer at all in order to hide their igno-
rance or they'd point to one door after another. To this
very day I haven't yet been able to find her house. Time
and again, either guessing on my own or following
guides, I'd go up to certain doors with the feeling that
this time I've surely found it, and the throng of people
going in and out, all with solemn faces and impressive
carriage and expressions of deep thought, seemed proof
enough. I'd join the crush and go in. There I'd see some
woman who was no innocent little lass in spite of the
way she had gotten herself up to look like the picture
of naïve simplicity. I'd notice right off that the apparent
deshabille of her hairdo hadn't been all nature's doing
and that the lady hadn't exactly been negligent about
the way her dress was draped. It was perfectly clear
that negligence was her particular way of decking her-
self out, that the apparent carelessness was to enhance
her looks. You could make out the powder and the
rouge, and her talk was very much like a courtesan's.
She'd revel in her lovers' compliments on her beauty
and her hand was out for their gifts; she'd seat the
wealthier ones by her side and wouldn't even bother
to look at the poor ones. Often, when her dress would
open as if by accident, I'd get a glimpse of a gold
necklace thicker than a dog collar. I'd forthwith back
out the door, my heart full of pity for those poor devils
she was leading, let's say by the beard rather than the
nose; like Ixion, they were making love to a phantom
instead of the real Hera.[14]

PLATO. One thing you say is true: there's nothing special about her door, and not everybody knows where it is. But we don't have to go to her house. We'll wait for her here in the Potter's Quarter. She'll come by soon on her way up from the Academy to take her stroll in the Stoa; it's her daily routine. As a matter of fact, here she comes now. See? The neat woman, so nicely turned out? Walking slowly there, deep in thought? The one with the kindly look in her eyes?

LUCIAN. I see a lot of women all turned out the same way, all with the same walk, and all wearing the same coats. Yet only one of them, certainly, is the real Lady of Philosophy.

PLATO. True. But she'll show you who she is. All she has to do is speak.

PHILOSOPHY. Dear, oh dear! Plato, Chrysippus, Aristotle, all the rest, the biggest names in my field, what are you doing up here? Why have you come back to life? You certainly do look angry. Was something below giving you trouble? And who's this fellow you're leading under guard? A ghoul? A murderer? A blasphemer?

PLATO. That's it, Philosophy, a blasphemer. They don't come any worse. He tried to run down not only you, the holiest of goddesses, but all of us who have handed on to posterity what you taught us.

PHILOSOPHY. You mean you're angry because somebody called you names? Yet you know the sort of things I have to listen to from Comedy at the Festivals of Dionysus, and you know that, in spite of it, I've always considered her a friend and never once took her to court or attacked her or held it against her. It was the usual playing around you expect at the festivals, so I overlooked it.[15] You see, I know that jokes never do any harm. On the contrary, they'll make a thing of beauty gleam more brightly and stand out the more, like gold hammered clean at the mint. I don't know why, but

you've all turned surly and bad-tempered. You're stran-
gling this man! What for?

PLATO. We got permission to come up for this one day
so we could get to this fellow and give him what's
coming to him for all he's done. Through rumors we
got word of the things he said in public against us.

PHILOSOPHY. You mean you're going to kill him without a
trial? Without hearing his defense? The man obviously
wants to say something for himself.

PLATO. No, we're putting the whole business in your hands.
Whatever you decide will settle the case once and for
all.

PHILOSOPHY. And what do *you* say?

LUCIAN. I agree absolutely, Lady Philosophy. After all,
you could discover the truth even without anybody's
help. As a matter of fact, it was only with a good deal
of trouble and after a lot of begging that I managed to
have the case reserved for you.

PLATO. So, damn your hide, she's "Lady Philosophy" to
you now, is she? But just the other day, with all those
people looking on, you completely and utterly disgraced
her by hawking specimens of each of her schools, one
by one, for a half a dollar apiece.

PHILOSOPHY. Careful now. This man may not have been
running down philosophy but the quacks who practice
a thousand and one vices in my name.

LUCIAN. You'll know soon enough. Just be willing to hear
my defense.

PHILOSOPHY. Let's go to the Areopagus.[16] No, make it the
Acropolis itself—we can get a fine panorama of the whole
city from there at the same time. Ladies, will you please
walk around the Stoa in the meantime? I'll meet you
there as soon as I've heard this case.

LUCIAN. Who are these women, Philosophy? They seem
as nice as you.

PHILOSOPHY. This mannish-looking one is Virtue, the one there is Good Sense, and next to her is Justice. The one in front is Education, and that faint figure whose coloring is so hard to make out is Truth.

LUCIAN. Which one are you talking about? I don't see her.

PHILOSOPHY. Don't you see her there? The plain, naked one? Forever dodging and slipping away?

LUCIAN. Now I can just make her out. But why don't you take them all along so I can have a plenary session for my trial? I certainly would like Truth to take the stand and testify for me.

PHILOSOPHY. Very well. Will you all please follow me? It won't be any hardship to hear a single case, particularly one that's going to involve us personally.

TRUTH. You others go. I don't need to listen to things I've known about and understood all along.

PHILOSOPHY. But, Truth, we'll need you. You should share the bench so as to keep us informed on every point.

TRUTH. Then may I take these two little handmaids of mine? They're very, very dear to me.

PHILOSOPHY. Of course. Take as many as you want.

TRUTH. Independence! Frankness! Follow me. We have to see if we can save this poor man who loves us so dearly. He's in danger of his life for no just reason. Argument, you wait here.

LUCIAN. Oh no, dear Lady, he must come if anyone does. The fight I have on my hands is not with any ordinary wild animal but with shysters who aren't easy to argue down, the sort that can always find some loophole to slip through. So Argument's a must.

PHILOSOPHY. An absolute must. Even better, take Proof here.

TRUTH. Follow me, all of you, since you seem such musts for this trial.

ARISTOTLE. Philosophy, look! He's got Truth on his side to use against us.

PHILOSOPHY. My dear Plato and Chrysippus and Aristotle, what are you afraid of? That she'll lie for him? She's *Truth!*

PLATO. No, not that. But he's an out-and-out rascal and he's got a smooth tongue. He'll talk her into things.

PHILOSOPHY. Don't worry. Justice is here with us. Nothing unjust can happen. Let's go. You there, what's your name?

LUCIAN. Me? Frank Talk. Father's name I. Telltruth, grandfather's I. Refute.

PHILOSOPHY. Birthplace?

LUCIAN. Syria, Philosophy, on the banks of the Euphrates. But what does it matter? I happen to know that some of my opponents are no more Greek than I, yet you can't tell from their behavior or education that they came from Soli or Cyprus or Babylon or Stagira.[17] Even if a man talks a foreign language, it shouldn't count the least bit against him in your eyes, so long as his mind is honest and decent.

PHILOSOPHY. You're right. The question was irrelevant. But what's your profession? That's something worth knowing.

LUCIAN. I'm a fraudhater, cheathater, liehater, humbughater. I hate the whole damned breed. And there are plenty of them, as you know.

PHILOSOPHY. My, oh my, that's quite a "hateful" profession you practice!

LUCIAN. True. And observe the number of enemies I have, and the risks I run, because of it. However, I'm also good at its opposite, I mean the things that end in -lover. You see, I'm a truthlover, beautylover, simplicitylover, and whatever else goes with loving. But there are so few to practice this profession on! Now the clientele for its counterpart, the candidates for hatred, are legion.

I'm afraid I've already forgotten the one because I use it so little and have become an expert in the other.

PHILOSOPHY. Yet you shouldn't. They're two sides of the same coin, as the saying goes. Don't split your profession in two. There may seem to be two, but the two are really one.

LUCIAN. You know best about these things, Philosophy. I'm the sort of person who applauds and loves good people and hates good-for-nothings.

PHILOSOPHY. Well, here's where we want to be. Let's hold the trial somewhere in this porch of Athena's temple. Priestess, please set up the benches for us. While she's doing that, let's all offer up a prayer to the goddess.

LUCIAN. Goddess of the City, be my ally against the frauds. Forget not all the perjury you hear daily from their lips; you are the Watcher over the City, only you observe what they carry on. The moment has come to repay them! If you see that I am losing, that the black-balls are in the majority, add your vote and save me!

PHILOSOPHY. All right, my philosophers, we're seated on the bench, ready to hear what you have to say. But there's no way for all of you to talk at once, so choose the one you think will make the best prosecuting attorney, and let him present the charges and submit the evidence. After that, Frank Talk, you'll present your defense.

CHRYSIPPUS. Let's see, who's the best one to handle our case? You, Plato. A marvelously noble mind, a beautiful and wonderfully pure diction, charm that's so persuasive, understanding, precision, arguments that carry such conviction at the critical moment—all these you have to offer in abundance. Take over the prosecution and, on behalf of every one of us, say what should be said. Refresh your memory of all those famous works of yours and make a mixed grill of your arguments against Gorgias and Polus, Hippias and Prodicus;[18] this man here is even cleverer. Add a sprinkling of Socratic irony, give him those tricky, rapid-fire questions, and, if you think it's a good idea, stick in somewhere that line of yours about "Great Zeus who drives his winged chariot across the heavens";[19] say he'll be angry if this fellow doesn't get what's coming to him.

PLATO. No, not me. We should pick someone more violent, Diogenes here, or Antisthenes, or Crates, or even yourself, Chrysippus. This is the time for courtroom and debating technique, not for beauty or a clever prose style. Frank Talk's a lawyer!

DIOGENES. *I'll* conduct the prosecution. If you ask me, just a few words are all that's needed. Besides, he insulted me the worst of all—the price he put on me the other day was fifty cents.

PLATO. Philosophy, Diogenes will be our spokesman. My dear fellow, as you prosecute, remember this: don't talk only about your own case; keep our common interests in view. If it so happens we don't agree with each other in our writings, you needn't go into that. And you needn't discuss at this time which of us has more truth on his side. Just rage about how Philosophy herself has been foully insulted and maligned by Frank Talk's dialogues, and fight for what we all have in common, forgetting about the points on which we disagree. Don't you see? You're our sole representative. We're risking all we stand for on you now: either it will appear noble and good or the conviction will remain that it's just as this fellow has made it out to be; it's up to you.

DIOGENES. Don't worry. I'll speak for all of us; I won't leave out a thing. Even if Philosophy weakens because of what he has to say—it's her nature, you know, to be easygoing and kindhearted—and decides to let him off, I won't fail you—I'll show him that we Cynics don't carry sticks for nothing.

PHILOSOPHY. None of that. No sticks; words—they're much

better. But get started. The water's been poured in and
the judges are all looking at you.[20]

LUCIAN. Philosophy, let the rest of these philosophers sit
on the bench and vote along with you. Diogenes can do
the prosecuting all by himself.

PHILOSOPHY. Aren't you afraid they'll vote against you?

LUCIAN. Not at all. As a matter of fact, I want them; it'll
help swell my margin of victory.

PHILOSOPHY. Very handsome of you. All right, you may all
sit down. Diogenes, the floor is yours.

DIOGENES. Philosophy, you know very well what kind of
men we were while we lived; there's no need for me to
go into the matter. Myself aside, Pythagoras here, Plato,
Aristotle, Chrysippus, all the others—who is not aware
of the benefits they gave to the world? What I *will* take
up now, however, are the insults men such as we have
suffered at the hands of this damned Frank Talk. You
see, he says he was once a lawyer. Well, after he quit
the satisfactions of the courtroom, all the verbal craft
and power he had acquired there he turned loose on us.
He not only forever runs us down by labeling us as
cheats and frauds; he also talks people into laughing at
us and looking down on us as nonentities. Even worse,
he's made people despise you, Philosophy, as well as us,
by calling all that you stand for nonsense and drivel and
by expounding the gravest matters you taught us just
to ridicule them. As a result, audiences give him their
applause and cheers and us their boos.

You see, that's the way most people are: they enjoy
a mocker and jeerer, particularly when he's tearing apart
what is accepted as noble and lofty—just as they en-
joyed it in bygone days when Aristophanes and Eupolis
put Socrates here on the stage as a butt and wrote some
preposterous comedies about him.[21] Yet those two dared
do this to only one man, and during the Festival of

Dionysus at that, when this sort of thing was allowed and jokes were considered part of the occasion:

Perhaps the god was pleased—he likes a laugh.[22]

But not this fellow. After a great deal of thought and research, after filling a thick book with his slanders, he assembles audiences of the best people and, at the top of his lungs, rains down insults on Plato, Pythagoras, Aristotle, Chrysippus, me, every one of us—not only without a festival to give him license but without ever having suffered personally at our hands! After all, we could have forgiven him what he was doing if he had been acting in self-defense instead of being the one to start the fight.

But, Philosophy, here's the very worst. In doing all this he uses your name as camouflage; he has seduced Dialogue, our own sister, made her join his troupe, and assigns her roles against us; and he has even talked Menippus,[23] our colleague, into playing in a number of his comedies—Menippus, the only one who betrayed the common cause and isn't here to join in this prosecution.

The man should pay the penalty for all these crimes. After tearing to shreds before so many witnesses what is most noble in life, what could he possibly say in his defense? As a matter of fact, it will be highly instructive for said witnesses to see him punished: it will give them the proper respect due philosophy. For, if they see an insulted party hold his peace and do nothing, they naturally will put it down, not to self-control, but to cowardice and stupidity. And who in the world could tolerate that last thing he did? Just as if we were a bunch of slaves, he put us on the block, appointed a hawker, and, as we get the story, sold us off, some for a big price, some for a hundred and fifty dollars, and me, damn his hide, for fifty cents. Everyone there got a good laugh. That's why we've come back to earth. Our temper's up. We've suffered the worst possible insults. We demand that you give us revenge; it's our right.

PHILOSOPHERS. Bravo, Diogenes! You spoke for all of us and said everything that had to be said.

PHILOSOPHY. Stop the cheering, please. Pour the water in for the defendant. Frank Talk, your turn now. The water's running, so get started.

LUCIAN. Philosophy, Diogenes hasn't charged me with all he could. I don't know why, but he left out most of my criticisms and the more serious ones at that. Now, far from denying them or coming before you with an elaborate defense of them, I think I'll include right now any he didn't mention or any I haven't previously made. This is the way for me to make you realize just who the men were that I sold on the block and ran down by labeling as cheats and frauds. You must keep your mind on only one thing: whether or not I'm telling the truth about them. And, if what I'm going to say sounds slanderous or shocking, I think it would be fairer to put the blame on them for carrying on the way they do rather than on me—I'm simply submitting evidence.

You see, as soon as I realized the ugly things lawyers had to go in for—tricks, lies, bluster, browbeating, throwing their weight around, and a thousand others—as you'd expect, I made my escape. I headed, Philosophy, toward the good things you had to offer and decided to spend whatever days were left to me under your sheltering hand; it was like hastening from the wind and waves to a peaceful harbor. A single peep at what you stood for and—it was inevitable—I was overcome with awe at you and all these gentlemen here: they were the founding fathers of the good life; they reached out their hands to help all who were striving toward it; they had the finest and most useful counsel to offer—provided a man didn't slip or go against it but kept his eyes glued on the rules you set forth and arranged and guided his life accordingly, something which, god knows, few people nowadays will do.

On the other hand, I also noticed many who were not philosophers for the love of it but simply hungered for the public acclaim they could get out of it. In what was obvious and common and easy for anyone to ape— I mean length of beard, impressiveness of gait, and cut of clothes—they were a very good facsimile of men of virtue. However, in what they did with their lives they went completely counter to their appearance, practicing the very opposite of your preaching and dragging in the mud the dignity of your profession. The sight of all this infuriated me. The whole business made me think of some flabby, effeminate actor of tragedy in the role of Achilles or Theseus or, still worse, Heracles; someone who couldn't talk or walk like a Hero and who minced and simpered under his mighty mask, someone even Helen and Polyxena[24] couldn't bear as he overplayed their roles, to say nothing of Heracles—who, if you ask me, would immediately flatten the fellow out, mask and all, with a whack of the club for disgracing the Conquering Hero so by making a woman out of him.

Gentlemen, I saw that all of you were suffering such impersonations at the hands of these people. I couldn't stand the shameful act they were putting on. How dare these apes don the mask of Heroes? How dare they imitate that ass from Cumae, the one which, by putting on a lion's skin and emitting astonishingly fierce brays, passed itself off as a lion around Cumae where one had never been seen, until a stranger came along who, having seen both lions and asses often enough, demonstrated the truth of the matter with a few wallops?

However, Philosophy, the very worst thing I noticed was this. When people saw the scoundrelly or ill-mannered or lewd ways of any of these specimens, without exception they put the blame on you, Philosophy, and on Chrysippus or Plato or Pythagoras—whichever of you had furnished the name the misguided failure had appropriated and the words he was mimicking. From his living bad example people drew ugly conclusions about all of you long since dead. There was no way to compare him with what you were when alive. You were nowhere about, while he and his shocking behavior were in the clear view of all. So you were dragged down into the same slander and were condemned in absentia along with him. I couldn't bear the sight of this. I exposed them. I drew the line between them and you. And you, who ought pin a medal on me for this, hale me into court!

If I see some initiate of the Mysteries[25] giving away the secret ritual and going through the dances in public, and I get angry and show him up, are you going to consider *me* the wrongdoer? You can't; it's not right. When our theatrical directors order a flogging for some actor who hasn't done justice to the role of Athena or Poseidon or Zeus and hasn't played it as a god deserves, neither Athena, Poseidon, nor Zeus gets angry at them for putting the whip to a man dressed up in heavenly garb and wearing a mask with divine features. I rather imagine the gods would get satisfaction out of the punishment: if a servant's part or a messenger's is bungled, that's not so serious, but heaven deliver us from an actor who doesn't give the audience a proper Zeus or Heracles—that's a crime!

The most preposterous part of the whole situation is this. Most of these specimens know every word you've written. Yet, from the way they live, it looks as if they had read and studied them for the sole purpose of doing exactly the opposite. Everything they preach—how they scorn money and fame, consider beauty the only good, are above anger, look down their noses at celebrities and address them as equals—god knows is fine and wise and wonderful, very much and truly so. But they teach these very things for pay! They worship wealth, their mouths

water for money, these creatures who are more snappish
than curs, more timid than rabbits, more fawning than
monkeys, more thieving than weasels, more lascivious
than jackasses, more quarrelsome than cocks. That's why
nobody can keep from laughing at them as they push
and shove in their money-grubbing, or elbow each other
on the doorsteps of the rich, or join in the great banquets
—where they pass vulgar compliments, gorge themselves
indecently, grumble at their portions, hold raucous and
unlovely philosophical discussions in their cups, and take
their drinks straight without being able to hold them.
The non-philosophers at the party naturally laugh at
them and are disgusted with philosophy for producing
such scum.

The most shocking thing of all, though, is this. Every
one of them will talk about lacking nothing and even
shout to the housetops that the only rich man is a wise
man. But then a minute later he will come up to you
to ask for money—and fly into a rage if he doesn't get
it. It's as if someone in a king's robes with a diadem
and tiara on his head plus all the other marks of a mon-
arch were to stop his inferiors in the street and beg from
them. Whenever any of them has occasion to accept
money, then there's much talk about "Wealth should be
shared," "Money is a matter of indifference," "What's
gold or silver? No different from the pebbles on the
beach." But, whenever some old and dear friend is in
need and asks for just a little of the plenty they have,
what does he get? Silence, embarrassment, blank looks—
a complete recantation of all their statements. Those in-
cessant speeches of theirs about friendship, their "vir-
tue," their "honor"—it's all gone and flown off some-
where, winged words for real, not uttered in earnest but
just part of the verbal shadowboxing of their daily de-
bates. The brethren are friends only so long as no gold or
silver comes between them. Just show them a dollar bill
and the peace is shattered, war to the death breaks out,

the books are rubbed out, and Virtue runs for her life; they act like a pack of hounds who have had a bone tossed in their midst—making a simultaneous leap, they snap away at each other and howl at the one who's quick enough to grab it.

There's a story that a king of Egypt once taught some apes to do a dance. The animals, excellent mimics of men, learned very quickly. Dressed in purple robes and wearing masks, they went through the steps and, for quite a while, put on a very good show. Then some jokester in the audience who had a handful of nuts in his pocket tossed it among them. One look and the apes forgot all about the dance, reverted to what they really were, apes and not ballet dancers, smashed the masks, ripped up the robes, and started to scrap with each other over the nuts. The troupe fell apart at the seams and the audience hooted.

These people are like those apes. They were the ones I called names—and I will never, never stop exposing and ridiculing them. But heaven keep me from ever being so insane as to say anything slanderous or stupid about any of you or your like—for there are, there actually exist, people who practice true philosophy and abide by your precepts. What could I find to say, anyway? What in your lives can be compared to theirs? However, these godforsaken frauds I hold it is right to despise. Pythagoras, Plato, Chrysippus, Aristotle—what do you say? That these specimens have anything in common with you? That their lives display some relationship, some resemblance to yours? Damn it all, about as much as Heracles does to a monkey, as the saying goes! Just because they have long beards and long faces and claim to be philosophers, must this make them like you? I might have put up with it if they were at least convincing in their role. As things stand, however, a vulture could sooner play a nightingale than any of them a philosopher.

This is all I have to say for myself. Truth, will you please testify to its veracity for them?

PHILOSOPHY. Frank Talk, would you step aside? A little farther, please. Well, what shall we do? How do you feel about what he said?

TRUTH. Philosophy, all the time he was talking I was praying to sink into the earth. That's how true it all was. As a matter of fact, as I listened I kept recognizing the culprits and I kept fitting names to his statements: "This applies to so-and-so; that's what so-and-so does." All told, he's given us a description of these people that's as clear as any picture, and not only of their bodies but of their very souls as well. Perfect likenesses too.

GOOD SENSE. And I blushed deep red, Truth.

PHILOSOPHY. And what do you say, gentlemen?

PHILOSOPHERS. Dismiss the complaint and declare him our friend and benefactor. What else is there to do? We've done the same thing the Trojans did: goaded this tragedian here into reciting the woes of Troy. Well, let him deliver his lines. Let him act out these enemies of heaven to the hilt.

DIOGENES. I must join in the praise for the man, too, Philosophy. I retract the charges. He's a hero; he's my friend.

PHILOSOPHY. Congratulations, Frank Talk. The verdict is unanimous: not guilty. We assure you, from now on you are one of us.

LUCIAN. I just this minute offered up a prayer of thanks. But wait—I think I'll do it a little more in the tragic style. It's more impressive.

> Holy goddess of victory,
> May my life ever be in your hands,
> May you never deny me your crowns.[26]

VIRTUE. Let's start on a second round now. Let's try those frauds too. Let's make them pay, each and every one of them, for their insults. Frank Talk will be prosecuting attorney.

LUCIAN. Well said, Virtue. Syllogism, lean out over the city and announce this to the philosophers.

SYLLOGISM. Hear ye, hear ye! All philosophers are to report to the Acropolis to defend themselves before Virtue, Philosophy, and Justice.

LUCIAN. See? Only a few have understood the call and are coming. Besides, these creatures are afraid of justice. And most don't have the time; they're busy with their rich friends. If you want them all to come, make your announcement this way——

PHILOSOPHY. No, Frank Talk. You call them yourself. Do it whichever way you want.

LUCIAN. Nothing hard about that. Hear ye, hear ye! All persons who claim to be philosophers or consider themselves connected in any way with philosophy are to report to the Acropolis for a handout. Each will receive three hundred dollars and a sesame cake. A bonus of a fig cake for all who can show long beards. Good sense, feeling for justice, or self-control not a prerequisite; if not available, not essential. Five syllogisms, however, required of everybody; it's not allowed to be wise without same:

> There in the midst stands an ingot of gold weighing fully two talents—
> Prize for the one who is best of them all in the chopping of logic.[27]

Wow! Look at the road leading up here—full of them pushing and shoving. All they had to do was hear about the three hundred dollars! And some are coming up by the abandoned wall, some by Asclepius' temple, even more along the Areopagus, some by Talus' tomb, and some have thrown up ladders and are clambering along the Temple of Castor and Pollux.[28] Whole hives of them,

[42–44

by god, or, to use Homer's expression, "whole clusters,"
like a swarm of bees. On this side hundreds and on that
> Thousands, as thick as the blossoms and leaves that
> emerge in the springtime.[29]

It's been just a few minutes, and already the Acropolis
is full of them "noisily perching"; wherever you look,
nothing but sacks, beards, fawning, shamelessness, staffs,
gluttony, logic, greed. The few who came here at the
first summons have disappeared and can't be seen;
they've been swallowed up in the mob of these others,
and there's no making them out since everybody looks
the same. As a matter of fact, this is the most terrible
thing of all, and you're chiefly to blame, Philosophy:
none of them have any distinguishing marks. Often the
fakers are more convincing than the real philosophers.

PHILOSOPHY. I'll take care of it later. Right now let's greet
them.

PLATONISTS. We Platonists should get ours first!

PYTHAGOREANS. No! We Pythagoreans first. Pythagoras has
seniority.

STOICS. Ridiculous. We Stoics are the best.

PERIPATETICS. No, sir! Where money's concerned, we
Peripatetics should be first.

EPICUREANS. We Epicureans don't mind waiting till last to
get the money—but hand over the pastry!

ACADEMICS. Where are those two talents? We Academics
will show how much better we are at picking arguments
than anyone here.[30]

STOICS. No, sir! Not with us Stoics around.

PHILOSOPHY. Stop this wrangling! And you Cynics—stop
shoving and whacking each other with those sticks!
Now hear this: you were called here for a totally
different reason. I'm Philosophy, and here are Virtue and
Truth. We're going to try you all, right now, to see
which are the real philosophers. Any we find who have

led their lives according to our principles will be judged perfect examples and will live happily ever after. Any we find to be fakers who have nothing in common with us we will bring to a bad end to stop them, quacks that they are, from laying claim to what's beyond them. What's going on here? What are you running for? Oh, my god, most of them have jumped over the cliff! The Acropolis is empty except for this handful who stayed behind because they weren't afraid to be tried. There's a sack some miserable Cynic dropped in the rush. Will you pick it up, please, my servants? Let's see what's in it. Beans, maybe, or a book, or some cheap bread?

LUCIAN. No! Look—gold, perfume, a razor, a mirror, a set of dice.

PHILOSOPHY. Oh, fine. What a noble specimen! So this was the way you equipped yourself for your profession, eh? With these in your pocket you were going to castigate the world and be the custodian of other people's morals, eh?

LUCIAN. That's how they are. Your job is to figure out a way to end their incognito so that anyone who meets up with them will be able to tell those who are good from those whose lives are anything but good.

PHILOSOPHY. You do it, Truth; it's in your own best interests. Find a way to keep fraud from getting the upper hand over you and good-for-nothings from taking advantage of ignorance and posing as decent people without your knowing it.

TRUTH. Philosophy, if it's all right with you, let's give that assignment to Frank Talk himself. We've seen that he's a good man, that he's a friend of all of us, and that, above all, he worships you. Let him take Argument and go around to all who claim they're philosophers. Whoever he finds is genuine he's to give a wreath of ivy and free meals for life at City Hall.[31] If he finds any of those damned impersonators—and their number is legion—he's to rip off their old coats, clip their beards to the skin with a pair of goat shears, and tattoo a mark on their foreheads or brand one between their eyes. The mark can be a fox or an ape.

PHILOSOPHY. Bravo, Truth. Frank Talk, use the type of test we're told eagles do. I don't mean, of course, to classify those creatures by having them actually look at the sun like eaglets.[32] I mean put gold and reputation and pleasure in front of them. Anybody you see who's not drawn to the sight and pays it no attention gets a wreath of ivy; anybody you see who goes goggle-eyed and reaches out a hand for the gold gets his beard snipped off and then gets packed off for branding.

LUCIAN. I'll do it just that way, Philosophy. Pretty soon you're going to see most of the faces tattooed with foxes and apes and just a handful topped with wreaths. But, if it's agreeable with you, by god, I'll even bring some of them back to this spot!

PHILOSOPHY. What are you talking about? Bring them back? They've run away!

LUCIAN. I'll do it, all right—if the priestess is willing to let me use that hook and line there for a moment, the one the fisherman from Peiraeus dedicated to the goddess.

PRIESTESS. Here it is; take it. Take the rod, too, then you'll have a complete outfit.

LUCIAN. Priestess, could you bring me some cakes and a little gold? And hurry, please.

PRIESTESS. Here you are.

PHILOSOPHY. Whatever is he thinking of doing?

PRIESTESS. He's baiting the hook with a cake and the gold. He's sitting down on top of the wall. Now he's lowered the line into the city.

PHILOSOPHY. Frank Talk, what is this? Thinking of fishing up the stones from the abandoned wall?

LUCIAN. Shush! Wait till they start biting. O Poseidon,

holy god of the catch, and dear Amphitrite, I pray you
—send me lots of fish. Ah! I see a shark, a nice big fel-
low. Wait—it's a goldfish.

ARGUMENT. No, it's a dogfish. It's got its mouth open—it's
going toward the hook—it smells the gold—it's coming
near—it's nibbling—got it! Let's haul it up.

LUCIAN. Give me a hand with this line, Argument. Up at
last. Well, let's see who you are, my fine fish. It's a dog,
all right.[33] My god, what teeth! So, my hero, you were
caught gorging yourself around the rocks where you
thought you could sneak in with nobody seeing you, eh?
Now everyone's going to get a good look at you hanging
by the gills. Let's pull out the hook and bait. What's
this? The hook's bare! The cake and gold are already
stuck down in his belly.

DIOGENES. Damn it all, make him throw up so we can use
the bait over again.

LUCIAN. There we are. Tell me, Diogenes, do you know
who this is? Has he anything to do with you?

DIOGENES. No, sir!

LUCIAN. Well, how much would you say he's worth? The
other day I put a price of fifty cents on him.

DIOGENES. Too high. He's inedible; tough and putrid—not
worth a penny. Toss him headfirst over the cliff. Argu-
ment, let down the hook and pull up another. Watch
out for one thing, though, Frank Talk: don't let the rod
bend too much; it'll snap.

LUCIAN. Don't worry, Diogenes. They're all lightweights.
Weigh less than a flounder.

DIOGENES. Flounder—that's just the word for them, by god.
Well, pull them in, anyway.

LUCIAN. Look! What's this other one? It's like a plate, a
fish sort of sliced lengthwise. Sole, maybe. It's making
right for the hook, mouth wide open—took the bait—
got it! Heave up.

DIOGENES. Who is it?

ARGUMENT. He says he's a Platonist.

PLATO. Damn you! Going after gold, too, are you?

LUCIAN. What do you say, Plato? What'll we do with him?

PLATO. Over the same cliff with him too.

DIOGENES. Go after another.

LUCIAN. I see a beauty coming—so far as I can tell; it's pretty deep down. Rainbow-colored with some gold stripes on the back. See it, Argument? It's one of the school that pretends to follow Aristotle. It came right up and then swam away again. It's looking around carefully. Now it's back—its mouth is open—got it! Haul it up.

ARISTOTLE. Don't ask me about him, Frank Talk. I don't know who it is.

LUCIAN. Then he goes over the cliff too. Look! I see a whole lot of fish all alike—same color, full of spines, and skin rough all over; harder to handle than sea urchins. We'll need a net for them, won't we? But we don't have any. Well, let's just pull up one out of the school; that'll be enough. The nerviest one there will certainly take the hook.

ARGUMENT. Lower away if you want. But first put on a long iron leader. Then they can't bite through the line once they've gulped down the gold.

LUCIAN. The line's down. O Poseidon, give us a quick catch! Wow! They're scrapping over the bait! One bunch is nibbling around the cake and another hanging on for dear life to the gold. Well done! You hooked a big, strong one. All right, you, tell us whose name you go under. Isn't this ridiculous of me? Trying to make a fish talk! They're dumb, of course. Argument, you tell me who this one's master is.

ARGUMENT. Chryippus here.

LUCIAN. I think I know why: because there's gold (*chry-*

sion) in the name. For god's sake, Chrysippus, tell me, do you know these specimens? Do you teach them to behave the way they do?

CHRYSIPPUS. Damn it all, that question's an insult, Frank Talk. What makes you think I'd have anything to do with the likes of these?

LUCIAN. Bravo, Chrysippus, you're a gentleman. So head-first with this one too, just where the others went. He's so thorny I'm afraid anyone who tries to eat him will puncture his gullet.

PHILOSOPHY. Enough fishing, Frank Talk. There are so many, one of them might get away with the gold and the hook and then you'd have to make good to the priestess. Well, we ladies will be off for our stroll. And it's time for all of you to go back where you came from; you don't want to overstay your leave. Frank Talk, you and Argument make the rounds and give out wreaths or brands as I instructed you to.

LUCIAN. I will, Philosophy. Good-by, gentlemen. Argument, let's go down and carry out our orders.

ARGUMENT. Where should we go first? The Academy or the Stoa? Or should we start with the Lyceum?

LUCIAN. It won't make any difference. Wherever we go, I know we'll need plenty of brands and very few wreaths.

NOTES

[1] A parody of *Iliad* 2.363.
[2] A parody of *Iliad* 6.112.
[3] See p. 211, n. 9.
[4] Pentheus was torn to pieces by the fanatical female followers of Dionysus whose worship he had banned, Orpheus by the women of Thrace whose advances he had rejected.
[5] *Iliad* 22.262.
[6] A patchwork, with changes, of *Iliad* 6.46, 6.48, and 20.65.

[7] A parody of *Iliad* 10.447–48.

[8] Neither this nor the line Lucian quotes in his next speech are from extant plays.

[9] *Orestes* 413.

[10] *Bacchants* 386–88.

[11] *Iliad* 3.57.

[12] Two famous mythological examples of presumption. Thamyris was a minstrel from Thrace and Eurytus a king of Oechalia in north Greece.

[13] The trial with Philosophy on the bench is inspired by the famous scene in Aeschylus' *Eumenides* in which Orestes defends himself against the Furies in a court presided over by Athena. His jury was hung, and this gave Athena the right to vote; she cast hers for Orestes and thereby set him free.

[14] See p. 107.

[15] Greek comedies were put on as part of the program of events during the Festival of Dionysus. The nature of the holiday apparently permitted playwrights unusual freedom of speech.

[16] The hill where Athens' first and most famous court held its sessions.

[17] Chrysippus had been born in Soli in Asia Minor, Zeno, the founder of Stoicism, in Cyprus, Diogenes the Stoic (not the famous Diogenes) in Seleuceia near Babylon, and Aristotle in Stagira in Macedonia.

[18] Sophists whose ideas Plato refuted in various dialogues.

[19] Plato, *Phaedrus* 246e.

[20] Courtroom speeches were timed by a device that used water somewhat the way an hourglass uses sand.

[21] Aristophanes' *Clouds*. Eupolis was a contemporary of Aristophanes; none of his plays have survived.

[22] From some unidentified comedy.

[23] See p. 174.

[24] One of Priam's daughters.

[25] See p. 193, n. 9.

[26] The closing lines of three of Euripides' plays: *Iphigenia among the Taurians, Orestes, The Phoenician Women.*

[27] A parody of *Iliad* 18.507–8.

[28] The abandoned wall, i.e., the old, prehistoric wall, and the Temple of Castor and Pollux were on the sheer north slope of the hill of the Acropolis, Asclepius' temple and Talus' tomb on the south, and the Areopagus to the west.

[29] *Iliad* 2.468. "Whole clusters" is from 2.89 and "noisily perching," below, from 2.463.

[30] I.e., the New Academics, whose position was very similar to that of the Skeptics (p. 333, n. 19).

[31] The award Athens gave to Olympic victors and others who had brought honor to the city. Socrates, in his celebrated trial, claimed that this is what he should have been sentenced to.

[32] There was a story that eagles tested their young by having them stare directly into the eye of the sun to see whether or not they could do it without blinking.

[33] See p. 174.

THE DEATH OF PEREGRINUS

At the Olympic Games of 165 A.D. a Cynic philosopher (cf. p. 174), Peregrinus, ended his life with a flamboyant suicide. If he meant to make headlines he certainly succeeded: contemporary writers discussed his death, and it was still worth mention even two hundred years later. In the guise of a letter to a friend Lucian gives what purports to be an eyewitness account.

Lucian may or may not actually have played all of the role he assigns to himself in this narrative. The point is irrelevant because this portrait, like the one he made of Alexander (p. 267), is drawn not so much from life as from his loathing of men like Peregrinus. Lucian was a dedicated adherent of a life of reason, calm, and moderation; Peregrinus was a rebellious, restless soul who spent his life in emotion and violence and ended it in a blaze of theatricality that was a very mockery of moderation.

The facts of the man's career are here—but you must often read between the lines to find them. He voluntarily gave away a large property to join the budding Christian sect and, obviously a man of ability, swiftly rose in its ranks. Christianity wasn't enough to satisfy him, so he switched to the Cynics, apprenticing himself to a particularly fanatical branch in Egypt. With this background he turned to preaching physical rebellion, first in Rome and, when thrown out of there, in Greece. Finally he left life as violently as he had lived it, in the garish glare of a pyre outside the great sanctuary of Zeus at Olympia.

A modern psychiatrist might very well have interesting and perhaps sympathetic comments to make on such a career. Lucian wasn't a psychiatrist; moreover, he despised all playing to the grandstand—and this suicide, whatever the motives, was a grandiose grandstand stunt. So, merci-

*lessly and masterfully, he blocks out his picture. He paints
a foreground of vivid immediacy, sketches the background
in a swift flash back, brings us to the climax with a tense
first-person narrative, and then adds, as a last superb
touch, the inimitable anticlimax.*

*The scene is first Elis, the town nearest the sanctuary,
then the sanctuary itself, and lastly a spot two miles east
of it.*

Dear Cronius,

That poor devil Peregrinus—or Proteus as he preferred
to call himself—has behaved just like his Homeric proto-
type.[1] He had already been through a thousand transfor-
mations; now he's even turned himself into fire—and all just
to be in the public eye; his passion for it was that great.
At this moment our paragon of virtue is cinders, carbonized
à la Empedocles[2] with this difference: when Empedocles
threw himself into the volcano he tried to keep it a secret;
our hero waited for the Greek festival that draws the big-
gest crowds, built an enormous pyre, and jumped into the
flames before an army of witnesses—after informing his
public about his plans a few days before the grand gesture
took place.

I can picture you getting a good laugh out of the drivel-
ing old fool—or, rather, I can hear you giving vent to the
things you naturally would: "What stupidity!" "What a
hunger for notoriety!" "What a . . . ."—whatever it is we
usually say about things like this. Much safer to make
the remarks where you were, far from the scene. I made
them right beside the fire and, before that, when sur-
rounded by a mob of listeners where I raised the hackles
of the old lunatic's admirers, though some there joined me
in laughing at him. I was almost torn to pieces by his pack
of Cynics the way Actaeon was by his own pack of hounds
or his cousin Pentheus by the Maenads.[3]

Let me give you the whole stage setting for this per-
formance. The playwright and what he's like you know,

and you know the great tragic scenes, better than anything by Sophocles or Aeschylus, that he kept putting on all his life. I got into the act as soon as I arrived at Elis. I was walking across the training grounds when I caught the loud, unlovely accents of some Cynic bawling out the usual street-corner nonsense about virtue and reviling all and sundry. The peroration of his bellowing concerned Proteus, and I'll try as best I can to repeat exactly what he said. You'll recognize the stuff, of course; you've stood around and heard these ranters often enough.

"Some people," he vociferated, "have dared to say that Proteus is a publicity seeker. O heaven! O earth! O sun! O streams and seas! O Heracles, god of our fathers! Proteus? The man who went to jail in Syria, who gave away fifty million dollars to his home town, who was banished from the city of Rome? The man more brilliant than the sun, the rival of Olympian Jove himself? Just because he has decided to make a fiery exit from life, certain people will have it he's seeking publicity! Didn't Heracles go this way?[4] Didn't Asclepius and Dionysus die in the lightning's blaze?[5] Didn't Empedocles leap into the volcano?"

When Theagenes—to give our bellowing friend his name —had delivered these remarks, I asked someone in the crowd what Heracles, Empedocles, and this business about fire had to do with Proteus. "He's going to cremate himself at the Olympic games fairly soon," I was told. "How?" I asked. "And why?" The fellow tried to tell me, but the Cynic was yelling so, it was impossible to hear anyone else. I listened to the rest of his bilge which included some marvelous hyperboles: after rejecting Diogenes, his master Antisthenes, and even Socrates himself as fit competition for Proteus, he called on Zeus to step into the ring. But then he figured he'd better divide the honors, so he ended up like this: "I give you the two finest masterpieces the world has ever seen: the Zeus of Olympus[6] and Proteus, the one designed and fashioned by Pheidias and the other by Nature. But now this work of art will wend his way from men to the gods on a chariot of fire, making orphans of us all." Having delivered himself of this in a rain of sweat, he burst into a fatuous fit of tears and started tearing at his hair—taking care, however, not to tear too hard; finally some of his Cynic brethren led him off, ministering consolation to his blubberings as they went.

The next minute, without giving the crowd time to break up, someone else[7] took over the platform and poured cold libations on the flaming sacrifice we had just been offered. First he laughed long and hard, a real belly laugh obviously, and then he said, "Since that damned Theagenes finished off his nauseating remarks with Heraclitus' tears, I'll match him by beginning with Democritus' laughter."[8] And he doubled up in a second fit so infectious that most of us couldn't help doing the same. Then he straightened up and spoke as follows.

"Gentlemen, how can you help laughing when you hear such unmitigated nonsense and see old men all but turn somersaults in public for a bit of filthy notoriety? If you want to know what this work of art that's going to incinerate itself is really like, listen to *me*. I've observed his character, I've followed his career, and I've found out a thing or two from the people of his home town and from others who had reason to know him well.

"Now, then, this bright product of Nature's design and craftsmanship, as soon as it arrived at man's estate, was caught in the act of committing adultery somewhere in Armenia, was given a thorough beating, and only got away by jumping off the roof and taking to his heels in spite of the radish up his anus.[9] Next he perverted a handsome young boy and, since the parents were poor people, bought them off to the tune of five thousand dollars; otherwise they'd have had him up before the governor of the province. But I think I'll skip all this sort of thing; after all, the clay was not yet modeled, the finished work of art hadn't yet been fashioned. What he did to his father is worth hearing, but you all know the story—you've heard how he

strangled the old fellow; the man was already past sixty
and Proteus was getting impatient. But then, when a
clamor arose over the affair, he held his own trial, reached
a verdict of banishment, and took to the road, constantly
moving from one place to the next.

"During this period he apprenticed himself to the priests
and scribes of the Christians in Palestine and became an
expert in that astonishing religion they have. Naturally, in
no time at all, he had them looking like babies and had
become their prophet, leader, Head of the Synagogue,[10]
and what not, all by himself. He expounded and com-
mented on their sacred writings and even authored a num-
ber himself. They looked up to him as a god, made him
their lawgiver, and put his name down as official patron
of the sect, or at least vice-patron, second to that man they
still worship today, the one who was crucified in Palestine
because he brought this new cult into being.

"Well, Proteus was arrested for being a Christian and
thrown into jail, an event which set him up for his future
career: now he had standing, a magic aura, and the public
notice he was so passionately in love with. Once he was
behind bars, the Christians, who considered this a catas-
trophe, moved heaven and earth to get him free. When
this proved to be impossible they went all out to do ev-
erything else they could for him. From the crack of dawn
on you could see gray-haired widows and orphan children
hanging around the prison, and the bigwigs of the sect
used to bribe the jailers so they could spend the night
with him inside. Full-course dinners were brought to him,
their holy scriptures read to him, and our excellent Pere-
grinus—he was still going under that name at the time—
was hailed as a latter-day Socrates. From as far away as
Asia Minor, Christian communities sent committees, pay-
ing their expenses out of the common funds, to help him
with advice and consolation.

"The efficiency the Christians show whenever matters of
community interest like this happen is unbelievable; they

literally spare nothing. And so, because Peregrinus was in jail, money poured in from them; he picked up a very nice income this way. You see, for one thing, the poor devils have convinced themselves they're all going to be immortal and live forever, which makes most of them take death lightly and voluntarily give themselves up to it. For another, that first lawgiver of theirs persuaded them that they're all brothers the minute they deny the Greek gods (thereby breaking our law) and take to worshiping him, the crucified sophist himself, and to living their lives according to his rules. They scorn all possessions without distinction and treat them as community property; doctrines like this they accept strictly on faith. Consequently, if a professional sharper who knows how to capitalize on a situation gets among them, he makes himself a millionaire overnight, laughing up his sleeve at the simpletons.

"As it happened, Peregrinus was released from jail by the governor of Syria. The governor had a penchant for philosophy and, fully aware that Peregrinus was enough of a lunatic to welcome a death that would give him a martyr's acclaim, set him free without considering him worth even the customary flogging. Peregrinus went back home. Here he discovered that the matter of his father's murder was still a sore point and that any number of people were threatening to bring charges against him. The bulk of his property had been made off with while he was away, and all that was left was the farm land, worth in the neighborhood of a hundred thousand dollars. The entire estate the old man had left was worth about three million and not the fifty million that that boob Theagenes talked about. You wouldn't get that much if you sold off all of Parium[11] plus its five neighbors and threw every man, woman, cow, and piece of equipment into the bargain.

"Starting an action and bringing charges against him was still a hot issue, and there was every chance that before long someone would do something about it. The townspeople as a group particularly had it in for him: they took it hard that a fine old gentleman—so those who had seen him said—had come to such an ungodly end. Now note the solution our canny Proteus came up with for all his troubles, including the dangerous spot he was in. He arranged to appear before the whole citizen body of Parium. By this time he had grown a crop of long hair and dressed like a character out of some tragedy: an old coat on his back, a sack over his shoulder, a staff in his hand. In this getup he appeared before them and announced he was donating the whole estate his poor, dear father had left him to the public. The minute they heard this the townspeople, a poverty-stricken bunch watering at the mouth for a handout, shouted to the heavens that here was the only true philosopher, the only true patriot, the only true follower of Diogenes and Crates. His enemies were muzzled; anyone who tried to bring up the matter of the murder was promptly stoned.

"So Peregrinus took to the road for a second time. For travel expenses he had the Christians—with them as his guardians there was nothing he had to do without—and he kept himself going this way for some time. Then he committed some sort of outrage against them, too—I think he was caught eating the things they're not supposed to —and, since they would no longer have anything to do with him, he was hard up. So he decided he had to recant and ask the city for his property back. He filed a petition, confident that the emperor would order restitution of the gift. It didn't do him any good: the city filed a counter-petition, and he was ordered to abide by his original decision since he had taken it of his own free will.

"The aftermath was a third departure from home, this time to Agathobulus in Egypt where he took lessons in that master's astonishing discipline. This involved shaving half his head bare, smearing his face with mud, masturbating in front of crowds of spectators to demonstrate 'stoic indifference,' flogging and getting flogged on the buttocks with canes, plus lots of other violent hocus-pocus. So prepared, he sailed for Italy and, the minute he got off the ship, started reviling all and sundry. His special target was the emperor;[12] knowing full well he was the mildest, gentlest ruler on earth, Peregrinus was able to show his nerve without any risk. The emperor, naturally, didn't give a second thought to this foulmouth; he hardly felt it necessary to punish some pseudo philosopher for mere words, particularly one who had raised name-calling to the status of a profession. As a result, Peregrinus' reputation began to grow: to the man in the street, at least, his lunacy made him a hero. This went on until Peregrinus made too much of a good thing; then the Prefect of Rome, who was a man of sense, packed him off with the comment that this was one kind of philosopher the city could do without. But even this redounded to his fame: everybody started to talk about the philosopher who was thrown out because he was too outspoken and independent. In this way he joined the honored company of Musonius, Dio, Epictetus, and others who had found themselves in a similar situation.[13]

"So he set sail for Greece. Here he busied himself, one day handing out insults to the townspeople of Elis, another trying to convince the Greeks to rebel against Rome, a third attacking a particularly prominent and cultured man. Why him? Because, among other benefactions to Greece, he had arranged to have water piped into Olympia and thereby keep the crowds at the festival from dying of thirst.[14] Proteus tore into him for making women out of the Greeks: spectators at the games *should* put up with going thirsty—and, damn it all, they *should* die like flies of the epidemics which, up to then, used to break out when the crowds were there because the place was so dry. And he said these things while drinking that very water! The audience made a rush and was on the point of doing him in with stones when our hero saved his skin by taking refuge at the altar of Zeus.

"The following four years he spent putting together a speech and, at the next Olympic games, delivered it before

the public, a panegyric on the man who had brought wa-
ter there and a defense of his own hasty departure at the
time. But by now nobody paid him any attention; he was
no longer the celebrity he had once been. Everything about
him was old stuff and he hadn't been able to work up any-
thing new, some move that would sweep all who came his
way off their feet and make him a public figure, the cyno-
sure of all eyes—this had been his passion, his consuming
passion, from the day he was born. So he thought up the
grand final gesture of the fire. Immediately after the last
Olympic games he announced to the public that, at the
next Olympics, he would burn himself alive. So now he's
going through this hocus-pocus we're hearing about: dig-
ging a pit, collecting wood, promising a spectacular show
of fortitude.

"Now it's my opinion that a man should by all means
await his death and not run away from life. However, if he
decides that he must, at all costs, make his escape, neither
fire nor any other sort of theatrics is the way; let him
choose some other kind of death—there are thousands of
them—and make his exit. If he must play Heracles and
jump blissfully into a fire, why in the world didn't he walk
off without saying a word to a soul, pick some well-
wooded mountain, and incinerate himself there with no-
body else around except someone like that Theagenes to
be his Philoctetes? But not he; he's going to roast himself
at Olympia when the crowd for the games is at its height,
practically on the stage of a theater. And, so help me
Heracles, if atheists and parricides are to pay for their
crimes, he has it coming to him. As a matter of fact, look-
ing at it that way, it seems very late in the game for this
final act of his: he should have paid his debt to society in
full years ago—and by being dropped into Phalaris' bull[15]
instead of executed instantly with a whiff of fire. For that's
what I'm told, that there's no quicker way to go than by
fire: all you have to do is open your mouth and a second
later you're dead. But, if you ask me, he's thinking of the

spectacle it will make: a man cremated on hallowed ground
where to bury even those who happen to die there is a sin.
You probably have heard that long ago there was someone
who wanted to make a name for himself and couldn't do
it any other way, so he burned down Artemis' temple at
Ephesus.[16] Peregrinus has a similar idea in mind—so deep
in his vitals is this passion to be a public figure!

"Of course *he* tells us he's doing it for mankind, to teach
us to scorn death and be strong in the face of adversity.
Now I'd like to ask a question, not of him, but of you.
Would you want criminals to take lessons from him in this
business of being strong and scorning death, the stake, and
similar terrors? I know very well you wouldn't. Now, then,
how is Proteus going to draw the line? How is he going
to help the good without making the good-for-nothings
more reckless, more ready to run risks than ever? Let's
grant the possibility that only people intending to see it
for healthy reasons will turn out for this affair. Then I'll
ask you another question: would you like your children to
follow the lead of a man like Proteus? You would not. Yet
why do I have to ask?—there isn't one of his own disciples
who'd follow him! That's what I particularly have against
Theagenes. He's aped everything else the man has done.
Why doesn't he follow his master and keep him company
on his voyage 'to Heracles' side,' as he puts it? Why,
Theagenes can achieve eternal bliss in no time at all: just
join the jump into the fire.

"Following a leader isn't a matter of sacks and staffs
and old coats. All this is safe and easy; anybody can do
it. Theagenes must follow him right to the end, through
the finale; he must build a pyre of fig logs, the greenest
he can find, and asphyxiate in the smoke. Fire? Heracles
did it that way, so did Asclepius; what's more, you can
see any number of temple robbers and murderers go that
way, thanks to a judge's sentence. Smoke's much better;
it's unique—you can call it all your own. Besides, if Heracles
actually did make a grand gesture of this sort he did so,

as we know from the play,[17] because he was sick: the
Centaur's blood was devouring his flesh. Just why is friend
Peregrinus tossing himself into the flames? 'By god, to set
an example of fortitude like the Brahmans.' Theagenes,
you see, feels he must compare him to the Brahmans—as
if there can't be publicity-mad morons in India too! A
Brahman, eh? Then let him act like a Brahman. They don't
simply jump into a fire—Onesicritus, Alexander's navigating
officer, saw Calanus burn himself, and we have his de-
scription of what they do.[18] After they set up the pyre
they stand alongside and, holding themselves motionless,
broil awhile; then they climb up, lie down, and very dig-
nifiedly burn up without shifting position the slightest.
What's Proteus doing that's so great if he simply jumps
in, bursts into flame, and dies? And I wouldn't put it past
him to jump out again half-cooked—but, no, rumor has it
he's arranging to put the fire deep down in a pit.

"Some people claim he's changing his mind and talking
about certain dreams to the effect that Zeus won't let him
defile hallowed ground. Don't worry about *that:* I'll take
my oath there isn't a god in heaven who'll raise a fuss if
Peregrinus comes to a bad end. As a matter of fact, it's
not very easy for him to back out at this stage. The rest
of his pack are hounding him: they're shoving him into
the fire; they're egging him on; they're not going to let him
show a yellow streak. And, if he takes a pair of *them* along
as he makes the jump, it would be the one pleasant fea-
ture in his whole performance.

"I hear he doesn't consider Proteus a good enough name
any longer; he's changed it to Phoenix, since the Indian
Phoenix also leaps into a fire, so the story goes, when it
gets along in years. He's even making up his own legends
and has produced some prophecies, hoary with age of
course, to the effect that he's to become a divine watcher
of the night; obviously he already has a yen for altars of
his own and expects that posterity will erect a statue of
him in gold. So help me, with all the fools there are in this

world there's every likelihood some will be found to claim
that he cured them of a fever or that one night they ran
into our divine night watchman. And, since Zeus's Proteus,
first holder of the name, had the gift of prophecy, I sup-
pose those damned disciples of his will arrange to have an
oracle and a holy of holies set up on the site. You take my
word for it: he'll have his own priesthood—priests of the
whips or the branding irons or some such hocus-pocus; by
god, he might even have a secret cult founded for him on
the site, a nighttime affair with a torchlight parade around
the pyre. Why, just the other day Theagenes, according
to what I hear from one of my friends, announced that
the Sibyl had issued an oracle about all this. My informant
says it went:

> Yet, when the time comes that Proteus, finest of all of
> the Cynics,
> Kindling a fire on the soil set apart for great Zeus of the
> thunder,
> Into the embers shall leap and depart thence for lofty
> Olympus,
> Then do I bid all you mortals who feed on the fruits of
> the harvest,
> Honor this greatest of Heroes, this spirit that roams
> through the darkness,
> Seat him alongside Lord Heracles, seat him alongside
> Hephaestus.

This is what Theagenes claims he heard from the Sibyl.
But I have another oracle on the same subject to give him
from Bacis.[19] Bacis said—and very well, too:

> Yet, when the time comes that he with the most names
> of all of the Cynics,
> Into the embers shall leap with his heart stirred by
> fame's driving fury,
> Then must the rest of the jackals, all those who have
> been his disciples,

> Copy the fate of their master, the wolf who hath gone
> off and left them.
> One who doth cowardly flee from the fiery might of
> Hephaestus,
> Him all Achaeans must quickly belabor with stones till
> he perish.
> Else the cold fish will attempt to climb up on his crowd-
> heating soapbox,
> Lugging a sack full of gold—he makes many a loan at
> good interest;
> Thousands in cash does he have on deposit in prosperous
> Patras.[20]

What do you say, gentlemen? Is Bacis any worse at hand-
ing out oracles than the Sibyl? So it's high time Proteus'
glorious pack of disciples started looking around for a spot
to dissolve themselves into thin air, to use their expression
for the burning."

The man finished talking and, while the whole crowd
shouted, "Let them burn! They deserve it!" climbed down,
smiling. However, their

> cry escaped not the hearing of Nestor.[21]

Theagenes, as soon as he heard the shout, came on the run,
climbed up, began his bellowing, and hurled down a few
thousand imprecations on the last speaker (I'm sorry I
can't give you his name; he was a very fine fellow). I left
him splitting his lungs and went off to see the athletes,
since the word had gone round that the referees were al-
ready taking their places.

Now you know what happened at Elis. At Olympia,
when I arrived there, I found the rear of the temple full
of people arguing about Proteus. Both pro and con were
represented, so most were settling the matter with their
fists. This went on until, right after the contest to pick the
announcers, Proteus came along with an enormous en-
tourage and launched into a speech about himself: what
sort of life he had lived, what risks he had taken, what

hardships he had endured for philosophy. He had a lot to say, but I heard only a little because of the mob. Pretty soon I began to worry about getting squashed in all the crush, as I saw happening to a number of others, so I bid our death-happy sophist a long farewell and left him delivering a pre-demise version of his funeral eulogy. This much, though, I did hear: that he wanted to "put a crown of gold on a life of gold"; that, since he had lived like a Heracles, he must die like a Heracles and dissolve into thin air; and, "I want to help all men by showing them the way to scorn death. All men must be my Philocteteses." At which point the sillier ones in the crowd blubbered and bawled out, "No! Save yourself! For Greece's sake!" while the hardier spirits shouted, "Finish what you started!" This staggered the old fellow completely; he was expecting that everybody would clutch him and, instead of consigning him to the flames, force him to stay alive—much against his will, of course. But that "Finish what you started" was a bolt from the blue. It made him paler than ever—and he already was the color of a corpse, started his knees knocking, and stopped his mouth. You can imagine what a laugh it gave me. After all, there was no call to pity anyone that desperately in love with being in the limelight, more so than all others hounded by the same curse. In any event, he went off with a mob at his heels and was getting his fill of public attention as he surveyed the ranks of his admirers; the poor devil didn't realize that criminals headed for the hangman or the cross draw even bigger crowds.

The games finally ended, the finest I've ever seen, and I've been to them four times. With everybody leaving all at once it was impossible to find transportation so, although I didn't want to, I had to stay behind. Proteus, after endless postponements, had finally announced the night on which he would stage his cremation. One of my friends invited me to go along, so around midnight I got up and went straight out to Harpina where the pyre was.

You leave by the race track, and it's a good two miles east of Olympia. As soon as we got there we saw that the pyre had been set up in a pit about six feet deep. To make sure it would catch fire at once, it was mostly torchwood with kindling stuffed in the cracks.

When the moon rose—she, too, had to witness this glorious act—Proteus came forward. He was wearing his usual garb. By his side marched the Cynic bigwigs with our hero from Patras, a torch in his hand, prominent among them; he played the second lead in this drama and up to the hilt. Proteus also had a torch. They went up to the pyre and set it afire, each at a different point. With all the torchwood and kindling it burst into a sheet of flame. And now, Cronius, follow me closely. Proteus put down his sack, his coat, and that Heracles-sized stick of his and stood there in an unimaginably filthy shirt. He asked for incense to throw on the fire. Someone handed it to him and he tossed it on. Then he faced the south[22]—even the south had to get in this tragic act of his—and cried, "Gods of my mother! Gods of my father! Be gracious to me!" With these words he leaped into the blaze and disappeared from sight, swallowed up in the towering mass of flame.

Again I picture you laughing, friend Cronius, at the finale of this drama. When he bawled out, "Gods of my mother," on my honor, I had no great bone to pick with him. But when he added, "Gods of my father," it brought to mind the story of the murder, and I couldn't keep from guffawing.

The Cynics, who were standing about the pyre, didn't break down and cry but did display some grief by staring at the flames in silence. This went on until I blew up at them and said, "Let's leave, you fools. There's nothing pleasant about watching an old man roast and breathing in this stink. What are you waiting for? Some artist to come along and paint you looking like the disciples in those pictures that show them surrounding Socrates in his cell?" This raised their hackles and they began to swear at me; some even made for their sticks. But, when I threatened to grab a few of them and heave them into the fire so they could follow their master, they quit and peace was restored.

On the way back, Cronius, I thought over a variety of things. I reflected on the nature of the yen for glory. It's the one passion none of us can escape; if even men who seem to be without flaw can't, how could someone like Proteus whose life, in every other respect, was lunacy and madness and deserved to end in the flames?

After a while I ran into a lot of people coming from Olympia to see the sight; they thought they were still in time to find him alive since a rumor had gone round the day before that he would greet the sunrise—this, of course, is the way we're told the Brahmans do it—and then mount the pyre. My announcement that the act was over headed all of them back except the few enthusiasts bent on seeing the actual site and on snatching some souvenir from the ashes. Then, friend Cronius, I had my hands full answering all their questions as they quizzed me on every detail. Any person of taste and sense I gave the plain facts as I've done with you. But, for the fools who listened open-mouthed, I went in for some tragic dramaturgy myself: I told how, as soon as the pyre burst into flame and Proteus threw himself in, first the earth trembled and rumbled, and then a vulture sprang from the blaze and flew up to heaven, crying out in a human voice:

The earth I've left. To Olympus I go!

Their jaws dropped and they fell on their knees, shuddering. "Did the vulture go off toward the east or the west?" they asked. I gave them the first answer that came into my head.

Back in town I stopped to listen to a gray-haired old gentleman who, to judge by his face with its long beard and reverend air, was someone you could have complete faith in. He was holding forth about Proteus and, among

other things, reported that, after the cremation, a little
while ago he had caught sight of Proteus dressed all in
white and, not more than a minute ago, had left the vision
strolling in the arcade, radiantly happy and wearing a
crown of ivy. Then, on top of all this, he added the vulture,
swearing that he saw it fly from the pyre with his own
eyes. *My* vulture, the one I had put into flight just a while
back to poke fun at the ways of fools and dumbbells! You
can just imagine the sort of things that are certain to hap-
pen for friend Proteus in time to come: all the bees that
will alight on that hallowed spot, all the crickets that are
going to sing there, all the crows that will treat it like
Hesiod's tomb and fly to it, and so on and so forth. When
it comes to statues, I know that Elis and the other places
he said he had written to will have plenty of them up in
no time. The story is he sent letters to just about all the
important towns, a sort of last will and testament plus sug-
gestions and rulings. He even appointed certain of the
brethren with the titles of "Messengers from Death" and
"Couriers of the Grave" to do the delivering.

This is how poor Proteus ended. To put it briefly, he
was a man who never once looked truth in the face, whose
every word and deed were for public attention and the
plaudits of the crowd—to such a point that he leaped into
a fire where, deaf to them forever, he was never to enjoy
the cheers.

I have one more thing to tell, which will hand you a
big laugh, and then I'll stop. You've always known—I told
it to you myself as soon as I arrived from Syria—what hap-
pened when I sailed on the same boat with him from
Troas: how during the crossing he had every luxury in-
cluding the company of a good-looking young boy whom
he had talked into becoming a Cynic so he, too, could
have an Alcibiades,[23] and how, when we were bothered
by a squall that hit us one night in the middle of the
Aegean and kicked up a tremendous sea, this marvel who

was too strong to fear death started wailing along with the women. Well, a little before his end, about nine days or so before, he vomited during the night, probably because he had overeaten, and came down with a high fever. I got the story from Dr. Alexander who was called in to examine him. Alexander reports that he found him rolling on the ground and pleading passionately for a drink of cold water, since he was burning with fever and wasn't able to stand it. Alexander told him no and then added that, if Proteus wanted death so badly, here it was accommodatingly knocking on the door; how simple it would be just to obey the call and then there'd be no need of the fire. Proteus' answer was, "Anyone can go that way. There won't be the same glory in it."

That's what Alexander had to tell. I saw Proteus myself a few days before he died. He was smeared with a strong salve to make his eyes water. You understand, of course, that Aeacus[24] won't accept anybody with sore eyes. Eye salve! It's like bandaging a bump on a finger just before you're to mount the gallows. What do you think Democritus would have done if he had seen *that*? Given the man the laugh he deserved? But where could he have gotten that much laughter! You, my friend, you laugh, too —particularly when you hear others marvel.

NOTES

[1] Proteus, a sea-god with prophetic powers, was able to change instantly into any shape whatsoever.

[2] See p. 211, n. 9.

[3] Actaeon was so punished because, while hunting, he had the misfortune to catch sight of Artemis in her bath; for Pentheus, see p. 361, n. 4.

[4] A Centaur that Heracles had fatally wounded smeared a robe with his own blood, which was poisonous. Heracles was tricked into wearing the robe; it began to eat away his flesh,

so, to end the agony, he climbed on a pyre which Philoctetes then kindled for him.

⁵ Asclepius, the gifted doctor, had restored the dead to life, which understandably upset Zeus, who destroyed him. It was Dionysus' mother, not Dionysus, who was thunderbolted; Theagenes doesn't bother about details.

⁶ See p. 10, n. 3.

⁷ No doubt Lucian himself—if the speech was ever actually delivered.

⁸ See p. 332, n. 8.

⁹ The standard ancient punishment for the offense.

¹⁰ Lucian, like many pagan writers, probably confused Jews and Christians to a certain extent.

¹¹ Peregrinus' birthplace. It was a small town—but no one-horse village—on the Asia Minor side of the Dardanelles.

¹² Antoninus Pius.

¹³ C. Musonius Rufus, a Stoic, had been banned by Nero (66 A.D.), Dio Chrysostom and Epictetus, Cynic (at least in later life) and Stoic respectively, by Domitian (82 and 89 A.D.).

¹⁴ The man was Herodes Atticus. Impressive remains of many of his benefactions, including the aqueduct at Olympia, are still visible.

¹⁵ Made of bronze and constructed like an oven so a victim could be slowly cooked to death.

¹⁶ Herostratus, in 356 B.C. The temple was one of the seven wonders of the ancient world.

¹⁷ Sophocles' *The Women of Trachis*.

¹⁸ Besides being Alexander the Great's chief navigating officer, Onesicritus was a Cynic philosopher and a historian. Calanus was an Indian in Alexander's retinue who, when old and sick, stolidly did away with himself.

¹⁹ A prophet of considerably lower rank than the Sibyl.

²⁰ Patras was Theagenes' home town.

²¹ *Iliad* 14.1.

²² Probably another of Peregrinus' Hindu touches: the South, in Indian literature, is the region of the dead.

²³ Cf., p. 211, n. 15.

²⁴ See p. 173.